Good Food

D1290406

Good Food

Grounded Practical Theology

Jennifer R. Ayres

BAYLOR UNIVERSITY PRESS

© 2013 by Baylor University Press
Waco, Texas 76798

All Rights Reserved. No part of this publication may be repro-
duced, stored in a retrieval system, or transmitted, in any form or
by any means, electronic, mechanical, photocopying, recording
or otherwise, without the prior permission in writing of Baylor
University Press.

Cover Design by Charles Brock, Faceout Studio
Cover Images © Shutterstock/Ronald Sumners, Yellowj, Tom
Wang, CCat82, B Brown, yukibockle, and Davide Mazzoran
Book Design by Diane Smith

This paperback edition was first published in November 2020
under ISBN 978-1-60258-985-8 and includes a revised preface.

Library of Congress Cataloging-in-Publication Data

Ayres, Jennifer R.
Good food : grounded practical theology / Jennifer R. Ayres.
247 pages cm
Includes bibliographical references and index.
ISBN 978-1-60258-984-1 (hardback : alk. paper)
1. Food—Religious aspects—Christianity. 2. Agriculture—Religious aspects—Christianity. I.Title.
BR115.N87A97 2013
261.8'32—dc23

2013012317

In loving memory
of the women who have shared with me
the joy of growing, preparing, and eating good food:

Carol Ayres, Margie Ayres, and Martha Jenkins

Contents

Preface

SEEDS PLANTED

Complete quiet took over the van on the ride back to the dormitory. The ten high schoolers in the back of the van, participants in Candler School of Theology's Youth Theological Initiative summer academy, had quickly settled into silence once we departed the Hartnett community garden in the Oakland City neighborhood of southwest Atlanta. All were exhausted after spending the first half of the day gleaning produce, with the July midday heat descending upon the group. The community garden was expansive and fecund, yielding several hundred pounds of produce that morning.

It yielded other fruit as well.

As the youth finished their work in the Hartnett garden, they excitedly took photographs of all of the produce they had picked. When we took the obligatory group picture, they insisted on holding the tomatoes, zucchini, and even green beans, which were still damp from the morning dew. Just what was it that they were trying to capture with their cameras? Since they were adolescents, we might chalk it up to the proclivity to photo-document everything.

But being present with young people as they put their hands in the dirt, placed their bodies in the midst of a resilient community, pulled fruit directly from the land, and collapsed in laughter from the sheer joy of it demands a different telling. In touching the earth in that garden, students confronted issues of hunger and nutrition, food policy, environmental justice, and economic disparity. They also, however, experienced a kind of transformation in that garden, a transformation that cries out for theological interpretation and an embodied ecological spirituality. Gleaning in an urban garden is just one of countless religious practices of food justice, practices that demand analytical, theological, and moral attention. This book, born in that garden, is an invitation to this work.

Across the United States, Christians and people of conscience are putting into action their concern for our food system, and thereby demonstrating an authentic quest for good food. This book is for them, for their religious leaders, and for all of us who long for a more just, healthy, and flourishing food system for all.

GOOD FOOD
GROUNDED PRACTICAL THEOLOGY

Like those young people in the garden, this book begins in, and perpetually returns to, the ground. The quest for good food described in these pages is examined through the lens of what might be called a grounded practical theology. It is grounded in two senses of the word. First, in a material sense, a quest for good food necessarily brings to the fore questions about agriculture— from the backyard garden to the corporate farm, from soil to animals (including humans), from independent farmers to exploited laborers, from city sidewalks to rural rolling hills. A practical theology of food requires sustained attention to the land, and all of its inhabitants. It must be grounded, in that sense.

A practical theology of food is grounded in another sense, as well. Like the methods of grounded theory in sociology, grounded practical theology emerges from intimate and close observation of everyday life.[1] The theological and moral questions posed in this book are thus prompted by analyzing and reflecting upon concrete social, political, and ecological realities. Conversely, a grounded practical theology also issues in practices that respond faithfully to these realities, while expanding Christian theological imagination.[2] This dance—from material realities, to theological and moral reflection, to engagement in religious practices—is reflected in the unfolding of the chapters of this book.

ON WRITING A FOOD BOOK

Preparing and eating food is a universal human experience, and every family has its own traditions, preferences that shape what they understand to be "good food." Every culture holds particular foods to be nutritionally, agriculturally, and culturally significant. And every community has its own particular hopes, challenges, and strategies for seeking a just food system. Truth be told, everyone has ideas about food. As I discussed *Good Food* with groups around the country, earnest conversation partners shared with me their deep concerns and creative ideas for responding to our food system. Many of them are the same questions that appear here. Some of them remain in the background.

Thus, a brief word about the scope of this book is in order. The analysis, theological reflection, and practices here described are inspired by the efforts of Christians in the United States to respond faithfully to the global food system. As such, the social analysis and practices necessarily include some attention to global dynamics and the effects of economic globalization, but the focus remains the responsibility and practice of U.S. Christians in light of these realities.

Similarly, although the scope of issues that could be addressed is vast, much of the grounded practical theology of food that follows is oriented toward a particular point of creative tension: the balance between economic and food security, on one hand, and sustainable agriculture, on the other. Sometimes these two emphases evoke tension between activists who might otherwise agree that we have a broken food system. For example, at a 2012 conference on food justice, sponsored by the Institute for Agriculture and Trade Policy, more than one critique was levied against activists in the sustainable food movement for failing to care as much about workers and poverty as they do about the land.

The practices examined here stand in this tension between social justice and ecological sustainability: churches that economically support farmers who are using sustainable agricultural practices, congregations in food-insecure areas growing their own organic fresh produce, Christians from the United States learning about the effects of globalization on indigenous agricultural practice, and a college work program preparing a new generation of farmers and activists. There are many other faithful practices that address this particular intersection in the global food system, and even more that address other dimensions of it.[3] Already, important books have been written about some of those practices, and others are waiting to be written. My hope is to be a conversation partner in this ongoing social and religious movement. Many religious communities are discerning that now is a moment to respond to pressing issues in their local food systems. Church leaders, religious activists, and theology students will find in these pages an invitation to reflect holistically about these issues: deepening their social and political analysis, integrating a theological vision for good food, and grounding this work in material practices saturated with theological and moral significance.

WITH THANKS FOR GOOD FOOD

This grounded practical theology of food has been nourished around many, many tables. One of the great benefits of exploring this topic with religious leaders and activists is that they are eager not only to tell their story, but to show it: inviting me into their homes, workplaces, communities, and churches. Being so welcomed into the lives of the people whose stories are told here has been a remarkable privilege for which I hardly know how to express my thanks.

For all of the communities and organizations who invited me into their lives for a time, welcoming me among them so that I could observe firsthand their practices of engaging the food system, thank you: Faith in Place (Chicago, Illinois), where I spent a few months as a scholar-in-residence; the Chicago Religious Leadership Network on Latin America (CRLN); the Cuernavaca Center for Intercultural Dialogue on Development (Cuernavaca, Mexico); Warren Wilson College (Swannanoa, North Carolina); the MANNA Food Bank (Asheville, North Carolina); and Georgia Avenue Community Ministries (Atlanta, Georgia). In each of these places, kind people also sat down for conversations with me about their work, and so I offer them my thanks, in particular: Clare Butterfield, Erika Dornfeld, Veronica Kyle, Abby Mohaupt, and Brian Sauder of Faith in Place; Erica Spilde of Chicago Religious Leadership Network; Mallory McDuff, Carol Howard, and Julie Lehman, all faculty and staff of Warren Wilson College; Chase Hubbard, Nathan Ballentine, and J. Clarkson, alumni of Warren Wilson College; and Chad Hale of Georgia Avenue Community Ministries. I am particularly happy to have been so warmly welcomed—and, indeed, put to use—at Faith in Place, spending hours in the office, in a car, on a bus, at the state legislature, and in church basements. The members of the Faith in Place staff have become colleagues and friends. Likewise, Mallory McDuff received me into her home and shared her work with me. I hope that this is the beginning of a long professional collaboration with a "natural saint."[4]

The book was born in the course I taught on globalization for Candler School of Theology's Youth Theological Initiative, and our class' collaboration with the Atlanta Community Food Bank. It was nurtured and clarified in the "Food and Globalization" course I co-taught with colleagues Deborah Kapp of McCormick Theological Seminary and Kate Blanchard and Catherine Fobes of Alma College. Other friends and colleagues have kept me company and shared many delicious and, of course, sustainably produced meals with me while I was working on this project. They have heard more about this project than should ever be inflicted upon anyone, and I am grateful: Lib Caldwell, Ted and Paula Hiebert, Ken Sawyer, Deborah Kapp, Beth Corrie, and Kate Blanchard have witnessed some of the intellectual labor pains. Aaron and Lauren Mathews, Amy Packer and Rachel Huehls, Benjamin Porter, and Beth and Brownie Newman were wonderful hosts and shared many wonderful meals with me during my time in western North Carolina. In addition, both Aaron and Beth were kind enough to help me make contacts in the area.

I must also express my gratitude to the institutions that have supported this project, both financially and with release time. I began this project during my first research sabbatical granted by McCormick Theological Seminary in Chicago, Illinois. For an early career scholar, this gift of time was more valuable than I can express. I also was granted a reduced teaching load in the first semester at my current institution, Candler School of Theology at Emory University in Atlanta, Georgia. They also supported this project with a travel and research grant in the summer of 2012. Finally, I owe a debt of gratitude to the Lilly Foundation for a Research Expense Grant, awarded through the Association of Theological Schools, which funded much of the travel for the research described in this book.

This book would not exist, however, if not for the capable editorial work of Carey Newman at Baylor University Press. Good-humored, frank, and encouraging, Carey has been a wonderful person with whom to collaborate on this project, as has the entire staff at Baylor.

He has read more drafts than anyone should ever be asked to read. The book is stronger for Carey's editorial wisdom, and I hope that I have not too severely depleted his store of metaphors.

A NOTE ON THE PAPERBACK EDITION

Since I first published *Good Food* in 2013, so much has changed, but so much has remained the same. As I write this, the United States is in the grip of a pandemic, its food supply—particularly meat processing and distribution—vulnerable to shortages, slow-downs, and most morally concerning, severe outbreaks among low-paid workers now deemed "essential" and required to report to work in sometimes unsafe conditions. The United States Congress has passed into law two new Farm Bills, in 2014 and 2018, which restructured economic support for the U.S. agricultural system, shifting the balance of support for farmers from commodity payments (payments for growing very narrow set of crops) to crop insurance subsidies (payments to support farmers in the case of agricultural loss). In each Farm Bill negotiation, nutritional assistance is repeatedly placed on the chopping block. Rural communities in the heart of the country's agricultural heartland continue to struggle economically and with regard to infrastructure and human services. And securing access to healthy food continues to be a fight against racial and economic injustice and disinvestment in communities neglected and exploited by the industrial system of food distribution.[5]

I still have hope, however, because I keep meeting the ongoing collaborators for this book: people of faith who are, together, imagining a just and flourishing food system. Some of you I met in the process of writing the book, some of you I have met since its publication, and the rest I anxiously await the opportunity to meet. I hope that this book will strengthen and deepen your work.

A Grounded Practical Theology of Food

FOOD MATTERS

In the summers of a southern childhood, whole meals are made of fresh vegetables from plants in the backyard or the roadside produce stand. Suppers taken out on the back porch might boast a steaming cob of Silver Queen corn, some cucumbers sprinkled with vinegar, a slice of Vidalia onion, and the ubiquitous tomato sandwich. Thick slices of misshapen ruby-hued tomatoes rest upon white bread, dressed only with Duke's mayonnaise and a gracious amount of cracked pepper. Mopping up the tomato juice dribbling down their chins, family members share laughter and tall tales, reveling in the late evening sunlight. Such meals fortify the affective bonds between sisters and brothers, between parents and children.

A few miles away, in a downtown farm-to-table restaurant, a couple may be enjoying an exquisite five-course chef's menu, prepared from ingredients gathered from local farmers and ranchers. With each bite, expressions of surprise and appreciation give way to contented sighs. They might enjoy a visit from the chef to their table, in which they learn about the ingredients and the farms and farmers that produced them. Their meal is of the sort reserved for special occasions, an extravagance that signifies a moment of celebration or major life event. A meal like this is a celebration of beauty, a delight in the earth's good gifts of food and wine.

In a local church basement, that same evening might be the designated time for the monthly fish fry, where congregation members take turns at the fryers and broilers, comparing recipes and techniques. As the earthy scents of greens and cornbread mingle with piquant fish and spices, the hall fills up with older members of the congregation and the broader community. For a few of the diners, this meal might be the most substantial they have had in the last few days. For many of them, it offers a too-infrequent opportunity to gather with other people for a shared meal. In this meal, participants build community and extend care to its most vulnerable members.

Food matters. Whether crafted from the simplest of ingredients or with the expertise and artistry of the most inspired chefs, meals are essential to human life.[1] Beyond its immediate nutritional content, food is an avenue for strengthening affective and familial bonds, celebrating life events and delighting in artistry, and building community. When families, friends, and communities of faith gather around tables to break bread together, they are reconnected with one another. This simple assumption has been the premise of many meal scenes in films, from the community-healing meal at the center of *Babette's Feast* to the family-reconciling feast in *Soul Food*.[2] Where, with whom, and what we eat matters, beyond the nutritional calculus of calories and nutrients. The act of eating is constitutive of human living and is pregnant with meaning and identity-shaping power. The lavish and evocative images from these films testify to the emotional and social meaning of eating, and are representative of a growing consciousness of food, its preparation, and its sourcing. These days, particularly in the United States, it is cool to be a "foodie."[3]

THE QUEST FOR GOOD FOOD

But not every meal is *Babette's Feast*. To be a "foodie" might be understood as a luxury afforded only to the economically privileged, those who have the time and resources to shop at farmers markets and organic grocers, dine in farm-to-table restaurants, and study the elaborate techniques and recipes taught in fancy demonstration kitchens or printed in exhausting detail in *Cook's Illustrated.* Self-proclaimed defenders of the "foodie" identity acknowledge that in the last three decades "the food world was shifting on its tectonic plates, and that perfectly sane people had suddenly become obsessed with every aspect of food."[4] The time and disposable income to support an obsession with food are available to a relatively slender portion of the United States population. Just the same, the cultural conversation happening around "good food" is expanding, in part thanks to cable television and countless food websites. A quest for "good food," however, cannot be built solely on aesthetic or cultural grounds, particularly for people of faith. To call food "good" demands a moral analysis of how food is produced, distributed, and consumed in society. Otherwise, the ideal of good food is reserved for the farmers market set, a snobbish exercise of privileged self-expression now so recognizable that it is caricatured in popular culture.[5]

People of faith, too, are concerned about good food, and they bring to bear their theological and moral sensibilities:

> You cause the grass to grow for the cattle,
> and plants for people to use,
> to bring forth food from the earth,
> and wine to gladden the human heart,
> oil to make the face shine,
> and bread to strengthen the human heart.[6]

A seemingly countless number of biblical texts describe faithful relationships to land, animals, agriculture, labor, and the poor.[7] The quest for good food requires moral attention to farmers and laborers who struggle to forge a sustainable and meaningful life in an increasingly industrialized food system. It requires moral attention, likewise, to the poor in rural and urban communities who struggle to find healthy food at an affordable price. It is a broad social and environmental movement that addresses the deepest needs of the poor, the laborer, and the earth.[8] This is good food.

In the United States, many meals are eaten alone, out of the microwave or from a take out bag. These meals conceal not only the origins of the food consumed, but also the hands that prepared it. The emotional connection established between cooks and diners is absent, as is the delight in a meal lovingly prepared. Even more, some meals are not meals at all, but small doses of calorie-dense yet nutritionally wanting snack foods purchased at the corner store—when there is money to do so. Likewise, most producers and distributors of food in the United States work in a context that is a far cry from the bucolic images of small farms and produce stands. Rarely encountering a family buyer, today's agricultural work resembles something more like a factory than a farm.[9] This is not good food.

In most Christian communities, the core liturgical act is a sacred meal: the Eucharist, the communion of the faithful. In shared meals, God's presence is revealed. It was only after sharing a meal with the Risen Christ that the disciples recognized the divine in their midst: "When he was at the table with them, he took bread, blessed and broke it, and gave it to them. Then their eyes were opened, and they recognized him."[10] While shared food is a source of divine revelation in Scripture, its absence or manipulation is also is a source of human suffering and environmental degradation. The most vulnerable members of society—widows, orphans, migrants—are susceptible to poverty and hunger, and a society that allows this to happen is subject to divine judgment.[11] Similarly, the land is to be tended with care and reverence, and its misuse too is subject to divine judgment.[12] If cultural interest in "good food" means nothing more than aesthetics and sentimentality, then it ignores these serious moral demands of the Christian life, to the peril of us all.

BUILDING A GROUNDED PRACTICAL THEOLOGY OF FOOD

Within every meal—and in the paradigmatic meal of the Eucharist—is embedded an invitation to both divine encounter and moral responsibility. In the food itself, the earth that yields it, the labor that prepares it, and the social relationships formed around it, Christians are confronted with both God's presence and God's demand. It is an embodied confrontation, with multiple layers of meaning, and it refuses both theological abstraction and simplistic responses. Instead, what is needed is a grounded practical theology of food.

A grounded practical theology of food requires a willingness to wade through and respond to these ambiguities, identifying within them pressing theological and moral questions, and opportunities for embodied and meaningful practices of faith. A far stretch from the lavish feasts depicted in film and on the Food Network, a grounded practical theology of food makes its home in the mundane, excavating theological and moral significance in each bite taken, each hour labored, and each seed planted. It is "concerned with the embodiment of religious belief in the day-to-day lives of individuals and communities,"[13] a reflective kind of theology practiced by everyday Christians, religious leaders, and scholars concerned about the state of our food.

Primer on the Global Food System
People, Places, Planet, Policies

Although Christian traditions, in all their diversity, orient them-selves around a sacred meal, a grounded practical theology of food cannot bypass the struggles, ambiguities, and systemic issues that are present in and underneath *every* meal. There are many thorny issues to address, and the web connecting seeming disparate issues is very strong and easily tangled: for example, one can hardly speak of issues in urban food sources without traversing the terrain of hunger, nutrition, economics, labor, human dignity, environment, and so on. Sometimes it may seem that just as progress is made on one issue, another challenge emerges: sustainable agriculture advocates, for example, have been surprised by charges that they care more about the land than about the animals and people who labor upon it. Likewise, community food security advocates have been drawn up short when their efforts to secure an affordable and stable food supply are critiqued as perpetuating the demand for environmentally destructive practices of industrial agriculture.[14] Each earnest effort to address imbalances and seek flourishing in relationship to food is necessarily limited and subject to critique.

While admittedly such efforts will always be perspectival and limited, a grounded practical theology of food begins with a clear, unflinching, and systemic analysis of the *global food sys-tem*. "Food systems" are complex and interdependent patterns of food production (what food is grown and by what methods), dis-tribution (how food is processed and transferred from producers to consumers), and consumption (what kind of food persons and communities eat).[15] And no person is unaffected by this system. "The food system . . . is unusual in its universality: Everyone eats," writes Marion Nestle.[16] Furthermore, in recent decades food systems have become increasingly global: food grown in one place is processed in another place—sometimes in another country—and shipped across thousands of miles. Food availability and prices in Mexico and South Africa are affected by weather events in the U.S. Midwest, and vice versa. To eat is to implicate oneself in this complex global food system. Even a study situated in the United States must take into consideration the global dimensions of this struggle.

Take, for example, the tomato: the one that graces the simple sandwich described above. For families who have not the time, the expertise, or the green space to grow a tomato, making a tomato sandwich is actually quite complicated. In some rural areas and urban neighborhoods, a fresh tomato might be somewhat difficult to come by. Perhaps the family needs to shop in a convenience store, because the nearest proper grocer is a couple of miles away, with no direct bus line to it. They might find a tomato in that convenience store, but the hue would an anemic shade of pink, and the flesh dry and mealy. What's more, this fruit, barely recognizable as a tomato, might cost twice as much as it would in a grocery store.[17] (Of course, an heirloom variety proffered at a local farmers market would be financially out of the question and the transportation issues even more complicated.) For their money, perhaps they would do better to purchase hamburgers in the fast-food outlet next door, which would get them a dose of protein in addition to the puny lettuce and tomato garnishes. One member of the family might even work at that fast-food restaurant, earning less than one thousand dollars a month in her minimum wage job, where she is offered only an unpredictably scheduled thirty hours a week, and thus is not eligible for benefits. Her wages are so low that she can hardly afford or find time to prepare a healthier meal than the ones available on the "value menu" at her workplace.[18]

Setting aside, for a moment, the question of why a hamburger, produced from an animal fed with vegetables, is cheaper than the vegetable itself in this particular community, one might consider the slice of tomato that appears on that hamburger. Like the pale, flavorless (and nutritionally compromised) single variety of tomato available in the convenience store, this tomato was shipped from far away—Florida, perhaps—and grown in chemically fertilized soil, subjected to large amounts of pesticide, and picked early so that it would survive the transport all the way to a midwestern city. The person who picked it from the vine might be an undocumented migrant worker who not only works twelve hours a day performing this backbreaking labor, but also fears abuse, wage theft, and even deportation at the hands of his employer. Undoubtedly, this agricultural laborer would prefer to be with his family in Mexico, perhaps farming corn as his parents and grandparents did. With less land available to small farmers in Mexico and market prices for corn too unpredictable to sustain a family (as a result of international trade agreements), however, he takes the risk to bring his agricultural expertise to the United States. Despite constant fear in an unfamiliar place, he feels it is the only financially responsible thing to do in his situation. All of these complexities are resident in that anemic slice of tomato that garnishes a fast-food hamburger.

A brief analysis of even the simple tomato quickly betrays the complexities and injustices resident in the global food system. An awareness of these injustices and a vision for a different way have given rise to the movement for *food justice*. Briefly defined, food justice means "ensuring that the benefits and risks of where, what, and how food is grown and produced, transported and distributed, and accessed and eaten are shared fairly."[19] This standard helps people of conscience to identify and analyze food injustice, wherever it is present. Thus, the first step toward food justice is an analysis of the global food system.

The task of analysis is a daunting one. The mountains of available data on the global food system, an avalanche of texts, films, magazine articles, and blogs can threaten to overwhelm even the most committed and savvy activist. In part, this is due to the quantity and complexity of the data available: keeping apprised of new developments might be a full-time job! More fundamentally, however, U.S. Christians who seek to respond faithfully to the global food system might find themselves, understandably, at the brink of despair. Simple quests to address local problems quickly yield to an ever-deepening awareness of not only the complexity of the issues, but also the structural injustices that so frequently exacerbate and sometimes even directly cause instances of local suffering.

Despair creeps in when efforts to increase the availability of affordable food in a community eventually demand that one also consider the low wages paid in neighborhood low-price grocery outlets. Despair creeps in when one realizes that an independent farmer cannot make a sustainable living selling produce at a price that the working poor can afford to pay. Despair creeps in when hunger grows in the same rural communities that are producing the most food. Despair creeps in when one is confronted with an ecosystem that is groaning under the weight of human interventions and in which animals are subjected to cruel and inhumane treatment for their entire short lives. And despair creeps in when one confronts the reality that U.S. farm and trade policies stack the deck against indigenous farmers in other parts of the world. In other words, despair works its way into human consciousness whenever efforts toward good food are thwarted by stubborn structural injustices. The global food system is rife with deep and seemingly intractable problems, and thus the work of social analysis always presents the risk of despair.[20] The quest for good food necessarily, then, entails a degree of risk, and a willingness to dwell with ambiguities: "The search for guarantees and for single comprehensive solutions is often paralyzing," admits ethicist Sharon Welch.[21]

Making Room at the Table
A Theology and Ethics of Food

Inasmuch as despair is a shared human experience, however, it presents a particular theological challenge to Christians. Confessing that God is active in the midst of even the worst human suffering and the worst human expressions of sin, greed, and injustice, Christians are called to embody hope in the face of despair. As long as people are hungry, yearning for agricultural work with dignity, seeking to restore their rural and urban communities, and longing to honor and reconnect with the land, Christians concerned about the global food system cannot give up. A trenchant social analysis must not give way to despair, but fuel Christians' hopeful work toward a different way: a different way of relating to the hungry, the laborer, and the earth.

Christians who recognize the seeming intractability of the global food system might justifiably ask, How do we do that? How do we cling to hope that God is indeed redeeming creation, feeding the hungry, and making a way for justice in the food system, despite all evidence to the contrary?

In the midst of very powerful and death-dealing forces in the global food system, the table around which Christians regularly gather—the Lord's Table—stands as a witness to God's abundance, God's presence in the material gifts of the earth, God's delight in the nourishment and enlivening of earthly bodies. Each time we share the bread and cup, we testify to God's presence in the simple acts of eating and drinking together. And while a grounded practical theology of food must begin with a clear-eyed assessment of the concrete realities in the global food system, it also is rooted, established, and nurtured around the eucharistic table. This way of thinking about food requires a perpetual return to the table, where partakers of the sacred meal are fed, bonds are reestablished, and imaginations are ignited. The fullest expressions of this meal around the eucharistic table reveal it as a source of sustenance and social connections for all, regardless of social situation. They express reverence for the gifts of grains and fruits of the earth. They honor the work of the farmers and laborers who commit long and physically demanding hours to the tasks inherent in producing food. Around the table, we might see—indeed, taste—a different way.

A faithful response to the global food system is nurtured by a return to the eucharistic table, but it also sometimes demands a rebuilding of it: expanding and reshaping it in light of human encounters in the world. Each time Christians gather around the table, they bring with them their experiences of the global food system, their complicity in it, and their efforts to resist it. These experiences thus shape how they perceive the sacred meal, and imbue it with new layers of meaning.

Food Practices
Toward a Different Way

In the face of all the bad news, people of faith across the United States—and around the world—are yet embodying real hope in real practices of resistance. They are prefiguring another way in which agricultural work has dignity, in which enough healthy food is available in every community, in which communities can afford to support sustainable agriculture, in which all life is honored, and in which the land is tended with respect and care. While their efforts are small and unlikely, on their own, to stem the tide of the global food system, they do represent small miracles. These practices of resistance testify to another biblical meal image: "You prepare a table before me in the presence of my enemies."[22] That is, in the midst of powerful forces that exacerbate hunger, poverty, exploited labor, soil degradation, animal abuse, and climate change, they are windows of grace. They display real and yet fragile goodness.

Finally, then, a practical theology of food cannot be founded solely upon reports, analyses, books, or another documentary. It also cannot be founded solely upon eucharistic practice or even biblical testimony. A grounded practical theology of food requires knowing, touching, and caring about real people, the earth, and its wondrously diverse cultures. When Christians participate in these "food practices"—supporting farmers, growing food, learning about trade and agriculture, advocating for just policies, and establishing agriculturally and economically sustainable lifestyles—they place their bodies and their full selves in postures that engage their senses and emotions. Intellectual and theological analysis, on their own, cannot do this. Through these practices Christians do not only imagine but *discover* a different way: inhaling fresh earth, tasting lovingly prepared food hot off the stove, stroking the bristly coat of a farm animal, being enveloped in the boisterous sounds of a farmers market—or the silence of acres of rural farmland. With each tiny, fragile act, these faithful responses to the global food system are changing human relationships to food, to the land from which it comes, and to the laborers whose work brings it forth. Each practice further changes the shape and arrangement of the eucharistic table, expanding its meaning and complicating its moral significance. They are, in short, embodiments of good food.

Hope persists in the most unexpected places, if we know where to look.

PART I

CHAPTER ONE

Primer on the Global Food System
People, Places, Planet

In October 2008, just before the presidential election, Michael Pollan published an open letter to the soon-to-be president elect in the pages of the *New York Times Magazine*. The letter, cleverly entitled "Farmer in Chief," issued this simple charge: "Food is about to demand your attention."[1] Pollan argued that the food system in the United States touched most of the core issues in that year's presidential campaign: climate change, energy independence, healthcare. To that list, one might add economic, trade, and labor policy. The ways in which food is produced, distributed, and consumed in the United States add up to a massive and complex system that has global implications. Of course the next president would need to attend to these realities. Indeed, food demands our attention.

Attention to the complexities of the food system is not, however, a simple matter: a cacophony of voices are vying to frame the issues affecting the production, distribution, and consumption of food in the United States and around the world. Michael Pollan is very popular these days: between *The Omnivore's Dilemma* and *In Defense of Food*, as well as his appearances in films like *Food, Inc.*, Pollan has been a key figure in a new national conversation about the global food system. But of course, he is not alone. A constellation of popular culture purveyors, celebrity chefs, and policy wonks have entered the fray—including the ABC television show *Jamie Oliver's Food Revolution*, Alice Waters and the Slow Food Movement, Michelle Obama's campaign to eradicate childhood obesity, policy think tanks like the Institute for Food and Development Policy and the Institute for Agriculture and Trade Policy, and the quickly multiplying shelves in bookstores across the country that are dedicated to the emerging field of "food studies"—and they all testify to the cultural, political, and economic weight of the conversation. It seems as if everyone has an opinion about food.

The global food system is dizzyingly complex, and prone to evoke paralysis or even despair in even the most committed religious "foodies."[2] A grounded practical theology of food requires at least a sketch of some of the major contours of the global food system, including the economics of food production and distribution; the relationship between class and access to fresh, "real" food; trade and labor issues in the global food system; animal welfare; food policy; and the environmental implications of current patterns of production, distribution, and consumption. At every point in this cycle, communities, vulnerable populations, and ecosystems are at risk. Furthermore, policies both exacerbate and ameliorate the effects of the global food system. One might sort these multivalent concerns and many others into four very broad categories—people, places, planet, and policies—in order to describe the developments in and effects of the broad sweep of the global food system. This chapter takes up issues facing persons, communities, and the ecological context, while the next chapter examines the political dimensions of the system.

Of course, these concerns are neither discrete nor easily divided into such categories, but examining each facet of the system, while keeping in view the complex whole, provides the clearest analysis of the system. The task is aided by examining its consequences for individuals and families, for the economic and sociocultural lives of communities, for the ecosystem, and for common political life. From the most intimate of family meals to the around 170 billion dollars U.S. Americans spend on fast food per year, the food system touches every aspect of human life.[3]

PEOPLE

Human life around the world is bound up in the global food system. Clearly, other forms of life—other animals, plants, earth, and air—are also implicated in the complex web that is the food system. Human beings, however, are uniquely implicated and affected at every point in the production, distribution, and consumption of food: from farmers and laborers to shareholders and consumers.

Farmers

The documentary *The Real Dirt on Farmer John* depicts young farmer John Peterson as he watches his family farm auctioned off, one tool at a time, in the early 1980s.[4] He is consumed by a deep and devastating depression, tormented by his sense of shame and failure. But he was not alone. Many middle-income farmers lost farms that had been in their families for generations, accruing massive debts and living the reality of Secretary of Agriculture Earl Butz' motto, "Get big or get out."[5] This philosophy has deeply influenced agriculture policy and practice for the last forty years, emphasizing efficiency, consolidation, and commodification. As a result, over the past half-century, small-scale farmers have struggled to thrive independently; they may have joined up with large-scale operations and begun to grow just one or two crops—like corn and soybeans—not for local sale and consumption, but as "cash crops."[6] Furthermore, even as farmers have turned to income-producing crops, the demands of keeping up with technological advances are quite costly.

In 2010 testimony before the U.S. Senate Agriculture Committee, Secretary of Agriculture Tom Vilsack expressed his concern about the future of farmers in the United States. In particular, he lamented the exodus from rural communities and the decreasing number of young adults entering the farming vocation. Arguing that farmers are as central to our society as teachers and police officers, he asked, "Why not set as a goal for the 2012 Farm Bill the ability to add at least 100,000 additional farmers in the area of the small farming and commercial operations? Why not establish local advisory councils in communities across the country to identify, recruit, encourage, and assist young people to consider a life of farming? . . . [We need] young farmers. The sad reality is that the farming community is aging."[7] It has become increasingly difficult for farmers to make a living pursuing this vocation, and even those who farm cash crops for large-scale corporations find that their debt-to-income ratio quickly becomes unmanageable.

Workers

As much as small-scale farmers are suffering in the United States, migrant workers here—as well as farmers in other countries— suffer even more. In fact, many migrants in high-risk, low-wage, and low-security agriculture jobs here in the United States are in those jobs because they were no longer able to farm their own land in their home countries as a result of unregulated economic globalization.[8]

In any case, the laborers in the processes of production and distribution of food are perhaps the most vulnerable of all persons in the global food system: agricultural workers who do backbreaking work in the heat of summer for substandard wages, workers in packing and processing plants who experience some of the most unsafe labor conditions since Upton Sinclair's *The Jungle*, and workers in the fast-food industry—particularly workers of color— who rarely see wage increases or promotions. In all of these types of work, one finds a large number of migrant workers, many of whom are reluctant to advocate for better wages or conditions for fear of being discovered as undocumented workers.

Agriculture in the United States has always relied on the work of migrant labor. In Edward R. Murrow's historic 1960 news report *Harvest of Shame*, U.S. viewers were confronted with the stories of rural white families from Appalachia and African American families in the mid-twentieth century migrating north as the harvesting season progressed, working the fields in abysmal conditions.[9] On the other side of the country, the agricultural sector in California relied on East Asian and then Mexican immigrants.[10] In 1942 the United States established the formal Bracero Program, sponsoring nearly 4.5 million guest workers from Mexico to support U.S. agriculture. Not quite legal, not quite undocumented, the farmworkers who entered the United States under this program were exceedingly vulnerable: "*Braceros* were used when needed, were under federal authority (but saw only limited intervention by the government regarding conditions on the ground), and were fearful of complaining, given the real possibility of deportation."[11] Now, in the early part of the twenty-first century, U.S. agriculture still relies on largely undocumented migrant farmworkers (about one-third of all agricultural workers), who work under much the same conditions: withheld wages, no breaks, sexual harassment, child labor, and prison-like housing conditions.[12]

It is tragically ironic, furthermore, that agricultural workers are also more than twice as likely as the national average to face food insecurity,[13] a condition in which families report reduced quality, variety, or desirability in their diets and/or disrupted eating patterns and reduced food intake.[14] Due to the necessity of relying on cheap, processed foods, they also report high rates of obesity and diet-related illnesses.[15]

Agricultural workers in our fields are not alone in their vulnerability, however. They are joined by the laborers in food processing and distribution. The documentation of oppressive and unsafe labor conditions in food processing plants is substantial,[16] as is the prevalence of low and sometimes withheld wages in the food service industry.[17] Persons of color, and particularly immigrants, are drastically overrepresented in these high-risk, low-paying jobs.[18]

Shareholders and Corporations

The food system clearly depends on farmers and laborers. As it is currently structured, it also depends upon very large corporations, corporations whose primary accountability is to their shareholders. The effects of the patterns of consolidation, whereby sometimes diffuse components of the food system are integrated and managed by large corporations, in United States agriculture are significant, and can be historically traced to the agricultural and economic developments of the mid-twentieth century.

In 1956 Harvard Business School professor (and former assistant agriculture secretary to President Dwight D. Eisenhower) John H. Davis argued that the clearest way to support farmers and correct food markets and "income anemia" for farmers was to phase out government support of agriculture and strengthen a then-burgeoning sector: agribusiness.[19] Agribusiness, he explained, is "the sum of all farming operations, plus the manufacture and distribution of all farm production supplies, plus the total of all operations performed in connection with the handling, storage, processing, and distribution of farm commodities."[20] Embracing the principles of agribusiness would allow for a more seamless "vertical integration" of the industry, whereby a more integrated relationship between farm production and the mechanisms of processing and distribution, for example, would allow for more efficiencies in the process.[21] Davis' admonitions would prove prescient.

Vertical integration in agribusiness, sometimes to the point of consolidation, is described as having an "hourglass effect" on the food system: a very large number of contract farms produce food that is processed and distributed by a very small number of companies to a very large number of consumers.[22] In August of 2011, for example, Cargill (one of the largest meat processors in the United States) recalled thirty-six million pounds of ground turkey after a major Salmonella outbreak.[23] In a food system in which so many aspects of the food-production process are controlled by a very small number of corporations, a serious outbreak of food-borne illness in just one processing plant can quickly create a very serious and broad public health crisis. Human health, as well as the economic livelihood of millions of farmers and laborers, is deeply bound to this structure.

Although it may be difficult to imagine a corporation as a "person" participating in the global food system, one can make two very important arguments about the personhood of corporations in the global system of food production, distribution, and consumption. First, as reaffirmed (and expanded) by the Supreme Court in 2010, corporations *are* in fact treated as persons under law.[24] It behooves people of conscience, then, to examine what motivations, norms, and outcomes guide the corporation's participation in the food system. Second, corporations are accountable to a specific set of persons—shareholders. In the context of corporate capitalism, food becomes a product for sale in the marketplace, and the profits from the sale benefit not just the farmer, but the shareholders in the corporations responsible for gathering, processing, and distributing the food.[25] This creates a dilemma for stakeholders in the food system, when market success frequently conflicts with economically and environmentally sustainable agriculture, on one hand, and nutritional and health outcomes, on the other.[26] For example, the Institute of Medicine has been studying the effects of food marketing on children and youth for the past several years. The 2005 study, requested by Congress and sponsored by the U.S. Centers for Disease Control, found that "current food and beverage marketing practices put children's long-term health at risk," and made many recommendations across diverse sectors of society to address the problem.[27] In 2011 a progress report indicated that very little progress has been made on these recommendations. This is no surprise: "Food companies cannot stop marketing junk foods to kids because the foods are profitable and their job as publicly traded companies is to grow profits every quarter."[28]

Farmers, laborers, and consumers are disadvantaged by corporations' singular focus on profits. In response, many food system experts, critics, and advocates argue for the necessity of external pressure, whether via public policy or coordinated consumer action.

Consumers

In a food system that places such a high premium on efficiency, cutting costs (even in wages), and increasing reliance on technology, one might expect that consumers would reap benefits from this arrangement. Perhaps they should be able to find more food, in wider varieties, at lower prices, and of more consistent quality. It is true, for example, that consumers in the United States spend, on average, a smaller proportion of their monthly income on food than their grandparents did.[29]

These paradigmatic changes in the system of food production and distribution, however, have not improved access to healthy and nutritious foods for many consumers in the United States and around the world. In many places, food security is tenuous at best. Agricultural workers—the people closest to our food—experience food insecurity at sometimes double the rate of others in the United States. In 2010 almost 15 percent of households in the United States experienced food insecurity (11 percent of households reported food insecurity in 2005). Perhaps more alarming is the fact that more than 21 percent of households with children under the age of six reported food insecurity. Households with children were more than twice as likely as those without children to experience food insecurity.[30] Food insecurity has been exacerbated by the 2008 recession: between 2008 and 2010, the number of households receiving Supplemental Nutrition Assistance Program (SNAP) benefits (food stamps) increased by 46 percent.[31]

A family's economic situation is not the only factor in food security, however. In many cities and rural communities across the United States and around the world, there are whole communities that lack access to fresh, healthy food at an affordable price. These communities are sometimes described as "food deserts."[32] This community phenomenon is described in detail below, but the reality of limited healthy food accessibility is experienced on a very personal level in the family home. Furthermore, many working-class families have little time to prepare healthy meals as they race between jobs and transporting children to school. This reality is made poignantly clear in the film *Food, Inc.* The Gonzales family, with limited resources and even less time, regularly purchases a meal for the family in one of the ubiquitous drive-through fast-food restaurants in their town. As mother Maria Andrea puts it, "Now that I know that the food is really unhealthy for us, I feel guilty giving it to my kids. But we don't have time to cook, because we leave at six. We don't get home until nine, ten at night. When you have only a dollar to spend, and you have two kids to feed, either you go to the market and try to find something that's cheap, or just go straight through a drive-through and get two small hamburgers for them, and 'Okay, here, eat them.' This is what's going to fill her up, not that one single item at the market."[33] Because the cheapest food frequently boasts the highest caloric value alongside the lowest nutritional value, malnourishment and obesity go hand in hand in the United States and, increasingly, other countries.

While families living in communities with limited access to fresh, healthy foods are particularly vulnerable to nutritional deficits, no one is immune to these challenges. The "cheap food" available in all kinds of food outlets is highly processed and nutritionally wanting. Although there are many ways in which this is true, two issues warrant mention here: genetic modification and the abundance of sugar in the U.S. diet. For the last ten years, an increasing proportion of foods purchased in the United States have contained ingredients derived from genetically modified plants. Genetic modification manipulates the DNA of plants to decrease drought vulnerability, increase crop yields, make plants resistant to otherwise devastating herbicides like Roundup, and even enhance cosmetic appearance.[34] Leaving alone, for the moment, the moral issues associated with patenting life forms and the global effects of developing supercrops in the United States that compete with more traditionally cultivated crops in places like Mexico, the presence of genetically modified ingredients in food products presents some anxiety for U.S. consumers.[35] Increasing concerns about what, exactly, they are eating have given rise to consumer initiatives to label food products containing these ingredients.[36]

Aside from concerns about "frankenfoods,"[37] conscious consumers are also raising questions about the high sugar content in many processed foods of the sort available in convenience and liquor stores. Even in supermarkets, 25 percent of the shelves are lined with sugary food products: soft drinks, candy, sugary cereals, juice beverages, and so on.[38] Recent studies correlate consumption of large amounts of fructose, such as the ubiquitous high-fructose corn syrup present in junk foods in the United States, with higher incidence of diabetes and heart disease.[39] Furthermore, high-fructose diets are correlated with obesity and insulin resistance. Consumption of fructose has a particular effect in the brain, as discovered by researchers at Yale University in a neuroimaging study: instead of promoting satiety and suppressing appetite (as with glucose), the ingestion of fructose actually stimulated brain activity associated with appetite.[40]

For consumers who want to know what is in their foods, avoid excessive processing, and limit unhealthy sugars, there is serious cause for concern. Even for the most nutritionally conscious, the food available in markets around the United States leaves many questions unanswered and many health considerations unaddressed. Even programs meant to improve nutrition are vulnerable to these challenges.

The National School Lunch Program (NSLP) was established in 1946 to address childhood nutritional deficiencies. In 2010, 31.8 million children received reduced or free lunches at schools and child-care facilities.[41] For some children, the meals they eat at school (sometimes both breakfast and lunch) are the only meals they eat. The meals subsidized by the program are required to meet federal nutrition standards, including the provision of key nutrients and limitations of calories from fat. Research indicates that while school lunches *do* improve the nutritional quality of children's diets overall, the amount of fat in these meals remains higher than the prescribed limit.[42] There are many challenges in meeting nutritional goals in the school lunch program, and this is in part due to the fact that it serves two "customers": domestic agriculture via commodity crop purchasing, and the school districts in which these products are distributed.[43]

PLACES

Where individuals suffer, whole communities suffer. What families experience in terms of limited resources, constrained options, and compromised health is mirrored in their larger communities, which face economic stress, limited public resources, and the exodus of large segments of their populations. The places in which persons live are at risk in the global food system.

Whole communities are affected by global patterns of food production, distribution, and consumption. Because there are about 922 million acres of farmland in the United States[44] and about 312 million persons living in the United States,[45] it might seem that there should be plenty of good, profitable agricultural work to go around, and an abundance of food to feed communities in rural and urban contexts. Strong and balanced food systems would support rural and urban communities here in the United States and globally. Instead, however, whole communities are struggling with high unemployment and underemployment in the agricultural sector, imbalances of food access in urban areas, and rapidly changing patterns of food production and access in global communities. Many scholars, agencies, and organizations that seek to address these imbalances advocate for "community food security," in which justice and health are sustained at every point, and in every place, in the food system. Community food security addresses, in a comprehensive approach, hunger, nutrition, community self-reliance, and economic health. It is "a prevention-oriented concept that supports the development and enhancement of sustainable, community-based strategies."[46]

Urban Communities

As noted above, in cities and towns across the United States, families with low incomes struggle to gain access to fresh and nutritious food. In addition to experiencing food deserts—a dearth of large or small grocery stores carrying fresh produce, healthy grains, and other nutritious food—these communities frequently also are home to a disproportionate number of fast-food restaurants and convenience and liquor stores.[47] This localized imbalance in urban food systems is frequently found within racially and economically marginalized communities, and is correlated with higher rates of chronic diet-related illness like diabetes and obesity. This presents not only an access problem with regard to nutrition, but also an economic problem in the local community.

One would be mistaken, however, to assume that the entry of a supermarket into a low-income community would solve food-access issues. In some cases, when supermarkets enter neighbor-hoods with limited options, they (perhaps inadvertently) squeeze out smaller, locally owned community outlets. The local economy is compromised, and the culture of the community is affected as well, because large-scale grocery outlets emphasize uniformity and bulk purchasing over cultural specificity: "Moreover, in an age of global retailing industrialization, supermarkets are increas-ingly focused on controlling their own long-distance supply chains and product selections, removing any vestige of the neighborhood-based, locally (and culturally) responsive food outlet."[48]

Finally, urban communities are affected culturally in one more way. With the increase in sales of highly processed, highly pack-aged food products, urban communities have become alienated from the process of food production. Many who have worked in urban gardening initiatives can attest to the expressions of surprise when an urban youth (or adult) first encounters a whole okra fruit or pulls a carrot from the ground. The distance between the con-sumer and the sources of milk and meat products is even greater. Wendell Berry describes this as a spiritual crisis: "These are reli-gious questions, obviously, for our bodies are part of the Creation, and they involve us in all the issues of mystery. But the questions are also agricultural, for no matter how urban our life, our bodies live by farming; we come from the earth and return to it, and so we live in agriculture as we live in flesh. While we live our bodies are moving particles of the earth, joined inextricably both to the soil and to the bodies of other creatures."[49] Alienation in the food system contributes to a number of problems, including a dimin-ished sense of agency and power in one's own life, as well as a cal-lous relationship with those who produce food and experience their own forms of suffering in their rural communities.

Rural Communities

While residents of cities are alienated from the process of food production, they also might imagine the farmlands to be idyllic, pastoral spaces. The reality is quite different. Farmers and farm laborers around the world are under tremendous economic stress. In some contexts, the stress has become so severe that farmers have chosen to commit suicide rather than face the shame of failing in agriculture or plunge their families into further debt.[50] Perhaps most dramatic was the case of Lee Kyung Hae, a Korean farmer who, as an act of political protest, committed suicide outside the 2003 meeting of the World Trade Organization in Cancún.[51] Farmer suicides constitute a social crisis. In India, for example, "These are not only individual tragedies, but social ones. . . . They become tragic ellipses in the struggle of a community. Within rural areas, there's mounting evidence to suggest that the burden of this tragedy is borne unequally. Women carry its brunt. . . . Even after [rare government compensation], rarely is there enough money to put the family back onto any sort of long-term footing. So mothers are pushed by many prongs to the cities, to become domestic workers, construction workers and sometimes sex workers."[52]

Around the world, we are seeing catastrophic effects of the economic pressures faced by farmers. Rural communities are facing "social tragedies," including the exodus of thousands of people from those communities in the United States. Between 2000 and 2008, 18 percent of "metropolitan" counties (with cities or urban areas of more than fifty thousand residents) witnessed population loss, while 56 percent of nonmetropolitan counties witnessed population loss.[53] In testimony before the House Committee on Agriculture, Secretary of Agriculture Tom Vilsack noted that the per capita income in rural communities is $11,000 below that in urban and suburban communities. Agricultural and manufacturing jobs are drying up in rural communities, and "[w]ithout viable employment opportunities, secure healthcare, modern infrastructure, and the growth of new industries, young people are choosing to leave their rural homes in search of jobs and opportunities elsewhere. As a result of these factors, the population of rural America faces significant challenges."[54]

Among these challenges are increased rates of poverty, decreased presence of community resources (such as medical professionals and retail outlets), and diminishing political representation. In legislative bodies determined by population, like the U.S. House of Representatives, declining population means less representation in Washington. Increasingly, the voices of rural Americans are drowned out in U.S. political negotiations.[55]

Global Communities

Globally, urban and rural communities face similar struggles to those faced in the United States, in terms of vocation and labor, economic vulnerability, and access to local and culturally appropriate food. In many parts of the world, the struggles of the farmer, the laborer, and the hungry are exacerbated by patterns of economic globalization. Food can travel great distances in very short periods of time, and foods formerly considered regional specialties are now accessible (and affordable) around the world. In Chicago, Illinois, consumers can trudge through snow-covered streets to purchase imported fresh mangoes, pineapples, and tomatoes in the middle of February. These foods, furthermore, are being produced in new places at lower costs. In fact, sometimes food shipped across seas is actually priced *lower* than food produced down the street.[56]

Globalized food products and distributors are changing the landscape of communities in almost every part of the world, dotting them with the familiar logos of corporate giants like McDonalds, Walmart, and soft drink companies like Coca-Cola and PepsiCo.[57] Multinational corporations are operating in communities around the world, sometimes jeopardizing the stability of local culture, agriculture, and economies.[58] So-called free trade agreements, in which parties commit to lower trade barriers in the interest of participating in global trade, make it very difficult for indigenous farmers to compete. In South Korea, for example, as trade barriers have steadily lowered, national food security has become increasingly dependent upon imports—not local production—and this phenomenon has devastated the farming community there. In 1970 approximately 44.7 percent of the population were farmers. In 2011 farmers make up only 7 percent of the population. Of course, some of this decrease can be attributed to the rapid industrialization in South Korea over the last fifty years, but it remains true that farming has become more and more difficult as global food imports have flooded the market there.[59] Current global economic structures favor production for trade—for export and import—rather than for local consumption.

Many agricultural activists find this shift to producing food for trade to be untenable, even as the shift is meant, in part, to address world hunger. They argue that efforts to establish food security, in which communities around the world have *access* to enough nutritious food, still place poor communities around the world at the mercy of wealthier countries and corporate models of food trade. Instead, a global movement of peasant farmers, largely led by the Vía Campesina network, calls for food sovereignty: " 'the right of each nation to maintain and develop its own capacity to produce its basic foods, respecting cultural and productive capacity,' as well as the 'right of peoples to define their agricultural and food policy.' "[60]

Wherever people live together in communities, they share both the risks and the fruits of the global food system. The brief stories recounted here point to the vulnerability of social groups in urban, rural, and global settings. While deeply troubling, however, the full story of the global food system is only partly seen in its human face. As it is increasingly practiced in many parts of the world, industrial agriculture profoundly affects the ecosystems of which human beings and human communities are a part. The health of agricultural workers is inextricably bound up with the health of the whole ecological spectrum: the very same pesticides and herbicides poisoning farmworkers have severe consequences for the land as well. The same brutalities experienced by chicken plant workers violate the lives of animals slaughtered in industrial farming operations across the United States. Even as communities seek economic and social justice, a thorough analysis of the food system also requires attending to the vulnerability of our planet. The very earth upon which people and communities live, work, and find their sustenance is threatened by these realities as well.

PLANET

Honored in 2012 by the National Endowment for the Humanities as the Jefferson Lecturer, Wendell Berry expressed his concern about our seeming failure to recognize the ways in which human and economic health are dependent upon the health of the land:

Industrialists and industrial economists have assumed, with permission from the rest of us, that land and people can be divorced without harm. If farmers come under adversity from high costs and low prices, then they must either increase their demands upon the land and decrease their care for it, or they must sell out and move to town, and this is supposed to involve no ecological or economic or social cost. . . . But land abuse *cannot* brighten the human prospect. There is in fact no distinction between the fate of the land and the fate of the people. When one is abused, the other suffers.[61]

Just as human beings and their urban, rural, and global communities are vulnerable in this global food system, so too is the earth. It is the first place, the place upon which all social places—communities, cities, small towns, and farmlands—depend. It is appropriate, then, to assess the health of the core place that sustains our food production, distribution, and consumption. People of conscience must consider, from time to time, how the global food system affects not only persons and human communities, but also the earth and all of the creatures that depend on its health. To do so is to broaden conceptions of "community," the circle of life in which human beings belong and to which they bear obligation.[62] In other words, humans belong to not only social communities, but also the land, in its deepest, most interdependent sense.[63] And yet, even those human beings who most long for a felt sense of relationship to the land find themselves alienated from it.

The film *Food, Inc.* opens with a very simple and yet stark claim—the ways in which consumers imagine or construct the pastoral farm in the United States bear little or no resemblance to the reality of farming in this country. Images on the packaging food products aid in this construction of the "rural": green rolling hills, a lone (and contented) cow, a simple red barn in the distance. The sanitized portrait of the countryside stands in stark contrast to the mechanized, large-scale, and forceful way in which agriculture is actually practiced in this age. Some assumed that agricultural advances and consolidation, managed by agribusiness, would benefit farmers, who could more seamlessly avail themselves of the seemingly unlimited benefits of research and technology to exert more control over the land: "We have improved livestock and plant characteristics, perfected insecticides, found ways of stimulating the growth of desired plants and retarding the growth of weeds, found better ways of managing soil, developed disease- and drought-resistant plants—the list could be extended almost without limit."[64]

Of course, sixty years later, exuberance over the promise of these technical "advancements" in agriculture is far more measured, to say the least. While many factors threaten environmental sustainability, the ways in which food is produced, distributed, and consumed are increasingly significant factors in the ecological crisis. As Michael Pollan wrote in his open letter to the soon-to-be-elected "Farmer in Chief," "After cars, the food system uses more fossil fuel than any other sector of the economy—19 percent. And while the experts disagree about the exact amount, the way we feed ourselves contributes more greenhouse gases to the atmosphere than anything else we do—as much as 37 percent, according to one study."[65] The ecological effects of industrialized agricultural practices might even be traced to the appearance, thousands of years ago, of the simple, oft-heralded plow, which allows human beings the power of literally "turning of the earth upside down."[66] In contrast with the modest plow, however, the contemporary agricultural practices that have developed since the mid-twentieth century are stunningly powerful and reflect humanity's seemingly unlimited capacity to manipulate the earth's resources.

Three of the major developments in agriculture that have had serious effects on the environment are the commodification of food and agriculture, the industrialization of agricultural practices, and mass food transport.[67] Some of these developments were introduced above, but here are examined according to their environmental effects.

Commodification of Food and Agriculture

When food is conceived as a product to be bought and sold, it becomes a commodity valued according to criteria such as price and convenience. This kind of calculus is in contrast with the lost days in which people ate what was grown near them, by farmers they knew, with methods that they understood, in a shared community context. The commodification of food is a serious challenge to understanding eating as a faithful expression of gratitude for and relationship to the earth and the food it produces: "the food many people eat is now purchased at a grocery store that imports its food from far away. . . . To receive food as a commodity means that a consumer's understanding and appreciation for the many social and ecological elements feeding into the food are fairly shallow. . . . This narrowing of a food imagination often leads to a narrowing of sympathies and care (for fields and farmers, for instance)."[68]

Commodification, however, is characterized not only by how those who eat understand their relationship to food. It also is characterized by how those who produce food understand their work. It affects the criteria governing the choices farmers make about best practices, production goals, and the communities in which the food they produce is consumed. The answer to these questions, in a commodified food system, frequently is reduced to the criteria of profitability and expanding the market. Here again, the agribusiness proposal put forward by John Davis in 1956 proves prescient. While many farmers would need to be helped in finding other kinds of work if they could not keep up with the pace of agricultural change, those who remained in farming would need to embrace agribusiness and the accompanying emphasis on mass production agricultural "commodities": "For those who elect to remain full time in agriculture and who give promise of success, we should concentrate on helping them to increase the size of their farms and to catch up with progress in terms of technical and managerial know-how."[69]

In a commodified agriculture model fixated on the profit motive, the producers and distributors of food must seek to provide the largest quantity of product that the market can bear, in the most efficient manner possible (i.e., lowered operating costs). The land and all of its living creatures, too, are understood differently in this model. They become "natural resources," from which humans extract goods that have monetary value. When the land is construed as a natural resource, or as a repository of resources, its conservation is in the interest of preserving more resources for humans' use. When animals are construed as natural resources, respect for their lives and well-being is secondary to their value as livestock, breeders, and dairy producers. The work of nurturing and cultivating a diverse and thriving ecosystem is understood instrumentally, insofar as the work enhances the ecosystem's capacity to yield more resources for human use and profit.

In this context, the commodification of food and agriculture has meant that ecological concerns are, at best, secondary to perceived economic concerns. Berry's admonitions to the contrary aside, farmers (and the corporations to whom they sell) are under economic pressure to produce as much (of the most profitable goods) as possible, as efficiently as possible. The effects of this pressure are many, but include an increasingly narrow spectrum of crops and an increasing burden on the soil.

The shift of agriculture from the production of food for local consumption to the production of commodities for sale has assumed an ever-expanding global market. It also has been built on an elaborate system of government programs, such as the Farm Bill, that have valued the production of just a few crops easily transported internationally.[70] Many farmers produce "commodity crops," often to sell to one of the agricultural consolidating giants like Cargill, Monsanto, or Archer Daniels Midland (ADM). Commodity crops assure the farmer (and the consolidator) at least some stability of income in the form of commodity payments from the USDA. They may choose to focus on one or two of these commodity crops, like corn and soybeans, utilizing industrial farming techniques including soil fertilization, herbicides, and pesticides.[71] For a farmer who depends on cash crops and high production yields for an already meager income, the financial risk of allowing the land to lie fallow for a year is just too great, as is the practice of leaving some land unfarmed at all times. The land has no rest. The commodification of food and agriculture has given rise to ever-increasing industrialization of farming practices.

Industrialization of Agriculture

In the film *Food, Inc.*, poultry farmer Vince Edwards describes what he considers to the be positive effects of farming for a corporate food company (Tyson): "[I]t's all a science. They got it figured out. . . . If you could grow a chicken in forty-nine days, why would you want one you gotta grow in three months? More money in your pocket."[72] Edwards' invocation of the themes of profitability and efficiency in farming exemplify the commodification of agriculture. The science and the calculus of "growing" (rather than raising) chickens also point to the ways in which the commodification of agriculture has issued in, reinforced, and been supported by another major change: the industrialization of agriculture.[73]

Industrialization has been changing the face of farming for the last century, beginning with large-scale wheat farming operations in California.[74] As early as 1929, agricultural economist Frank App was calling for the evolution of agriculture, from a "primitive" model, in which farming is confined to what the human farmer can do within the limits of the land being farmed, to an "industrial" model, which recruits capital and "nonfarm inputs" to increase and make more efficient the yield of the land.[75] Nonfarm inputs include skilled labor, fertilizers, pesticides and herbicides, feed for livestock (produced elsewhere), and machinery and technology. During and following the "Green Revolution" of the 1950s, organizations and aid agencies exported this way of farming around the world in an effort to increase production yields.[76] Advocates hailed these efforts to harness the power of technology as a "techno-political strategy for peace, through the creation of abundance by breaking out of nature's limits and variabilities."[77] These technological changes, accompanying the commodification of food, led to major shifts in agriculture, including a shift from growing food for local consumption to growing food for export. This form of agriculture has come to be termed "conventional" agriculture, but in reality, these practices have been the "convention" only for the last fifty to eighty years or so in the United States.[78] And the new convention presents major environmental challenges.

On many conventional farms, the use of chemicals, technology, and other manipulations of the environment enables farmers to focus on just one crop or one kind of livestock, and on a massive scale. In the 1950s farmers were already purchasing greater proportions of their farming supplies from business outlets, which were using emerging research to develop newer and more powerful products.[79] These techniques, while in some ways efficient, are in other ways highly inefficient and threaten the health of animals, the soil, biodiversity, and public health. Before industrialization and commodification made it possible (and indeed, desirable) to focus so narrowly on one agricultural product, farms grew vegetables and grains and raised livestock on a smaller scale. Farming has evolved from simple elegance to complex problem solving, laments Wendell Berry: "to take animals off farms and put them on feedlots is to take an elegant solution—animals replenishing the fertility that crops deplete—and neatly divide it into two problems: a fertility problem on the farm and a pollution problem on the feedlot. The former problem is remedied with fossil-fuel fertilizer; the latter is remedied not at all."[80]

In an agricultural context in which corn is one of the most reliably predictable and profitable crops, for example, many farmers have turned to corn production as a means to secure a more predictable and stable income. But when land is farmed for only one crop (and frequently only one variety of one crop[81]), season after season, the practice of monocropping strips the land of key nutrients and makes the crops, over the long term, vulnerable to any number of threats. In turn, this vulnerability requires the use of both chemical fertilizers and pesticides. Recognizing the risks of monocropping, many farmers now practice dual rotation, farming both corn and soybeans. Even with two crops, however, the soil requires artificial sources of nitrogen, via chemical fertilizers, to stay healthy. And without less profitable cover crops like grass and alfalfa, soil erosion is a real threat to long-term agricultural future, a problem exacerbated by severe storms. Soil erosion also threatens water quality, as runoff from conventionally farmed land carries fertilizers, pesticides, and herbicides into the water supply.[82]

In some ways, focusing on one or two crops is far simpler and more efficient than more diverse modes of farming, making larger-scale agriculture possible. With the advantages of technology and fewer tasks that demand human attention, farms can grow exponentially. Davis saw this as primarily a good thing for farmers, although he grossly underestimated the massive agricultural consolidation that we have seen over the past thirty years or so: "There may be a few phases of agriculture in which corporate farming will show an advantage over the family farm—particularly phases which require large investment for development or large space for economical use of equipment. However, there is little reason to believe this trend will become pronounced."[83] But corporate mega-farms *have* become the main producers of the food we eat, and bigger is not always better. Large-scale crop farming presents challenges with regard to soil health and threats to biodiversity. It is a far cry from biodynamic farming, in which a farm is treated as a self-sustaining living organism, free of most external manipulations, particularly products like synthetic pesticides and fertilizers.[84]

The case is perhaps even more pronounced when it comes to livestock farming. Take the case of hog farming in North Carolina, for example. As the tobacco industry was shrinking in the state, some economically stressed farmers—many of them African American, in the eastern part of the state—turned to industrial hog farming, forgoing the tradition of small and midscale independent farming that had characterized North Carolina agriculture. The development of concentrated animal feeding operations (CAFOs) in the 1980s, and their rapid expansion in the 1990s, introduced major ecological challenges previously unknown. CAFOs confine sometimes tens of thousands of animals in very close quarters for the production of milk, eggs, and meat products. Keeping large numbers of animals confined to small spaces raises both animal welfare and environmental concerns.[85] For example, the animals are fed in their confinement structures, "rather than the animals grazing or otherwise seeking feed in pastures, fields, or on rangeland."[86] In terms of environmental and public health effects, CAFOs must process solid and liquid animal waste in euphemistically named "lagoons," which are constructed and monitored according to EPA regulations. Reported incidents of lagoon collapses, however, present environmental and public health challenges, when millions of gallons of animal waste flood into nearby rivers and other bodies of water, contaminating the water supply.[87]

Along with these major spills, animal waste can enter water supply through small leaks, through runoff from excess precipitation, and from the wheels of farm equipment. The waste also contains pharmaceuticals given to the animals in order to prevent the infections that could spread in such confined quarters.[88] Apart from the major events that introduce contaminants into the water supply, studies have reported public health problems in the communities near large CAFOs, including asthma, allergies, pesticide poisoning, digestive problems, headaches, depression, and confusion.[89]

The rates of meat consumption have risen not only in the United States but in other parts of the world, too, raising the demand for animal products produced as cheaply as possible.

This consumer demand means that livestock farming has become progressively more inhumane and environmentally destructive. Industrial livestock farming, meeting the demand of increased meat consumption, contributes high levels of methane gas to the environment, the concentration of which is reported to have doubled in the last two hundred years. Methane gas plays a major role (more potent than carbon dioxide) in the trapping of heat in the atmosphere, and thus is a sometimes-overlooked factor in the debates over human causation of climate change.[90] Combined with the energy-intensive practices required to produce crops and raise livestock in industrial agriculture, Michael Pollan argues, this means that "when we eat from the industrial-food system, we are eating oil and spewing greenhouse gases."[91]

Mass Food Transport

Pollan's indictment that "we are eating oil" refers to the use of petroleum-based inputs in the agricultural system, such as fertilizers and the use of fossil-fuel-burning farm equipment. It also refers, however, to the environmental impact of what has been described as "food miles": the distance food travels from where it is produced or raised to the consumer. Since the late 1960s, the food miles for produce have been, in some cases, more than fifteen hundred miles.[92] In more recent years, in part thanks to trade agreements, produce shipped internationally has increased dramatically.[93] Although a relatively smaller proportion of industrial agriculture's carbon footprint, the practice of transporting large quantities of fresh produce over hundreds, even thousands, of miles indeed carries an environmental impact. It also complicates the picture of what constitutes sustainable agriculture: consumers must weigh the relative impact of eating an organically produced apple shipped fifteen hundred miles against that of eating a conventionally produced apple grown closer to home. Aside from the calculus of food miles, the mass transport of food has other environmental implications as well. In the last fifty years, food has increasingly been produced with the goals of "transportability, long store and counter shelf life, and uniformity of appearance."[94] The movement of food over great distances, along with the expansion of time and space between farm and table, requires more elaborate food preservation and packaging strategies. Discoveries of uses for polyethylene and polyvinyl chloride during World War II transformed the production and distribution of food, introducing into the food system "[p]lastic tubs, polyethylene jugs, all-aluminum cans, polyethylene-coated cartons, laminated plastic tubs, and plastic-foam cartons."[95] Both the production and the disposal of these materials present environmental challenges.

Emphases on convenience, efficiency, and scale in the global system of food production, distribution, and consumption have implications for the health of not only humanity and human communities but the earth as well. At every point in the global food system, human persons, communities, and the planet are suffering. Farmers struggle to pursue their vocations. Laborers work in dangerous and economically vulnerable jobs and face exploitation. Consumers struggle to find and pay for nutritious food. More broadly speaking, the places in which these individuals live are suffering, too: whole communities in rural, urban, and global contexts are struggling with population shifts, economic instability, food security, and alienation from the sources of food. Agricultural efforts to keep up with economic challenges and patterns of industrialization threaten animal welfare and put at risk the health of the soil, water, and air.

The human, social, and environmental costs of the global food system are great, and are disproportionately borne by the most vulnerable members of our society. Its effects on persons, places, and the planet are neither wholly market driven nor occur by simple happenstance, however. An analysis of some of the major policy arenas, from local ordinances to international trade agreements, reveals the ways in which they shape contemporary patterns of food production, distribution, and consumption.

CHAPTER TWO

Primer on the Global Food System
Policies

The vulnerabilities within the global patterns of food production, distribution, and consumption might be attributed to factors such as shifting levels of supply and demand, technology and the prioritization of efficiency, commodification and profit motives, human choice, migrations of people and communities, and so forth. Certainly, the global food system is dizzyingly complex, and discerning points of entry and faithful responses remains a deep challenge to people of faith. The complexity cannot, however, be wholly attributed to fickle markets, human greed, amoral technologies, or devastating shifts in population and industry.

All of the changes in agriculture, which have increased with mind-boggling speed over the past fifty years, have been accompanied, exacerbated, and complicated by constellations of policies on the local, state, federal, and international level. A "primer on the global food system" would be incomplete if it did not introduce at least some of the major policy developments affecting people, places, and the planet. The pages that follow examine the food implications of the policy priority of "cheap food" and farm bill and trade policy, and conclude with some comments on other smaller policy arenas.

"CHEAP FOOD"

A primary motivation for agricultural commodification and industrialization is ongoing demand for "cheap food." When the USDA began keeping statistics on food spending in the United States in 1929, families spent just above 23 percent of their disposable income on food (both groceries to be prepared at home and food purchased and consumed outside the home). In 2010 families spent on average just over 9 percent of their disposable income on food.[1] Poor people, however, necessarily spend a higher proportion of their income on food. In the United States, that proportion is as high as 20 percent.[2]

Just the same, many relish "boasting" about how little they spend on food.[3] Since the days of Agriculture Secretary Earl Butz in the 1970s, U.S. farmers have been encouraged, through policy changes, to shift to commodity crops, and in large quantities. These cheap commodity crops have played a significant role in lowering the cost of food: from grains to snack foods to meat and dairy products.[4] The food is deceptively and artificially "cheap," however, and the costs of this way of producing and distributing food are shifted to low-income workers, the ecosystem, and the health-care system.[5] A recent study, for example, suggests that analysis of the obesity epidemic in the United States should at least take into account the *kind* of calories found in "cheap food," namely calorie-dense and nutritionally deficient foods.[6] While the cost of fresh fruits and vegetable has risen, the cost of junk foods has decreased since 1985.[7] In the same time span, the daily diet of the average U.S. American has increased by 400 calories.[8]

THE FARM BILL

For any person committed to understanding the complexities of the global food system, a first stop in policy analysis is what is often called, in shorthand, the Farm Bill. "Farm Bill," however, is somewhat of a misnomer, in that the complex and unwieldy legislation includes everything from Supplemental Nutrition Assistance Program (SNAP), known in the past as food stamps, to international food aid. The more accurate, but not as easily remembered, official name for the legislation was the Food, Conservation, and Energy Act of 2008, and the working title for the Senate bill in 2012 was the Agriculture Reform, Food, and Jobs Act.[9] In recent years, public attention to the Farm Bill has surged as the expansiveness, cost, and relevance of the bill have become clearer to its stakeholders, a surprisingly broad constituency. Mistakenly considered to be innocuous, quaint legislation that affects and protects only farmers, the Farm Bill, in short, touches every person who produces, sells, prepares, and eats food in the United States (and many people who do these tasks in other countries, as well). The cost, variety, safety, and nutritional value of food are directly related to the structures of the Farm Bill, as are the environmental, social, and economic conditions under which it is produced and distributed. An interested follower of food policy debates, however, may find herself immediately frustrated when she tries to understand firsthand the exact contents and implications of the Farm Bill. The statute includes fifteen separate titles and at least as many discrete policy arenas, and it is virtually impossible for even an educated, well-informed reader to understand all eighteen hundred pages of specialist language and complex formulae. Although the pages that follow will do little to mitigate these complexities, they present some major patterns in the global food system, introduced above, that are of particular relevance in Farm Bill negotiations. First, however, a brief historical summary of the Farm Bill and survey of its landscape.

Farm Bill History and Scope

The original Agricultural Adjustment Act of 1933 was born during the farm crisis of the 1930s as an emergency measure to stave off farm foreclosures and support farmer income as food prices fluctuated wildly. The legislation tried to address market imbalances with regulation and price supports, and to address hunger through nutrition programs. By 1948, however, these emergency measures had become more permanent. Between the 1950s and the 1970s, aggressive efforts to broaden the global market for agriculture shifted the emphases of the Farm Bill to expanding foreign markets and large-scale production for export. These changes have progressively advantaged large agribusiness corporations over small and midscale farmers.[10] In fact, advocacy groups increasingly express concern about the leverage wielded by agribusiness giants in the drafting and discussion of Farm Bill legislation, and the diffusion of other, smaller groups that sometimes work at odds with one another.

With fifteen titles addressing discrete policy arenas, and a political climate that is rather hostile toward government spending, it is easy to see how groups that could collaborate sometimes find themselves in conflict. The piece of the pie allocated to everything *except* nutritional assistance (SNAP), commodities payments, and crop insurance is a mere 10 percent of the $289 billion bill.[11] This results in the perception, for example, that soil conservation programs come at the expense of programs to support underrepresented farmers. Recent efforts to establish more broad-based coalitions—addressing alternative and small-scale agriculture, community development, antihunger initiatives, environmental stewardship, labor, and other issues—have achieved some successes but struggle to develop a coherent food policy that is just for all.[12] It is clear, however, that precisely this kind of collaboration is needed to formulate a different comprehensive vision for agriculture and food in the United States. Furthermore, advocacy and policy analysis groups argue that the Farm Bill cannot, and should not, be the only mechanism leveraged to achieve a fair and sustainable food system. It does not address, for example, the treatment of workers, the increasing cost and concentration in ownership of agricultural land, animal welfare, or the increasing corporate control of the global food marketplace.[13]

On the other hand, the Farm Bill addresses many important issues of concern for people of faith who hope for a just food system. Among the many issues of concern are the government payment of commodity subsidies and crop insurance premiums, nutrition assistance programs, initiatives to support underrepresented (based on age, race, and gender) and small-scale farmers, and sustainable agriculture initiatives.

Commodity Payments and Crop Insurance Assistance

The 2008 Farm Bill allocated about $47 billion in government spending over five years to direct income support and loss mitigation.[14] Each time Congress renews and updates the Farm Bill, even ostensibly temporary measures to support farmers are reinscribed as permanent fixtures in the law.[15] The result is that the statutes now contained in Title I (Commodity Programs) and Title XII

(Crop Insurance and Disaster Assistance Programs) are incredibly complex, involving payments for what is being grown, what was formerly grown, and what is not being grown.[16] The intent of these financial supports is to provide economic stability to farmers in case of market fluctuations, in the form of commodity payments, and major financial loss due to disaster, in the form of crop insurance.[17] In the current U.S. food system, however, they have far more extensive reach than that. While one might think of these programs as a means to support poor farmers, in practice small and midscale farmers benefit very little from these payments, and in the long run, the food system (including farmers) may suffer.

Title I of the 2008 Farm Bill lists the following as commodity crops, eligible for direct (per bushel) and countercyclical (variance between expected price and actual market price) payments: "wheat, corn, grain sorghum, barley, oats, upland cotton, long grain rice, medium grain rice, pulse crops, soybeans, and other oilseeds."[18] Because commodity payments are made for only a narrow range of crops, many farmers are simply unable to take the risk of farming diverse crops.[19] In fact, farm policy has *penalized* farmers participating in commodity programs who plant noncommodity crops on the acreage enrolled in the commodity program. In the 2008 bill, a pilot program introduced some planting flexibility in a few states, allowing commodity farmers to farm a few other crops.[20] In the past, growers of specialty crops have opposed planting flexibility for commodity farmers, for fear that subsidized commodity farmers would easily undersell them in the marketplace. The 2008 Farm Bill included a new title for Horticulture and Organic Agriculture, which, among other things, allocates $1 billion over ten years to block grants for farmers of specialty crops.[21] The need to protect vulnerable smaller-scale produce farmers and the need to encourage more crop diversity within large-scale commodity-focused farming operations will require a delicate balancing act in the years to come.

It is not, however, only an issue of *which* crops are most heavily supported by the Farm Bill, but also an issue of *where and with whom* these supports are concentrated. Contrary to popular imagination, today's commodity payments tend to be concentrated among a relatively small number of large-scale farms and processors, rather than serving as a broad safety net for all farmers. Because commodity payments are calculated per acre, they have contributed to the concentration of crop production among the larger farms in the United States.[22] In an ironic twist on John H. Davis' 1956 proposals for strengthening agribusiness, major government spending persists, and most benefits the largest of the agribusiness corporations.[23] Furthermore, a loophole in current farm policy enables some operations to receive hundreds of thousands—even millions—of dollars in farm supports, as entities very loosely related to the day-to-day farm operations sometimes collect subsidy payments. Legislators could make one singular change to the Farm Bill that would significantly serve the interests of small and midsize farms: develop a clearer definition of what constitutes "active management" in farming. This clarity would help close the loophole that allows for these duplicate payments to mega-farms.[24] "It's one thing to support a family farmer. It's quite another to subsidize the expansion of a mega-farm operation that puts family farmers out of business," laments Farm Bill activist Daniel Imhoff.[25]

Finally, commodities payments and crop insurance supports contribute to what many have described as artificially cheap food. In some cases, food is sold for less than what it costs to produce, in part thanks to the preponderance of subsidized corn.[26] This is particularly true with regard to highly processed junk food, which is heavily dependent on corn. One can find corn in most high-calorie, low-nutrient foods. The most obvious examples are soft drinks (in the form of high-fructose corn syrup) and corn chips (processed cornmeal), but corn makes surprising appearances as a thickening agent, filler, and cooking oil used in the preparation of many cheap snack and fast foods.[27] While there are disagreements about how much subsidized corn affects meat prices, it is true that almost half of the corn grown in the United States is grown for cheap livestock feed, used in most CAFO operations.[28]

All of these issues raise questions about the production of real food in the United States, and whether the Farm Bill adequately addresses issues of hunger and nutrition. Alongside these considerations of what kind of food is produced in the United States and on what scale, the Farm Bill also addresses hunger and food security directly in its nutrition titles.

Nutrition Programs

Critics of "big agriculture" might be surprised to learn that the bulk of the Farm Bill expense is allocated not to commodity payments or crop insurance, but to nutrition assistance. The nutrition title of the Farm Bill includes SNAP benefits, food programs for schools and child-care facilities, and the special nutritional assistance offered through the Women, Infants, and Children (WIC) program.[29] In 2011 almost one in six U.S. Americans received SNAP benefits. Formerly known as the Food Stamp program, SNAP costs $75 billion per year.[30] Food stamps were introduced in New Deal programs and signed into law during the antipoverty legislative climate of the 1960s.[31]

Over the years, debates have emerged around the effectiveness and regulations of food assistance programs.[32] For example, in the 2012 Republican presidential primary season, former House Speaker Newt Gingrich repeatedly called Barack Obama the "Food Stamp president." Gingrich defended this claim: "more people have been put on food stamps by Barack Obama than any president in history."[33] Aside from critiques of the program, even its supporters sometimes find themselves in disagreement. For example, from time to time, antihunger and nutrition advocates disagree on how SNAP benefits can be spent.[34] Currently, SNAP benefits may not be spent on hot, prepared foods (even healthy vegan cuisine), but may be spent on potato chips or soft drinks. Increasingly, however, SNAP benefits are accepted and spent at local farmers markets.[35] One nonprofit organization, Wholesome Wave Foundation, offers grants for farmers markets to double the value of customers' SNAP benefits when purchasing fresh produce. At markets participating in the Double Value Coupon Program, the amount of SNAP benefits spent almost doubled between 2010 and 2011, from $1 million to $1.89 million, as customers were realizing more value for each SNAP dollar.[36] In a context in which the economic interests of farmers and consumers are sometimes in tension, this kind of initiative addresses the economic vulnerability of both, and offers an opportunity to establish relationships of mutual support.

Making Farming Possible for Vulnerable Groups

In 2010 USDA official Shirley Sherrod was asked to resign her position after video surfaced of a speech she delivered to the Georgia NAACP, in which she described a situation when she had wrestled with whether or not to help a white farmer who was struggling to keep his farm: "I was struggling with the fact that so many black people had lost their farmland, and here I was faced with having to help a white person save their land."[37] Conservative pundits immediately seized upon this supposed confession of bias. The real story that Sherrod was trying to tell, however, is how her work with the farmer, Roger Spooner, helped her to see how poor white farmers also have struggled to stay afloat in the midst of huge shifts in agriculture, and how wealthier groups (and, one might argue, powerful corporations) benefit from one vulnerable group being pitted against another.[38] "It's about the poor," she said. "It made me see it really was about those who have, versus those who don't . . . black, white or Hispanic."[39] Sherrod's frank comments expressed her own developing realization that most small and midscale farmers are economically vulnerable in the contemporary landscape of U.S. agriculture.

It is true, however, that some small and midscale farmers have struggled in greater proportion than others. There are many reasons for this, from outright discrimination to more complex structural barriers.[40] Women and farmers of color have historically struggled to gain access to federal resources extended in the Farm Bill. When applying for USDA loans, black farmers have been denied and delayed at higher rates, and received lower award amounts, than white farmers. Furthermore, historically, Latinos, Asian Americans, African Americans, and even Native Americans have been denied land ownership.[41]

Aside from outright discrimination, farmers from traditionally underrepresented groups face social and structural barriers to establishing economic security through farming. As African Americans moved away from the rural south in the Great Migration, they lost their agricultural roots.[42] As small-scale farming has become less and less sustainable as a vocation, fewer young adults have grown up in the farming culture, their families having left rural communities for more economic stability in urban areas.[43] As a result, many farmers from underrepresented groups who yearn to make a life in farming may lack the familial or cultural memory to do so.[44] But farm and food policy itself also implicitly discourages the most vulnerable farmers. For example, the crops that African Americans and Native Americans grow are more likely to be fresh produce distributed locally, rather than subsidy-eligible commodity crops for export. Even where they are eligible for Farm Bill support, beginning and socially disadvantaged farmers struggle to access those funds. While large farms and agribusiness operations may have the legal and professional resources to identify funding opportunities and write successful loan and grant proposals, a single family trying to make its way in agriculture has neither the time nor the expertise for this kind of work.[45]

The 2008 Farm Bill includes provisions for addressing the disadvantages facing farmers of color, women, and young adults. Advocacy groups hope that these initiatives will be strengthened in the 2012 bill. For example, the 2008 bill created the Office of Advocacy and Outreach, whose mission "is to improve access to programs . . . [and] the viability and profitability of small farms and ranches, beginning farmers or ranchers, and socially disadvantaged farmers or ranchers."[46] In the 2008 bill, programs for beginning farmers and ranchers were funded at $75 million, and programs for disadvantaged farmers were also funded at $75 million.[47] These are important steps. However, when one considers the relative proportion of this funding, it is a drop in the bucket. Commodities and crop insurance subsidies (which are limited to particular crops) dwarf these supports for the most vulnerable, small-scale farmers.[48] Those programs make up almost two-thirds of the budget not allocated to the nutrition title, while programs for beginning and disadvantaged farmers make up less than 1 percent.

Organic and Sustainable Agricultural Initiatives

As noted above, many beginning and disadvantaged farmers are not eligible for commodity or crop insurance subsidies because those funds are mostly reserved for particular crops.[49] In fact, a farmer who grows produce like tomatoes, carrots, and cucumbers grows "specialty crops," according to the Farm Bill.[50] The Institute for Agriculture and Trade Policy writes, "Existing Farm Bill programs are designed primarily for commodity production in the form of subsidies, research, crop insurance, and other risk-management programs. Similar programs are not available to small and mid-sized growers of fruit and vegetables and other, so-called 'specialty crops.' "[51] In a commodified agricultural context, and when commodity payments are reserved for particular crops, a farmer takes significant economic risks when he or she chooses to grow fruit or vegetables instead of corn or soybeans.

This is not to say, however, that there are no programs in the Farm Bill to support small and midsize farmers who want to grow produce, cultivate biodiversity, and otherwise engage in organic and sustainable agriculture. For example, the 2008 bill included, for the first time, a title on horticulture and organic agriculture.[52] Through that title's provisions, states could apply for block grants to support projects related to "specialty crops." The block grant program is funded at a rate of $55 million per year, more than initiatives for beginning and socially disadvantaged farmers and ranchers, but still a fraction of the supports extended via commodity payments and crop insurance supports.[53] The Farm Bill also contains a separate conservation title, including provisions for addressing soil quality and wetlands preservation in conventional farming operations.[54] The conservation title also includes the Environmental Quality Incentives Program (EQIP), which provides technical assistance and incentive payments to help farmers with environmental and conservation improvements. In 2008, for the first time, these funds were made available to farmers who transition to organic farming methods.[55] Unfortunately, despite its categorization as "mandatory funding," the amount appropriated for this title has been cut by nearly $3 billion since 2008.[56]

The Farm Bill contains many, many more provisions that affect the production, distribution, and consumption of food. This admittedly cursory glance at some of its major provisions relating to the domestic and global food system must be augmented, however, by at least some attention to the global effects of food and farm policy, which are intensified by contemporary "free trade" agreements.

FREE TRADE AGREEMENTS

The international trading of food is not new. In fact, one can trace it back centuries, to its role in patterns of colonization, imperialism, and the transatlantic slave trade. The increasing desire for salt and luxury spices, particularly among the elite, contributed to European military and political interventions to protect that trade in Asia and Africa.[57] The rapidity and complexity of global food trade, however, *is* new. Since 1994, the United States has entered into free trade agreements with eighteen countries.[58] These free trade agreements rest on the philosophical assumption that reducing restrictions on international trade will improve the economic situation of the people of participating countries. Global consumers, especially, should benefit from prices lowered by market competition. In reality, however, many factors complicate these anticipated outcomes. "Free trade" is perhaps a misnomer, in that the stipulations of these agreements frequently benefit a very small segment of the players in the global food system, threaten the livelihood of farmers and agricultural workers in a variety of contexts, and disrupt local and regional food systems. It is not necessary, however, to assume "a 'grand conspiracy' among agribusiness firms or governments to deliberately impoverish farmers or ruin domestic food markets in developing nations."[59] All the same, even unintended consequences of contemporary patterns of agricultural trade cry out for careful and critical analysis.

Transnational companies have played a large role in shaping agricultural trade policy, even as these policies have ostensibly been "in the interests of farmers," helping them to expand their markets.[60] As transnational corporations have emerged in the globalizing economy and are increasingly able to move capital and operations across borders, they also have gained a weightier voice in trade agreements.[61] Assumptions that free trade agreements would benefit small and midscale farmers or consumers simply must be questioned, given the drastic reductions in agricultural work and increases in poverty since the first free trade agreement entered into force less than twenty years ago. That first agreement was the North American Free Trade Agreement (NAFTA), and it is instructive in two very broad areas, here briefly addressed: the impact of free trade agreements on the agricultural sectors in developing countries, and the disruption of patterns of local food distribution and availability.[62]

Generally speaking, when a state enters into a free trade agreement, it concedes that the agreement will take precedence over domestic laws that may interfere with the trade liberalization process.[63] This is particularly true when it comes to the case of Mexico, in which two (among many) programs that have been eliminated in the process of implementing NAFTA are government support for poor farmers and subsidies for consumers.

After NAFTA was implemented, corn farmers in Mexico suddenly had to compete with very cheap (subsidized) corn coming from the United States. Within *one* year of NAFTA's passage, Mexican corn production fell by 50 percent.[64] Particularly for farmers who worked in *ejidos*, which were cooperative organizations on government-owned land, the elimination of government supports spelled the end of the farming life.[65] This exodus from rural agricultural life has contributed significantly to immigration in the United States, as former farmers move first to cities and then to the border regions to seek manufacturing and other kinds of jobs, and finally across the border to find agricultural jobs in the United States.

If farmers struggle under NAFTA, it would seem that consumers should benefit. Where farmers earn less for what they produce, one might assume that consumers would also be paying less. In fact, however, this has not come to be. Mexicans are now paying more for food generally, because while inputs into the food system are bought at the lowest cost (driving down corn prices and threatening the economic security of Mexican farmers), the products are sold at the highest price, now set in an international market.[66] In the tortilla crisis of 2007, prices for tortillas rose dramatically, in some places increasing threefold.[67] In part, the dramatic inflation of tortilla prices is also due to a policy change resulting from the implementation of NAFTA: price controls for tortillas. Price controls had kept tortillas, the nutritional and cultural heart of the Mexican diet, at an affordable price. In 1999 the price controls were eliminated and by 2007, a Mexican minimum-wage worker might spend a full third of her daily wages on tortillas.[68]

While the price of tortillas has been on the rise, other foods have become cheaper. Highly processed, heavily sweetened foods and beverages have flooded the market under NAFTA. While tortillas now cost twelve pesos per kilogram, some are turning to cheaper, less nutritionally dense products, such as noodles, as a substitute.[69] Since 1984 Mexicans' consumption of fat has increased by 28.9 percent, and their consumption of soft drinks has increased by 37.2

percent.[70] At almost 70 percent, Mexico now has the highest rate of obesity in the world, a rate that former president Felipe Calderón says has tripled in the last thirty years.[71] While in 1988, 33 percent of women were overweight or obese, by 1999 it was 59 percent.[72]

In short, the global food system is being radically altered by the combination of farm policy in the United States, which emphasizes commodity crops for export; the commodity subsidies to encourage farmers to focus on these crops; and trade agreements that frequently preclude government supports in the United States' partner countries. Among the many more dimensions of public policy that shape radical shifts in the U.S. and global food system, three smaller policy arenas affect local food consumption and distribution on a regular basis: school lunch programs, food safety regulations, and local food policy.

SCHOOLS, HOMES, PUBLIC SQUARES
FOOD POLICY IN DAILY LIFE

The Farm Bill and free trade agreements are broad, deep, and complicated policy arenas that shape the food system on a macro level. They affect what is eaten, how it is obtained, and what it costs. These challenges are critical to understanding the structural issues at stake in the food system. At the same time, there also are more immediate encounters with aspects of the food system that demand our attention. While attending to the global dimensions of food policy, one must not neglect the local dimensions: what children eat at school, what local artisans are able to produce and distribute in their communities, and the presence (or absence) of community voices in local government.

School Lunch Programs

During World Wars I and II, officials were alarmed by the large proportion of recruits who reported for duty in varying degrees of malnourishment.[73] Formalizing emergency measures in 1946 with the signing of the National School Lunch Act, President Harry S. Truman described the measure as aiding not only the "health of our children," but also the "welfare of our farmers," a dual-purpose mission echoed in the act's preamble.[74] Add to these dual objectives the expectation that childhood nutrition also contributed to our national security by fortifying military recruits, and one gets a sense for the complicated pathways of accountability for this historic program.[75] Childhood nutrition has improved as a result of the program, but much of the food provided in the school lunch program is still "cheap" food, predominantly produced from commodity crops.[76]

To some degree, the selection of foods for the school lunch program presents a philosophical argument in which some argue the program is a nutrition program, while others view it as a welfare program. When it is conceived as the latter, it is understood less as an investment and more as a handout. As such, discrimination persists against recipients of free and reduced-cost school lunches. For example, one Arizona school required children receiving free lunch to do extra "chores" in exchange for the meal.[77]

Given the challenges inherent in such a large-scale and commodity-driven program, food justice advocates have recently turned their attention to the development of relationships between schools and local farmers. For example, since 1996 or so, the Farm Bill has included the Community Food Projects Competitive Grant Program, which "unite[s] the entire food system, assessing strengths, establishing linkages, and creating systems that improve self-reliance over food needs."[78] Some communities have used these grants to fund Farm to School initiatives, and in 2010 the USDA implemented a new grant program dedicated to Farm to School initiatives.[79] Although each project is context specific, the goal of the Farm to School program is to "connect schools (K-12) and local farms with the objectives of serving healthy meals in school cafeterias; improving student nutrition; providing agriculture, health, and nutrition education opportunities; and supporting local and regional farmers."[80]

Food Safety and Cottage Food Laws

For centuries, societies have crafted ways to preserve food and prevent its spoilage. From salt curing and pickling, to refrigeration and freezing, to processing and canning, people have developed means to preserve food as it traveled further from its source and was stored for longer periods of time.[81] During the rapid urbanization of the early twentieth century, as more food needed to be shipped into growing cities, concern over spoilage and unsafe ingredients gave rise to the first food safety laws, such as meat inspection, pasteurization, and food-labeling requirements.[82]

These important advances in food safety had another effect, however: the requirements to meet the inspection and monitoring requirements have sometimes proved cost prohibitive for small operations. Particularly as food processing has become more concentrated, and the reach of a food safety breach ever broader, regulations have increasingly been designed for the largest of operations. With food justice activists, artisan producers protest being subject to ever more elaborate food safety regulations designed to protect consumers from contaminants more rapidly spread by mega-processing operations, arguing that they are not fair or even necessary to small-scale producers.[83] For example, artisan cheesemakers have worried in recent years about possible new regulations on the use of raw milk in cheese, despite the fact that just as many pasteurized milk cheeses as raw milk cheeses have been recalled.[84] While cheesemakers struggle to afford the time and financial commitments required to deal with complicated regulatory processes, small-scale bakers have had moderate success in supporting cottage food laws or regulations, which have been implemented in thirty-one states and are under consideration in eight more states.[85] Cottage food statutes allow for smaller food-processing operations, in which bakers, herb growers, and other artisans make food in their own kitchens for sale in their local communities, while at the same time providing some regulation.[86]

Local Food Policy Councils

Farm-to-school and cottage food regulation efforts are good examples of ways in which local and regional communities have worked to protect local foodways in the context of a global food system. At the same time, efforts are often disconnected, perhaps out of necessity, from broader systemic issues. The popular action approach to food justice is as "siloed" as federal food policy, with pieces lying in as disparate arenas as economic and tax policy, education policy, food and drug regulations, transportation policy, and environmental concerns.[87] Diverse groups affected by and implicated in the contemporary food system sometimes find themselves working at cross-purposes. The complexities of the food system demand a cooperative and comprehensive approach.

In response to both the increasing distance between federal food policy and local food needs and the diversity of perspectives and experiences present in each community, citizens have begun taking matters into their own hands, establishing local food policy councils. In some cases, councils are established by local governments, and in other cases, they are entirely grassroots-led. Similarly, some receive government funding and others nonprofit grant funding and still others operate on an entirely volunteer basis.[88] Food policy councils seek to integrate diverse needs related to the local food system, and comprise representatives from across the sectors in the local food system: production, processing, distribution, consumption, and waste management.[89] Their efforts represent the diversity of the food justice movement, bringing together community food security (or sovereignty) advocates and alternative agriculture advocates, making possible a conversation between allied but distinct food justice goals: sustenance for persons and communities, and sustainability for farmers and the earth.[90]

Even the most basic contours of our contemporary patterns of food production, distribution, and consumption illustrate the complexity of the global food system. These patterns affect and are affected by individuals, families, communities, and the environment—persons, places, and the planet—and political structures contribute to this system. One might, at this point, justifiably feel either unsatisfied by this cursory tour through the complexities of the food system, or overwhelmed and despairing at the sheer weight of it all. Or maybe a little bit of both. In the second half of this book, some of these themes—urban food sovereignty, economically viable means of sustainable farming, the interdependent character of global agriculture and trade policy, the reestablishment of bond of interdependence—will make a reappearance, embodied in the practices of people and communities of faith seeking to respond to these challenges. Their practices responsibly consider the contours and complexities of the global food system, but also breathe life into a practical theology of food that imagines the food system in a different way.

CHAPTER THREE

Making Room at the Table
A Theology and Ethics of Food

Standing amid piles of compost and rows of greens and broccoli in southwest Atlanta, Rashid Nuri smiles as if he has discovered a sacred secret. "Some people, when they get up and go to work in the morning, feel like they are going to hell. When I go to work in the morning, I know I am going to meet God in this garden."[1]

There is much to be said for the tangible, material benefits of Nuri's project, Truly Living Well farms. It is a nonprofit urban agriculture initiative that approaches community development through strategies designed to strengthen sustainable local food systems and provide basic horticultural education. Truly Living Well operates farms on a couple of campuses in the Atlanta region, and community members can purchase the produce with their Supplemental Nutrition Assistance Program (SNAP) benefits or by becoming members in Truly Living Well's community-supported agriculture (CSA) program.[2]

As impressive as they are, however, an abstract listing of the strategies and accomplishments of Truly Living Well farms does not communicate the profound integrity and beauty one apprehends when standing in the dirt there with Nuri. Far beyond the good and necessary material benefits pursued and attained by the work of Truly Living Well, one begins to discern a philosophical and theological commitment that creates, sustains, and enlivens that work. Indeed, the whole operation could be oriented around the possibility of divine encounter in that garden.

Like the garden, the table is a site for divine encounter. When we receive with gratitude food from the earth, prepare it with love and intentionality, and share it with friends and strangers at the table, we open ourselves to God's transformative presence in the world. "Food is itself a means of revelation," observes Shannon Jung. "Through eating together we taste the goodness of God."[3]

More broadly speaking, when religious people and communities engage in meaningful action in relationship to the whole system of food production, distribution, and consumption, they are confronted with the theological and moral significance of it all. Their encounters with struggling farmers, exploited laborers, abused animals, stripped soil, and abandoned communities necessarily challenge simple theological affirmations of divine encounter in the food system.[4] If God is being revealed in the food system as it is, people of faith might justifiably question whether this god is worthy of worship.

Truthfully, theological language has not always contributed positively to movements for social change or ecological wholeness. For example, otherworldly spiritualities have sometimes dulled calls for justice in the political and economic sphere, asserting that Christians' true home is not this world, but the next.[5] Even more troubling are arguments *against* caring for the environment, since this world is only "temporary" and such efforts distract Christians from preparing their souls for the next.[6] At a deeper and more fundamental level, Christian theology has been charged with an anthropocentrism that is embedded in one of the oldest stories of Scripture: the first creation account in Genesis, in which human beings are placed in the center of creation and instructed to exercise "dominion" over it.[7] In other words, theology does not offer an unambiguous "answer" to the problem of the global food system.

People of faith, however, must wrestle with the theological questions that necessarily arise when working on such thorny problems as the global food system. Patterns of growing, sharing, and eating food are a means of revelation in this sense, as well: they reveal something about the brokenness of humanity, and its social and ecological arrangements. This was true even for Christians who gathered for table fellowship in the earliest faith communities, and is perhaps an even more poignant reality for Christians today, in light of the global food system. We must ask, "What does it mean to work for justice in this world, even as we hope for a new creation?" Or, "What does it mean to be a human being in this context? What is our responsibility?"[8] These theological questions are present in a distilled form when Christians gather around the eucharistic table, where participants bring the full range of their humanity, where the gifts of the earth are transformed into divine presence, and where moral commitment is demanded.

The table, where we eat together, thus orients a theological framework for comprehending Christian responsibility and practice in light of the global food system. The table furthermore gives rise to four moral commitments that might ground faithful and just food practices. These commitments are dynamic, emerging from the theological framework, formed in deep engagement with liturgical, biblical, and theological roots. At the same time, however, they also are shaped and given life in the work of ordinary people of faith as they engage in a broad range of food practices. The theological framework, and its corresponding commitments, is always emerging, changing, and responding in relationship to the realities and complexities of the context of the global food system.

A NEW AND OLD TABLE THEOLOGY
EUCHARIST AND THE THEOLOGY OF FOOD

At the center of the Christian tradition sits a table. It was around tables that Jesus taught, loved, shared with, and challenged the disciples. At mealtimes, Jesus and the disciples shaped a beloved community, a community that understood sharing, hospitality, and attention to material needs to be at the heart of their life together. Even now, when the beloved community gathers around the table, we affirm that there we receive sustenance, we build relationships, and hear a challenge to seek flourishing in the world.[9]

Beginning with the very earliest Christian communities, when people of faith have gathered, they have celebrated the Eucharist, a unique meal that marks the presence of the risen Lord among the faithful. So central was the meal shared around the table in the earliest communities that Paul found himself regularly addressing conflicts that had arisen in regard to the norms and practices governing table fellowship in Corinth, Rome, and other places. These conflicts are instructive for Christians in light of the contemporary global food system. In a context of gross food insecurity, injustice for the most vulnerable in society (children, laborers, the poor), social and ecological alienation, and disrespect for the land and its life, biblical and theological accounts of the practice and meaning of table fellowship remain a touchstone for people of faith. For the first Christians, as for us, the table is the core of theological knowing and moral challenge.

Paul was concerned about the state of table fellowship in Corinth because while some approached the table with gluttony and drunken abandon, others went hungry. "Do you show contempt for the church of God and humiliate those who have nothing?" cried Paul.[10] The practice at Corinth—in which the most privileged individuals arrived first at the table, gobbling and slurping up everything laid out there with little concern for the poor and hungry in the community—flew in the face of admonitions to give thanks, "discern the body," and "wait for one another" in that shared meal.[11] In other words, one would be mistaken to assume that the only relationship that matters in the Eucharist is the relationship between the individual believer and God. At the table, we learn who we are: as individuals, but also as members of a community and even more, as members of God's creation.

Of course, the eucharistic table is only one site of shared meals, and only one kind of table. Given its social, moral, and economic contours, a grounded practical theology of food necessarily implies other kinds of tables as well. For example, it suggests a round table, as a site of mutuality and disruption of relationships of power; a kitchen table, as a site of work, contestation, intimacy, and solidarity; and a welcome table, as a site of hospitality and humanization: "A lot of community takes place at table, and the Christian heritage already has a long tradition related to table community, table sharing, table talk, and the like," Letty Russell writes. "At this table there is no permanent seating, and whatever chairs of authority that exist are shared. Christ is the host and bids everyone to come."[12]

Embedded in this expanded table theology are at least three core affirmations that orient the Christian faith: we each and together receive identities as members of the body of Christ and of God's creation; we worship a God who both provides gifts in abundance and demands their just distribution; and we encounter the nearness of the kingdom of God, and are invited to live toward that divine reality, even in the midst of social structures that seem at odds with this vocation.

Belonging and Membership

Christians approaching the eucharistic table might, in other meals, experience a great distance between their eating and the lives of farmers and laborers, agriculture, and even other people eating. Eating is something people so often do alone, perhaps out of a take out container, and one could hardly identify the origins of such a meal, or the conditions under which it was prepared. Eating can seem a solitary, even alienating, experience devoid of much awareness of all of the human labor and ecological sacrifices invested in the process. Christians might also bring this felt (but rarely articulated) distance and alienation to the Eucharist meal.

For Paul, however, the Eucharist held a deeply social meaning: in the Eucharist we are bound to one another. Paul's admonition to "discern the body" immediately follows his description of the church as the "body of Christ."[13] So while Christians always seek to discern the risen Christ at the eucharistic table, we also discern there the presence of Christ in Christ's *body*, the church. Sometimes the practice of receiving communion highlights the relationship between the individual believer and the person of Christ, focusing on the work of Christ in the forgiveness of sins memorialized in the sacrament.[14] This very personal dimension of the Eucharist can, if pursued to the exclusion of other dimensions of the practice, obscure the deep relatedness that resides within it. In fact, even as we remember the work of Christ, we are perpetually lured back into the community of faith. In an alienating world that *dis-members* the body of Christ, we are *re-membered*.[15]

In the shared meal, the body of Christ is embodied in the gathered community, and we discern among us God incarnate. "Through eating together," Shannon Jung writes, "we taste the goodness of God. . . . God intends food and eating to be for the purposes of delight and sharing."[16] Food is a means of revelation, and this theological claim is central to the practice of the Eucharist. God meets humanity there. At the same time, the gift of communion with

God and one another is paired with a moral obligation to actively seek interconnectedness. This is a serious challenge when so many aspects of the global food system obscure the bonds of relationship between the one eating a meal and the farmers, laborers, communities, and conditions that produced it. Food is a commodity, and at the most perfunctory level the responsibility of the consumer goes no further than paying a price for that commodity. The Eucharist, when encountered honestly, reveals the poverty of a commodified food system. Christians around the eucharistic table are not mere consumers. We are, together, members of a community.

About the social meaning of the Eucharist, the World Council of Churches has said, "The eucharistic celebration demands reconciliation and sharing among all those regarded as brothers and sisters in the one family of God and is a constant challenge in the search for appropriate relationships in social, economic and political life."[17] Indeed, as the church gathers around the eucharistic table, we are challenged to encounter one another there. Those who receive the meal, while giving thanks for its abundance, are to "discern the body," recognizing and strengthening human interconnectedness.

The abundance represented in the holy feast reminds us of God's open invitation, and our own moral responsibility to welcome friends and strangers to the table. There is always room at the eucharistic table, just as there is room at the tables of grandparents, dear friends, and raucous family reunions. It is similar to the unexpected abundance shared when Jesus (and, upon his insistence, the disciples) welcomed friends and strangers to stay and eat together after the Sermon on the Mount. Around abundant tables—or picnic blankets—there is always room. Everyone has a place. Everyone belongs. Everyone is re-membered: that is, everyone is incorporated into the community. No one is lost in the body of Christ: "Through the eucharist the all-renewing grace of God penetrates and re-stores human personality and dignity."[18] We receive at the table our identity as members of the body of Christ. In the African American tradition, the capacity of the abundant table to restore human dignity figures prominently. The "welcome table" is the site of membership and inclusion in a society bent on exclusion, and was embraced as a freedom song during the civil rights movement.[19] As the old spiritual goes, "I'm gonna sit at the welcome table . . . I'm gonna feast on milk and honey, one of these days." At the welcome table, none are outcast.[20] All belong.

So central to Christian identity is our membership in the body of Christ that Paul repeats the theme in several of his letters. It is increasingly prevalent in the later letters of First and Second Corinthians, and receives perhaps its fullest treatment in Romans. In the Letter to the Romans, Paul places the discussion of the body of Christ, and its relational implications, immediately after his exposition of election. "For as in one body we have many members, and not all the members have the same function, so we, who are many, are one body in Christ, and individually we are members one of another."[21] To say that the Eucharist reveals our interconnectedness is to say that, at the table, we also learn something about what it means to be human. We are members: members of Christ's body, of the gathered community, of the global communion, and indeed, members of creation.[22]

Just as we are bound together in our humanity, we also are bound to the earth, as we feast on its gifts of bread and wine. As physical beings dependent upon the earth's bounty, we are reminded in our eating that, among other things, "we are natural beings who are part of the ecological flow; . . . that we are dependent beings fed and nourished by soil."[23] Insofar as eucharistic eating is paradigmatic of all of our eating, when we fail to recall that the common loaf and cup depend upon the gifts of the land, we perpetuate a theological alienation from our ecological context. Recalling creation and divine provision in the sharing of the meal invites deeper communion with God and the rest of creation: "Food connects us to the memberships of creation and to God. Thoughtful eating reminds us that there is no human fellowship without a table, no table without a kitchen, no kitchen without a garden, no garden without a viable ecosystem, no ecosystems without the forces productive of life, and no life without its sources in God."[24]

Thanksgiving for Gifts and Just Distribution

After some eucharistic services, one sometimes finds a small group of people gathered around the table, continuing to feast on the bread remaining from the sacramental meal. Likewise, in traditions that restrict access to the Eucharist to members of that particular communion (Coptic Christians do this, for example), guests might receive some of the leftover bread at the conclusion of the service. The Eucharist extends beyond the immediate sacramental practice observed around any particular table. The Eucharist is also meant to materially and metaphorically feed those at the door of the church, and beyond. In other words, one would be mistaken to approach the table without perceiving *both* its abundance and its demand that we share that abundance justly. In the shared meal, we are invited to delight in what God provides, and instructed to share that which we have received, forsaking the temptation to hoard the abundance for ourselves.[25] Having tasted God's abundance, we are sent *from* the eucharistic table to ensure the distribution of God's gifts in the world. This sacred work necessarily entangles us in social, economic, and political realities. It means that Christians cannot ignore serious issues of food insecurity in poor urban and rural communities, or unjust wages and working conditions for agricultural laborers.

The writer of Luke-Acts describes the practices of the earliest Christian communities in the following way, illustrating the ways in which the obligations and benefits of their membership were quite visible in their shared practices:

> The believers devoted themselves to the apostles' teaching, to the community, to their shared meals, and to their prayers. A sense of awe came upon everyone. God performed many wonders and signs through the apostles. All the believers were united and shared everything. They would sell pieces of property and possessions and distribute the proceeds to everyone who needed them. Every day, they met together in the temple, and ate in their homes. They shared food with gladness and simplicity. They praised God and demonstrated God's goodness to everyone. The Lord added daily to the community those who were being saved.[26]

It is difficult to miss the commitment to mutuality in this description of the lives of early Christian communities: shared meals, shared everything![27] When contemporary Christians depart the eucharistic table and drive through communities with no place to purchase fresh produce, one must wonder about the meaning of sharing property and sharing food in places where corporate-owned supermarkets refuse to go and where liquor stores profit from the sale of overpriced junk food. Insofar as we apprehend and embrace the obligation inherent in our membership in the body of

Christ, we are sent into the world to share God's abundance, seek justice, and participate in God's saving work in the world. One cannot be Christian alone, and one cannot be Christian without practices of sharing. Membership is both gift and obligation.[28]

The Eucharist meal is a symbolic moment in this regard, in that the taste of bread and wine represents God's gift and challenge to Christians. The sheer abundance of God's provision is difficult to comprehend and trust, argues Walter Brueggemann. The great lie of which Christians have been convinced is that of scarcity. Despite the abundance of God's gifts, we are inclined to hoard, rather than to share.[29] The challenges of poverty, greed, and income inequality blur the relationship between God's abundant table and our economic and social relationships in the world. The tradition of World Communion Sunday, which originated in the Presbyterian Church, has sought to address this gap. When we celebrate the Eucharist, we are reminded "that the church founded on Jesus Christ peacefully shares God-given goods in a world increasingly destabilized by globalization and global market economies based on greed."[30]

The choice of bread and wine (or juice) shared in the Eucharist meal is thus economically symbolic. When they are the products of giant corporations, the situations of the wheat farmer and the agricultural laborer and the health of the soil are invisible. It need not be this way, however. One iconic image illustrates the rich relationship between the Eucharist and economic justice: a week before announcing his candidacy for president against incumbent Lyndon B. Johnson in 1968, Senator Robert F. Kennedy traveled to Delano, California, where he joined United Farmworkers leader César Chávez in receiving the Eucharist. Chávez had been fasting in protest of the treatment of migrant farmworkers in California. With that sacred meal, Chávez broke his fast after twenty-five days.[31] Within this image are layers of meaning that strengthen the social and moral implications of gathering around the table. As Kennedy and Chávez shared the bread and wine, they vividly represented the orientation of the Eucharist to worldly and material considerations: "As God in Christ has entered into the human situation, so eucharistic liturgy is near to the concrete and particular situations of men and women."[32]

Kennedy and Chávez demand that we consider the question "What has the Eucharist to do with the grape picker?" In fields and kitchens around the world, workers (often women) labor to set food on the table.[33] Contemporary rural families and agricultural workers disproportionately experience poverty, food insecurity, and health concerns. The agricultural workers in California in the late 1960s were no different. Chávez and the United Farmworkers were protesting the health and environmental risks posed by the widespread use of pesticides. One can hardly miss the irony of the fact, then, that the one who does the most backbreaking labor to produce the wine for the sacred meal is the very one most vulnerable in the global food system.[34] *Our sacred meal depends on the work of vulnerable, even exploited, agricultural workers.*

Living toward the Kingdom of God

The challenge to delight in and share God's radical abundance in the Eucharist, when taken with material and moral seriousness, is no small burden. In fact, if left only to modest human efforts, the expectation and struggle to meet it might leave people of conscience prone to despair. One becomes well acquainted with the ways in which social, political, and economic structures make this work very difficult. A range of limitations, both internal and external, constrains the work for justice. What prevents any of us from throwing our hands up in surrender, lamenting our failures, and abandoning the eucharistic challenge altogether?

The meals that Jesus shared with his friends served to "proclaim and enact the nearness of the Kingdom," making present to his companions an alternative future in which God restores relationships among persons, communities, and the earth.[35] So, too, Christians receive in the Eucharist a vision of the kingdom of God, and anticipate the establishment of the New Creation.[36] Participants in the sacred meal are offered a foretaste of God's alternative future, anticipating the "heavenly banquet" described by the prophets: "On this mountain the Lord of hosts will make for all peoples: a feast of rich food, a feast of well-matured wines, of rich food filled with marrow, of well-matured wines strained clear."[37] As God is redeeming, indeed, recreating the world, one of the primary images of the New Creation is a table feast!

The centrality of the table in eschatological images is depicted compellingly in Robert Benton's 1984 film *Places in the Heart*. In the film, Edna Spalding is trying desperately to cling to her family farm, home, and children after her husband dies in a tragic instance of violence. The young man who killed her husband is dragged to his death by members of the Klan. The film, set in the Depression era, depicts an agricultural community gripped by racism, conflict, and suffering. At the end of the film, however, Benton presents a eucharistic scene that makes clear the connection between the table and God's alternative future. As the church community gathers during worship, we see the characters receiving communion, one by one. This is no ordinary Eucharist, however: as the camera pans across the pew, viewers see Edna's husband, Ralph. And then they see the young man who killed him: all of them sharing the sacred meal together. The image of reconciliation and restored life is in sharp contrast to the animosity that characterized the community prior to and following their deaths.

In the Eucharist, even death does not have the last word. Where death and suffering are present in the global food system—in concentrated animal feeding operations (CAFOs); in the tomato fields of Immokalee, Florida; in the global pandemic of farmer suicides; in the economic decline of rural communities—even there, God's ongoing creativity demands Christians' perseverance and hope.

Throughout the biblical witness, testimonies to God's ongoing creative activity in the world point toward the goodness of the New Creation, even as they poignantly sharpen the distance between it and the current situation. Jürgen Moltmann describes the human experience of anticipating the new creation as a kind of *tension*, born of our responsibility in the world while trying to live toward the kingdom of God: "In this hope the soul does not soar above our vale of tears to some imagined heavenly bliss, nor does it sever itself from the earth. . . . It does not calm the unquiet heart, but is itself this unquiet heart in man. Those who hope in Christ can no longer put up with reality as it is, but begin to suffer under it, to contradict it."[38] In other words, real hope for the New Creation can by no means be escapist. It is the source of transformative tension in the present.

We bring these unquiet hearts, time and again, to Christ's table, seeking to taste the New Creation. We are commissioned there to share God's abundance and to embody Christ's ministry of reconciliation and justice in the world.[39] We envision, in this "table community," an "alternative world free of hunger, poverty and domination."[40] Remembering that God's active presence is bringing about this alternative world, we are invited to participate in that work in the world, which we glimpse and for which we are nourished in the Eucharist.

EUCHARISTIC THEOLOGY AND THE GLOBAL FOOD SYSTEM
FOUR MORAL COMMITMENTS

Insofar as Christian faith is oriented around a table (indeed, many kinds of tables), it is uniquely suited to speak authentically and prophetically to the realities of the global food system, even while recognizing that its theological grounding is necessarily fragile and subject to scrutiny. The meal around which the church organizes itself remains a source for moral imagination, demanding the examination of contemporary transnational patterns (and our complicity therein) of food production, distribution, and consumption with clarity and creativity. A moral imagination appropriate to our situation bears distinctive characteristics: given the challenges of the global food system and the grounded practical theology of food and table, particular moral commitments give rise to faithful and responsible food practices.

The formation of theological frameworks, and their associated moral commitments, is *always* in relationship to material and practical realities. That is, it is not simply a matter of getting the theology "right," which issues in clear moral directives, which then dictate appropriate practices that serve as an "application" of theology and moral commitments. Participants in food practices always are pushed to examine theological and moral commitments anew, in response to what they experience as they engage in practices. One of the most exciting aspects of practical theology is the rigorous work of renegotiating and reexamining theological frameworks and moral commitments in light of conscious engagement in the world. A grounded practical theology of food is no different.

Given that caveat, some preliminary moral commitments indeed present themselves for consideration. These commitments all respond earnestly to the contours of the global food system, draw upon the table theology outlined above (as well as the whole corpus of the biblical witness), and offer a foothold from which to develop practices that faithfully engage this context. Among the moral commitments at the core of food practices are the prioritization of the hungry, solidarity with and advocacy for those who work the land, the call to care gently for the land, and the reestablishment of bonds of interdependence between humans and the sources of our food.

Priority of the Hungry

When we receive the small taste of bread and the sip of wine, participating in the Eucharist might seem to bear only a distant and symbolic resemblance to the feast images found in the Bible. We ignore the more fulsome meals represented in the biblical narratives, however, at our own peril. To forget the hungry is to miss the central meaning of the meal. Feast and famine are at the heart of the Eucharist: "The simple, central action of the Eucharist is the sharing of food—not only eating, but sharing. The simple, central human experience for the understanding of this action is hunger."[41]

In some traditions, when the gathered community approaches the eucharistic table, each member opens her hands to receive the gift of the bread. This posture stands in contrast with other traditions in which participants might tear off a piece of the common loaf for themselves before dipping it into the cup: "It is a gift to be received. Not something that we grab."[42] The moral implications of this embodied understanding of the Eucharist are clear: in this meal, the proper posture is receptivity and thanksgiving, rather than self-sufficiency or, worse, greed.

Paul was very concerned that in the church at Corinth the community had lost the social sense of the Lord's Supper, in part because the wealthiest members brought their own "private meal," by which they "humiliate those who have nothing."[43] It is important to note that the Lord's Supper in the earliest Christian communities was celebrated in the context of a full common meal, likely in a gathering within someone's home. The requirement that everyone share the meal, eating together, also represented a reordering of social relationships in Corinth, where persons of privilege would have eaten the most and best-quality food.[44] It was not acceptable, in Paul's view, for members of the faith community with economic privilege to consume extravagant meals while members of their *own faith community* (much less the larger community) went hungry. It was difficult enough for the church at Corinth to keep in mind the relationship between the Lord's Supper and church members' responsibility to the hungry in their community, despite the fact that their Eucharist occurred in the context of a full common meal. How much more difficult it is for contemporary Christians to perceive the relationship of the sacred meal (with its representative tastes of bread and wine) and hunger in our time![45]

But perceive it we must.[46] That whole communities around our congregations are described as food deserts, and rural families living in the U.S. agricultural heartland are food insecure, is a scandal to the church. One means by which one might better understand Paul's concern about the exclusion of the hungry at the Eucharist is to read this text in broader biblical perspective. The biblical witness is full of admonitions, prophecies, parables, and stories that represent God's deep concern for—and human obligation to—the poor and the hungry. The text contains both metaphorical and material concern for the feeding of God's people. For example, farmers are admonished in several places to leave some of their crops for the poor and the refugee. Codes for harvesting appear twice in Leviticus, for example: "When you reap the harvest of your land, you shall not reap to the very edges of your field, or gather the gleanings of your harvest; . . . you shall leave them for the poor and for the alien: I am the Lord your God."[47] This admonition resonates in the story of Ruth, who meets Boaz when she arrives at his field to glean barley and wheat for herself and her mother-in-law, who have no source of income. The practice of gleaning—whereby the poor are allowed to take whatever is left after the harvesters have finished their work—appears to be a common model of charity operating in the background of these texts.[48] The texts take it a step further, either by direct admonition (Leviticus) or by attributing such practice to a "good man" (Ruth), *requiring* that landowners and their harvesters leave some of the bounty for the gleaners, as opposed to merely allowing the poor to glean once the landowner has sapped the land of its most profitable bounty. Likewise, another story about the prioritizing of the hungry appears in 2 Kings, where the offerings of first fruits to Elisha are repurposed for the feeding of the hungry.[49] Layering text upon text, the moral demand becomes clear: so long as we find the hungry among us, they are our priority—not offerings to kings or prophets, not our own profit from our land. The hungry come first.

Hunger, however, has grown in the places in which the most food is produced, despite the good intentions of the architects of the "Green Revolution," who hoped that increasing crop yields would insure an adequate food supply for a growing world population.[50] In the United States, 11 percent of households are food insecure, and rural areas report an even higher rate.[51] The same is true on a global scale. The shift from production of food to the production of feed and fuel also contributes to hunger. In 2000 only about 12 percent of corn grown in the United States was "consumed directly (e.g. corn chips) or indirectly (e.g. high fructose corn syrup)."[52] The rest—88 percent—went to feed and ethanol production. These already shocking numbers would be only more staggering today, as the cultivation of corn for ethanol production has quadrupled.[53] In the contemporary global food system, while many go hungry, large swaths of cropland are dedicated to cheap fuel and meat consumption.

Justice for Those Who Work the Land

In the order for worship for weekly community service of word and table at Candler School of Theology, there is an interesting attribution under "Worship Notes": bread baker. Each week, the bread received in the celebration of the Eucharist is made by a student, using a shared recipe published on the school's website. This practice evokes a sense of respect for the dignity of making food. By receiving both the bread and the cup, participants receive in their bodies the fruits of the labors of farmers and agricultural workers both here in the United States and around the world. When we think about all of the purposeful and bodily work undergirding the appearance of the bread and wine on our eucharistic table, ought not our hearts be filled with gratitude and awe for the sacred vocation of farming? In a moral sense, this gratitude and awe bear an obligation: to seek dignity and justice for the farmer and those who labor in all corners of the food system.

The farming life is a shared experience informing much of the biblical text. The whole biblical witness might be most properly read "through agrarian eyes."[54] In other words, the biblical writers knew agriculture. Some of them would have farmed themselves. In the very beginning, humanity's first vocation is to tend and keep the land.[55] The human being is created from the "arable soil" in Genesis 2, and humanity's very identity has its roots in this agrarian image.[56] Humanity's agrarian identity accompanies the people of God in the exodus and in exile, expressed poignantly in their cries and anxieties as they find themselves a landless people. As humanity's archetypal vocation, farming is holy work, and where it is impossible or precarious, a convicting moral question insists itself.[57]

Alongside the dignity of farming, biblical texts contain the demand to treat workers justly. Employers are to pay fair wages to workers, for example, and accumulating wealth from the labor of mistreated workers is a moral failure.[58] Jesus uses the agricultural day laborer as a character in the parable of the vineyard, in which the worker hired last is paid as if he had worked the full day.[59] Like today's day laborers, the worker in the parable likely would have been powerless with regard to when he was hired. The vulnerable worker, then, is dependent on a just employer: in a literal sense, the parable teaches that "those who are economically privileged, like the vineyard owner, are responsible for those who are not, while laborers are responsible to provide a full day of work unless prohibited by circumstances beyond their control."[60] Scriptural texts also address just treatment of tenant farmers, timely payment of laborers, the rights of laborers to eat the fruits of their labors, and the forgiveness of debt. The prevalence of these themes indicates a shared moral framework among hearers, one in which farming and agricultural labor are to be honored and protected by the community.[61]

We live in a time, however, in which the life of farming is increasingly at risk. During the farm crisis of the 1980s, many farmers lost their farms. Even for those who kept their farms, the sweeping changes in agriculture since the middle of the twentieth century have meant that family farms can no longer support all of the adult children who might want to farm. It has become increasingly difficult for farmers in the United States, and, indeed, around the world, to make a sustainable living pursuing this vocation. Many of them are shouldering staggering debt-to-income ratios as they try to compete in the large-scale market. Farmers are, on the whole, poorer than persons in other vocations. Small farmers in Africa make up 50 percent of the population described as "food insecure."[62]

The hardest and most unpredictable agricultural work frequently is performed by the most vulnerable members of our society: migrants. It is a sad irony that agricultural workers in the United States are more than twice as likely as the national average to face food insecurity, and report higher rates of nutrition-related illness.[63] In addition to these stresses, migrant laborers face the proliferation of anti-immigration legislation across the United States and the threat of being deported (and, in the meantime, exploited by employers who are keenly aware of migrants' precarious situation). While almost half a century has passed since Kennedy and Chávez shared the Eucharist, farmworkers continue in their struggle for civil and economic rights.[64]

When we take the bread and wine, we feast on the fruits of the labor of agricultural workers here in the United States and around the world. When we share in the sacred meal, we also are bound in the social and economic circumstances of those whose labor makes that meal possible. Where laborers are paid fairly and treated with dignity, our eating and drinking do justice. Where laborers are exploited, however, even the sacred meal is complicit in these structures of harm.

To Tend the Earth

They are the simple, common elements of a meal: bread and wine. Even more, they are simple, common fruits of the earth: wheat and grapes. Yet when we celebrate the Eucharist, we invite—and indeed, trust—the Holy Spirit to transform these elements into holy food. Insofar as the earth yields these fruits that we bless, break, and share, it demands gratitude and reverence, just as we offer gratitude and reverence to God when we say the prayer of great thanksgiving in the sacrament itself. We express reverence and gratitude for the earth when we recognize human dependence upon the earth, and apprehend the radical interdependence of all of life.

"We depend upon other creatures and survive by their deaths. To live, we must daily break the body and shed the blood of

Creation," Wendell Berry writes. "When we do this knowingly, lovingly, skillfully, reverently, it is a sacrament. When we do it ignorantly, greedily, clumsily, destructively, it is a desecration. In such desecration we condemn ourselves to spiritual and moral loneliness, and others to want."[65] Each act of eating implicates us in the destruction of the earth, and yet presents opportunities for practicing gratitude and reverence.

In eating, the line between sacrament and sacrilege is thin. At the heart of the matter is the theological and moral status of the earth and all of its inhabitants. Although many Christians would affirm John Calvin's description of creation as *theatrum gloriae*, the moral implications of this confession are not so clearly discerned.[66] Calvin describes God's wisdom as expressed in the "magnificent theatre of heaven and earth replenished with numberless wonders, the wise contemplation of which should have enabled us to know God."[67] Whereas Shannon Jung describes the act of eating as divine revelation, Calvin argues that even more fundamentally, God is revealed in all encounters with creation. We are enabled to know God when we contemplate God's work in creation.

Even so, God's revelation in creation might still be understood in an anthropocentric way: that God provides in creation the resources and backdrop for human activity. Karl Barth interprets creation as "the stage on which the drama of the divine-human relationship will take place."[68] In so doing, Barth exaggerates humanity's role in the drama of creation, when in reality "we are by no means the whole show," Anna Case-Winters argues.[69] This anthropocentric strand in Christian theology has perpetuated a dualism between humanity and nature, a dualism that has encouraged Christians to consider creation as the divine provision of resources for human use and consumption, rather than a web of interdependence in which we live and for which we bear moral responsibility. Furthermore, in 1967 Lynn White famously laid the blame for the emerging environmental crisis squarely at the doorstep of Christian theology, arguing that Christianity has even touted a biblical endorsement of human domination over nature.[70]

Domination is not the only way to construe biblical images of human relationship to the land, however. The Yahwist's creation story, presented in the second chapter of Genesis, makes clear the human being's dependence upon and moral obligation to the earth. In that story, the human person is formed from "arable soil" and commissioned not only to tend, but indeed to *serve* the earth.[71] An agrarian reading of biblical texts points not only to the dignity of the farming vocation, but to moral constraints on agriculture's use of land. While the context in which these admonitions were written is not the same as our own, they do commend a posture of restraint in working the land and in relationship to other living creatures, a posture increasingly difficult to maintain in the contemporary agricultural system. For example, farmers are to allow rest for the land, and not to reap "to the very edges of your field," and yet we live in a time of "fencerow to fencerow" planting and harvesting.[72] Other texts advocate the necessity for crop diversity, and yet we live in a time of monocropping and CAFOs, which require massive amounts of feed corn and are about as far from biodiversity as can be imagined.[73]

Without idealizing biblical images of agriculture, one can still reasonably contrast their norms of sustainability and restraint with contemporary intensive farming practices. At the heart of the matter, however, is the relationship of the human being to food sources. Each meal raises questions of identity, demanding consideration of who we are meant to be, in relationship to our food. In contrast to the radical interrelatedness described by the Yahwist between 'ădāmâ (arable land) and 'ādām (human being), the position of the contemporary human being in relationship to our food system reveals a relationship of radical alienation.[74]

Alienated No More

Finally, the moral commitments of prioritizing the hungry, seeking justice for those who labor in the food system, and tending the earth all rest upon one other moral commitment: cultivating and nurturing a keen sense of the interrelatedness of humanity and, indeed, all creation. If one receives no other moral demand from the eucharistic table, it is this one: having received the radical gift of membership in the body of Christ, the human's sacred obligation is to continually seek, tend, and nurture the bonds of connectedness in God's whole creation.[75]

The preceding moral commitments make clear the need for more just engagement in systems of food production, distribution, and consumption, but insofar as they emerge from a eucharistic identity, they assume a more elemental commitment, that human beings are obligated as members of creation. This obligation is rooted and given life in a spirituality of interdependence. Without this, one might very well pursue food for the hungry, justice for workers of the land, and preservation of the earth—but at a distance, as if one were not also implicated in the very same structures one seeks to change.

At the eucharistic table, however, Christians affirm something different: we affirm that this sacred meal connects us to the gathered community, both immediate and around the world; to farmers and workers from whose labor we have the gifts of bread and wine; to the land that yields them; and to God, by whose abundance we are sustained. When it is practiced with intentionality, we encounter this radical interconnectedness in the Eucharist: "Unless people participate organically in, rather than merely associate with, Jesus' life, they don't really know what it is to be alive. To be fully alive is to live sympathetically within the membership that the community is called to be, suffering with those who suffer and rejoicing with those who rejoice."[76]

It is not enough, then, to "do right" by farmers, laborers, the hungry, and the land. These efforts are good, but the Eucharist calls Christians beyond this, to a way of being that is "fully alive," founded in the deep trust born out of membership in creation. Cultivating an intentional consciousness of membership in creation aids in resisting and healing the alienation and "dis-membering" that mark the contemporary global food system.[77] We deceive ourselves when we imagine our lives to be self-sufficient. To be healthy, to be fully alive, we must understand ourselves as members: "[T]he community—in the fullest sense: a place and all its creatures—is the smallest unit of health and . . . to speak of the health of an isolated individual is a contradiction in terms. . . . We must consider the body's manifold connections to other bodies and to the world."[78] This spirituality of interdependence, and the moral obligation to tend that interdependence, is in direct contrast with contemporary patterns of alienation from agriculture.

One can point to any number of studies, or even personal encounters, in which one is confronted with the fact that children (and some of their parents) do not know the origins of their food.[79] The eggs on their individually and sterilely wrapped breakfast sandwiches appear magically before them, a far cry from the warm, brown-shelled prizes they might find nestled in hay on a local farm.[80] Food is now considered a commodity, something to be purchased (preferably at a very low price) in a supermarket, with little knowledge of its origins or the conditions under which it was produced. It is, at the root, a failure of imagination: "This narrowing of a food imagination often leads to a narrowing of sympathies and care (for fields and farmers, for instance)."[81]

A grounded practical theology of food must reignite religious "food imagination," nurturing and cultivating the connections between eating and the life and health of persons, communities, and the earth. It is not enough to learn *about* the environment, *about* agriculture, *about* the global food system. While this kind of knowledge is important, it will not have the effect of making us fully alive, conscious of the memberships that give rise to profound human identity. Instead, people of conscience must cultivate "that quality of mind that seeks out connections . . . [the capacity] to comprehend interrelatedness, and an attitude of care or stewardship. Such a person would also have the practical competence required to act on the basis of knowledge and feeling. Competence can only be derived from the experience of doing and the mastery of what Alasdair MacIntyre describes as a 'practice.'"[82] The cultivation of an ecological imagination demands learning *in* ecological context, *with* agriculture, and *through* authentic human encounters within the global food system.

And so the last thing that must be said about a eucharistic theology of food that issues in moral commitments of feeding the hungry, seeking justice for farmers and laborers, tending the earth, and reestablishing bonds of interdependence is this: it is embodied, given life, and reimagined in the midst of participation in ongoing practices of faith. Given this sketch of a theological framework from which people of faith might respond to the social, economic, and environmental challenges posed by the global food system, the categories and quandaries introduced here might be a first step in inspiring and awakening collective food imagination. This book, however, tells a different, deeper story: a story about people of faith coming alive, discovering the joy of a "certain kind of life," as they engage in a broad range of practices that seek to respond to the food system.[83] And there, too, they are being fed.

PART II

Given the intractability of the global food system, people of faith are confronted with a deep challenge to respond constructively to these issues, engaging them realistically without succumbing to despair. Embodying these four eucharistic moral commitments—prioritizing the hungry, seeking justice and dignity for those who work the land, caring gently for the earth, and reestablishing bonds of interdependence with the sources of their food—is no small thing in the midst of a food system that so frequently obscures the paths to these goals. Despite careful analysis of the facets of the global food system, and a reclaiming of theological table traditions for a just and faithful way of thinking about food, reformation of the food system remains a distant hope.

Indeed, many faithful people *are* working toward the reformation of the food system. From the mother who learns how to grow food in the backyard of her south Chicago church; to the small Presbyterian college advocating, innovating, and propagating sustainable agricultural practices in western North Carolina; to religious leaders and lay people alike who engage in political advocacy toward a more just food policy, Christians in the United States are joining with people of faith and conscience around the world in practices of hope and resistance. Together, they make up an international social movement toward food justice. The food justice movement is made up of discrete and diverse actors, communities, organizations, and practices, who share and are built upon commitments to the hungry, the farmer, the laborer, and the land. Some of them are responding to local needs without a great deal of global systemic analysis. Others of them are deeply aware of the global dynamics of local food and agriculture crises, and frame their responses according to the colloquial philosophical commitment to "think globally, act locally." All of their work, and the theological and moral insights born in their efforts, serve as an embodied testimony of the ways in which people of faith are responding to the global food system.

These stories are not merely interesting and inspiring, though they are certainly that. More importantly, they represent a different way of thinking theologically and morally about the food system. The analysis and frameworks presented in the previous chapters challenge people of faith to do the hard intellectual work of understanding, analyzing, and reconstruing human relationships to food and the system that produces it. Orthodoxy, or right theological thinking, however, will only accomplish so much. It remains at a level of abstraction and distance that can lull us into the misperception that getting the right intellectual framework is the key to solving these complex issues. The issues of hunger and nutrition, labor injustice, poverty, community decay, and environmental degradation, as well as religious and moral knowing oriented around a new table theology, however, present themselves in distinct and contextualized ways within each particular (and peculiar) community, each congregation, each constellation of players. To put it bluntly, thinking only ideationally about these matters simply will not do. Orthodoxy cannot, on its own, "answer" the challenges posed by the food system.[1] Broad social analysis and theological foundations must always be accompanied by the kind of knowing that is found only by getting one's hands dirty, to use an agricultural metaphor.

In discerning a faithful response to the global food system, then, people of faith must attend to ortho*praxis*—right practice—in the same way that they attend to orthodoxy. This is not, of course, to detract from the call to think critically and deeply about eucharistic faith in the face of serious challenges in our

patterns of food production, distribution, and consumption. It is
to say, rather, that theological and moral understandings of these
issues and commitments, as well as the capacity to act responsibly,
will be stunted if limited only to their intellectual dimensions.
It is to say that intellectual knowing must always be augmented
by the kinds of affective and embodied knowing that reside in
practice: the kinds of knowing discovered only by relating to
another human being, by placing our bodies in particular places
and positions, by smelling and touching and seeing. Engagement
in practices affords Christians a kind of knowing that is otherwise
"outside our ken."[2] This understanding of practices, and their
capacity to not only express but also shape our moral commitments (and thus our character), is central to conversations in both
ethics and practical theology.[3]

The first part of this book has framed a contextual, theoretical,
and theological framework for interpreting the global food system. In this second part, the questions become far more grounded,
embodied in the work of particular persons, communities, and
practices. This is not to say that the framework outlined thus far
recedes into the background. In fact, that analysis continually
insists itself into the conversation, resetting the stage for each new
practice introduced. Conversely, the practices themselves reinter-
pret and challenge the framework, repeatedly posing new insights,
new complexities, and new problems.[4] To the texts already considered—Scripture, policy analysis, law, philosophy, poetry—now
are added the sacred texts of human lives and activity, yielding
new invitations to people of faith.

And so, a book about religious responses to the global food
system would be incomplete without digging in the dirt: accompanying, as best one can in written word, people of faith as they
engage the questions, make mistakes, build relationships, influence their local food systems, and discover new ways of being
Christian in this time. People and communities seek to establish
food security in their neighborhoods and towns, build relationships between farmers and consumers, reenvision how humans
relate to the land, support the dignity and livelihoods of farmers
and laborers, and rediscover the meaning of being a neighbor. The
stars of the show, so to speak, are the practices themselves. Within
each practice, one encounters a variety of people doing their part

to be faithful members of God's creation: hearing their stories, examining more closely the challenges they seek to address, and considering the new theological insights and questions being raised by their experience. Their efforts are modest, and yet they constitute "little moves against destructiveness": imagining a different and just future for the food system, for human beings, and for the earth.[5]

CHAPTER FOUR

Church-Supported Farming
Building Relationships and Supporting Sustainable Agriculture

The fellowship hall of Faith Lutheran Church in Brookfield, Illinois, is bustling. Despite the icy February rain outside, the spirit inside the church is warm and energetic. For the first time, the congregation is hosting a winter farmers market, sponsored by Faith in Place.[1] Twice monthly through the long Chicago winter, farmers from as far as four hundred miles away descend upon local congregations. With help from confirmation classes, creation care committees, and other volunteers, the farmers set out their canned goods, pastries, eggs, fiber arts, spices, meats, and oils on tables around each space. The last hour before a market begins is marked by frenetic activity, as the volunteers await the arrival of each vendor, hope for a flood of eager shoppers, and occasionally offer up a quasi-prayer to the weather gods of the infamous Chicago winter.

These markets can be described as practices of church-supported farming, helping farmers extend their seasons in a region in which the usual selling season may last for only three or four summer months. They also invite shoppers—congregation members, neighbors, friends—into deeper relationship with the farmers who grow food and, through them, the earth that yields it. In each fellowship hall, church basement, or courtyard hosting a market, people of faith are seeking to close a gap: the gap between the economic security of farmers engaged in sustainable agriculture and the food needs of families who have become quite alienated from the real costs and processes of food production.

Around the United States, in rural and urban communities, religious communities are awakening to the ways in which the global food system alienates farmers, laborers, and consumers from one another. Perhaps they have financially struggling farmers in their midst, or families who are becoming increasingly concerned about the origins of their food. As they come to this awareness, they seek to make connections between the experience and struggles of farmers and every family's desire to eat healthfully, economically, and justly. These connections are severely obscured in the antiseptic aisles of the supermarket, where price tags are displayed prominently but ingredients and origins of foods are not. Cartoonish representations of contented animals, bucolic farms, and happy (mostly white) farmers on food packaging conceal the economic, environmental, and social realities of contemporary agriculture.[2] This degree of alienation is in direct contrast to the theology of interdependence represented in eucharistic life.

Practices of church-supported farming, like the market described above, seek to reestablish bonds of interdependence, finding means of connection and relationship where alienation abounds. The practices are innovative, but they also are a delicate balancing act. The creative tension of balancing sometimes-competing needs is not lost on Erika Dornfeld, Faith in Place's market coordinator. She fidgets, scurrying from the rain-soaked loading area to the coffee brewing in the kitchen to the sanctuary doors, peeking to see if worship is nearing conclusion. Walking away from the mushroom vendor's table, Erika wipes her brow with a silent "whew": "I tell you what—mushrooms are like the only fresh thing we have these days, so it just kills me if they don't come. But I also don't want them to come and not do well, so I'm torn that they showed up today." Although it is evident that she has planned and confirmed every detail, checked and rechecked the slate of vendors, and gently reminded the planners of the importance of publicity, Erika admits that she's always a little worried that something will go awry: whether all the vendors will arrive, whether roads will be passable in the Chicago winter, and whether people will come to the market and—more importantly—spend money there.

While it might seem a small thing that she's doing—these quaint markets—Erika's work is about standing in the gap that, niche restaurants aside, continues to grow between farm and table. Each church-hosted market embodies the connections that too easily are lost in the global food system. Although these markets—and other church-supported farming practices—are fragile, and their quantifiable effects are meager, they are nothing less than "little moves against destructiveness."[3] In the face of great structural injustice in the global food system, practices like these are remarkable seeds of resistance, and thus worthy of consideration.

A clear understanding of these practices requires, first, a deeper exploration of the contours of this alienation—the "gap" between farm and table—and the ways in which the current food system exacerbates these issues. Against this contextual backdrop, two church-supported farming practices—hosting markets and community-supported agriculture—emerge, accompanied by accounts of both their contributions and their fragility, as well as the personal stories of some of their practitioners. Joined together by their common quest for good food, congregation members, farmers, and local residents embody in these practices the kinds of interdependent relationships that resist the pervasive alienation that otherwise characterizes commodified food systems. By getting to know and supporting the farmers, participants honor the dignity of agricultural work, and also can trust the simple goodness of healthy, unprocessed foods. Together, the farmers and community members rediscover their identity as members of God's creation, and the concomitant demand to do whatever nurtures and respects the land. Practices of church-supported farming bear multiple effects on the global food system, on communities, and on the practitioners themselves.

MINDING THE GAP
FARMER AND CONSUMER NEEDS IN TENSION

The current arrangements of the global food system benefit a very small constituency. In the hourglass-shaped arrangement of food production, distribution, and consumption, a very thin band of food processors and distributors stands between farmers and consumers. While it would be a mistake to assume that consumers have no influence in the food that is available, the distance between farmer and consumer is not only greater than ever, but also filtered through that narrow band of processors and distributors.[4]

The growing gap between farmer and consumer is not only structural, however. It also presents a moral question for people of conscience. The mere fact that human beings become "consumers" by obtaining and eating food means that this gap is not a benign fact of life, but presents moral questions about the commodification of food, human relationship with the sources of food, and economic self-interest.[5] For Christians in particular, these moral questions are theologically charged as well, demanding attention to themes like divine providence, human vocation, and ecological care. In addition, for farmers the gap presents questions about the means of production, and their relationships with the communities in which the food is received. And they, too, must consider the role of economic self-interest.

In many ways, the gap between farmer and consumer is exacerbated by what appear to be competing interests. For a farmer to make a living, food must become either cheaper to produce or sold at a higher price. For a parent feeding several children, food needs to be as healthy as possible at the lowest price possible. People interested in creating a sustainable food system are challenged to consider whether farmer and consumer interests must always be at odds.

Just Farming
Risks of Sustainable Agriculture

The feasibility of sustainable agriculture is a lively question in current debates about global hunger, international development, food safety, and the economic viability of farmers in the United States.[6] One need not look very far, however, to see agriculturally productive and economically thriving small- and midscale farms incorporating sustainable agriculture practices. Many of these farmers quietly defy common assumptions about the altruistic, quixotic motivations of organic farmers.[7] When farmers make the commitment to transition from conventional to sustainable models of agriculture, even if production yields drop (and in some cases they do not), the higher price garnered by organic foods can often more than make up the difference.[8]

Some farmers in the United States and other countries are turning to alternative forms of agriculture in an effort to recover a more sustainable farming lifestyle.[9] Sustainability, in this case, is understood in the broadest possible sense, asking, "What is required to sustain life into the future?" A comprehensive understanding of sustainability entails what are sometimes called the "three e's": environment, economy, and equity.[10] Transitions to sustainable agriculture, in other words, should attend to the health of the earth (and particularly its soil); the economic security of farmers, workers, and communities; and the just distribution of both benefits and risks of embracing this alternative agricultural system. Of course, there are many risks in continuing with conventional agriculture as well. Some farmers tell stories about family farms that, as they began farming on an industrial scale, could no longer financially support the family, resulting in family members moving to urban areas for employment or taking on "off-farm employment" alongside the farm work.[11] The emotional and physical stress of farming on this scale and at this pace is significant as well.[12] Some who have grown up in farming communities know these risks quite personally, as they watched farms collapse under debt pressure, and farmers whom they loved become sick: "[W]hen we ask people to farm conventionally, we're asking them to poison themselves so that we can have cheap food. That's real for me. That's not just a theory," laments Faith in Place director Clare Butterfield.

For farmers who have already made the transition to sustainable farming practices, this integrated understanding (of economic and environmental sustainability) is at the heart of the diverse goals and benefits of alternative agriculture.[13] The transition from conventional to organic agriculture, however, can take as long as three to five years.[14] Farmers are economically vulnerable in the meantime, while they work conscientiously toward financial security in sustainable agriculture. Furthermore, there are particular risks associated with converting from conventional agriculture to sustainable agriculture.[15] Access to markets and crop insurance are two of the risks particularly relevant to the gap between farmer and consumer needs.

When farmers decide to transition away from conventional agriculture, one of the commitments they make is to find their own markets for the goods they produce.[16] While the promise of higher prices may allay some concerns about future markets for their goods, many farmers must first take the leap away from agribusiness, no longer selling their crops (or eggs or livestock) to one corporate buyer. As cash crop or contract farmers, they had to cultivate only one relationship; a move to organic and other alternative agricultural modes requires the establishment and nurturing of multiple relationships in order to market what they produce. Recently, for example, one of the Perdue contract poultry farmers featured in the film *Food, Inc.* made headlines by beginning a pastured egg farm, a total turnaround from her days raising chickens for Perdue.[17] She and her husband are now totally responsible for (and, on the bright side, totally in control of) establishing a market for the eggs they are raising. So far, they are selling the eggs to a local community-supported agriculture operation (CSA) and are working on a contract with a nearby major natural foods store.[18] Making these arrangements, however, is not always easy. Sometimes it even discourages collaboration between farmers, a risk that some farmers have creatively addressed by establishing farming cooperatives. As one founder of an Iowa meat marketing co-op put it, "As small producers, if we each tried to be a one-man show with direct marketing to the same customers, we would be working against each other."[19] Cooperatives offer social and technical support to farmers who are navigating the complexities of the market as small-scale producers.

Farmers also need support in another way. While growing commodity crops, farmers are eligible for subsidy payments and crop insurance. If they choose to transition to organic growing, for the most part they lose access to some government income supports and insurance assistance.[20] Farmers depend on crop insurance to get them through seasons in which weather, blight, or natural disaster severely affects production. One of the limitations of crop insurance subsidies is that they require neither that farmers take steps to mitigate the effects of climate change nor that they seek more environmentally sustainable farming practices. The ironic effect of these subsidies is that they perpetuate the very same environmentally destructive farming practices that contribute to crop failure, while abandoning farmers who want to change these patterns. In the absence of these guaranteed supports, farmers need insurance that they will not succumb to financial ruin if they make the transition toward more independence and sustainable practices. This is a place where communities of faith can support change: "If you want to change," Clare Butterfield imagines telling farmers, "we promise that your family will not be hungry." In other words, religious communities might provide alternative forms of "insurance" to farmers who want to find another way.

Establishing economic security, to a degree that supports ecologically sustainable and socially responsible farming practices, is the key to the viability of alternative agricultural models. This rests in part on supporting the financial stability of farmers. It also depends on the capacity of consumers to pay the real price of food produced by less-subsidized sustainable agricultural practices.

Just Eating
Consumers Trying to Do Good

For farmers and farmworkers to earn a sustainable income, consumers need both access and the resources to purchase the food at a fair price. Here, in many cases, is where the gap appears. Shoppers in the United States spend a far smaller proportion of their disposable income on food than their peers in other countries, and approximately one-third of what their grandparents paid for food.[21] Culturally, shoppers in the United States value frugality and can hardly resist revealing the low price they paid for something. Particularly during the economic recession at the beginning of the twenty-first century, many consumers are abandoning the supermarket to shop for groceries at discount stores like Walmart and Costco,[22] clip budget-friendly recipes from magazines and supermarket circulars,[23] and tune into the Food Network to watch *Diners, Drive-Ins and Dives* and *Ten Dollar Dinners*.

In many ways, frugality is a virtue. In economically challenging times, shoppers may need to make difficult choices between conventionally farmed eggs priced at less than one dollar per dozen and sustainably farmed eggs at prices sometimes topping five dollars per dozen. Many of them know, intellectually, that the latter are a better choice for the chickens, for the earth, and for the farmworkers. In the antiseptic environment of the supermarket, however, and with limited household budgets, the distance between the family dinner table and a farmer's livelihood may be just too great to overcome.

Even consumers who are willing to spend more on food that is justly produced frequently must rely on labels and other forms of communication from the food processors and distributors to make moral choices about the food they eat. "I think it is frustrating because really it is hard to know what the best choice, most faithful, ethical choice is," one pastor and mother of two laments. Echoing the concerns of many consumers who long for healthy food produced in just and sustainable ways, she is responding to a recent story about the National Organic Standards Board. The board has come increasingly under the influence of huge corporations, for most of which organics is only a segment of what they produce or distribute. The president of Eden Organics now refuses to put the certified-organic label on Eden's products, calling it a fraud: "The board is stacked. . . . Either they don't have a clue, or their interest in making money is more important than their interest in maintaining the integrity of organics."[24] Since 2002, the number of nonorganic substances allowed in "certified organic" foods has more than tripled. The Department of Agriculture is mandated to appoint three consumer representatives to the fifteen-member standards board. A report published by the Cornucopia Institute names at least two corporate executives (neither of whom were affiliated with any consumer advocacy group) who have been appointed to these seats.[25] Consumers reasonably may wonder whether their concerns are adequately represented in the setting of standards.

Consumers who want to make conscious decisions about the food that they purchase have relied on organic certification to guide them through the maze of options when shopping in local supermarkets. They are motivated by concerns about family health, the state of the planet, economic and worker justice, and animal welfare. They prefer to purchase, prepare, and share with their families foods that are free from toxins, have been produced in a humane manner, are grown and harvested in ways that are sustainable for the earth, and for which a fair wage has been paid to the farmer and the laborer. All of this information is virtually invisible in the supermarket. "Corporations just package things in brown and green, they call it 'natural,' and we buy it. They just slap a leaf on it!" laments one Presbyterian elder. While she is speaking hyperbolically, the truth of her statement holds true: consumers who want to make morally sound choices are often at the mercy of their food suppliers' willingness to share the very information they need to make informed decisions.[26] And when the regulating body itself is subject to question with regard to its motives, consumers may be tempted to give up altogether.[27]

When dealing with the complex structures of corporations, even well-meaning people of faith sometimes find the barriers between the consumer and producers too great to overcome. In some cases the distance between not only consumer and producer, but even distributor and producer, seems by design. In his efforts to uncover the origins of his favorite coffee drink, Tom Beaudoin discovered that "this company refused to take responsibility for living wages for their coffee farmers through a series of distancing measures, by employing layers of midlevel 'independent' operators to relate to farmers. Through a deft business mechanism, they pronounced themselves unaccountable to the workers they depended on the most."[28]

These "distancing measures" contribute a deep sense of alienation from the people and processes by which food is produced, distributed, and even consumed. Consumers may feel increasingly impotent when it comes to ensuring nutritious and safe food for their own children: even more so when considering their capacity to relate justly, compassionately, and honestly to farmers and the land upon which they work. People of faith who seek to address this distance are working to reestablish bonds of interdependence with farmers and farmworkers who otherwise might be anonymous to them and working lands that are invisible to them.

There are real tensions between farmer well-being and consumer well-being. Rather than attributing simple greed to either group, advocates for a just food system ask, Where is the common ground? Who can stand in the gap? In light of these realities, many communities of faith are working toward the reestablishment of bonds of interdependence and the reconnection of farmer and consumer.

IN IT TOGETHER
CHURCH-SUPPORTED FARMING

Practices of church-supported farming are a means by which people of faith are working to address these tensions and rediscover deep connections between farmer, land, and table. Religious communities offer a set of social and economic supports to farmers, including helping them to establish markets for the foods they grow and raise, interpreting to the broader community the value of purchasing goods from local farmers, and even (in the case of CSAs) paying a wage and benefits to farmers. These relationships also offer a set of social and ecological goods to the religious community, including the assurance of knowing the practices and inputs used to produce their food, the pleasures of relating more closely to the land and the food it produces, and a means to practice ecological sustainability. This chapter presents two such practices: religious communities hosting winter markets for local farmers, and a church that has started its own farm and community-supported agriculture program. The interfaith environmental organization Faith in Place has dreamt of and supported these practices across Illinois since its infancy. Before exploring these practices in detail, let us first situate them in the landscape of this organization.

Faith in Place and the Sustainable
Food Commitment

Since its origins in 1999, interfaith environmental organization Faith in Place has made "sustainable food" one of its four mission foci.[29] "Many of our faith traditions say something about how we eat, what we eat, how to grow food and how to give thanks for it. All of them say that we are charged with the love of our brothers and sisters," reads the rationale for the organization's commitment to sustainable food, reflecting the organization's commitment to both ecological and economic sustainability.[30] A commitment to sustainable food is a natural fit for the organization, situated in the agricultural context of Illinois. The commitment also, however, is deeply rooted in the biography and moral framework of Clare Butterfield, the organization's founder and executive director. She has witnessed the struggles of farmers in the central Illinois farming community of her childhood as well as hunger among the urban poor in a Washington, D.C., shelter. These experiences gave her "the sense that I was watching people drown and that I was in a safe place on the bank. And that just didn't feel like where I was supposed to be." The seeds for a ministry vocation grounded in the concept of sustainability were planted.

Whole communities, both rural and urban, suffer as a result of the arrangement of the contemporary food system. The way things are is not serving anyone, Clare argues: "You have to buy the whatever feeds your family well for the money that you have in your pocket. . . . [W]e attempt to solve this problem with cheap food, which still isn't working for you. . . . If the problem is poverty, let's solve poverty. Let's not impoverish another group of people—the ones who grow food." The sustainable food focus of Faith in Place is grounded in attention not only to the ecological dimensions of agriculture, but also to the social and economic dimensions of human thriving and human suffering. Theologically speaking, it requires tending the delicate bonds of interdependence that bind our futures, and the future of the earth, together.

Among the sustainable food programs organized in the past by Faith in Place have been a farmers market on the West Side of Chicago, which connected black farmers in rural Pembroke, Illinois, with Chicago's urban black neighborhood of Austin; summer urban gardening projects for children and youth; and an innovative eco-*halal* program called Taqwa. Taqwa was an effort to expand the concept of *halal* and to connect the Muslim community with a cooperative of organic lamb farmers who worked with trained and certified *halal* slaughterers to create a market of justly produced lamb.[31] As with many such efforts, however, the gap between farmer needs and consumer needs was just too great, and the eco-*halal* program struggled to find a stable market: "Oh, my goodness, it was hard. It was just crazy hard. We were trying to do so many things," Clare recalls. After six years, the organization handed the operation off to their partner, who has kept up the effort in collaboration with Whole Earth Meats. Once Taqwa ended, Faith in Place was in search of new sustainable food projects that offer a bridge between sustainable agriculture and community food needs, projects that address the economic security of farmers making the transition to sustainable agriculture and the increasing disconnect felt by consumers. Since 2009, two projects have emerged as creative responses to the needs of farmers and local communities: winter farmers markets and community-supported agriculture (CSA).

Winter Markets

Not unlike the Taqwa project, winter markets work toward diverse goals, supporting persons and communities at different points in the food system. Born in collaboration with a similar effort sponsored by the Churches' Center for Land and People in Wisconsin, the markets reflect the desire to promote mutual flourishing among farmers, consumers, and religious communities. The markets' goals are to "provide an additional source of income for vendors during the off-season; promote sustainable farming methods and economic justice for regional farm families; encourage healthy, wholesome eating; support the building of relationships between producers and consumers; and help farming families during times of crisis through the Farmer Crisis Fund."[32]

From these goals, it is clear that Faith in Place, in partnership with local faith communities, hopes that these markets will contribute to the closing of the gap between farmer and consumer. On alternating weekends each winter, market coordinator Erika arrives early in the morning, greeting member volunteers from the hosting religious community, from the Unity Temple in Oak Park, to the Jewish Reconstructionist Congregation in Evanston, to Bethany Lutheran on the South Side of Chicago. Slowly, the vendors pour into each space, turning empty rooms and tables into bustling, vibrant communities. Tables are piled high with mushrooms, herbal soaps and teas, pasta sauces, pastries, and yarn. Samples of lamb, salsas, and cheese abound. Coolers stocked with frozen meats, eggs, and cheese hum in the background. Sometimes musicians from the congregation show up. Other times, community members prepare a meal that is shared right in the midst of the market. One overhears conversations between the vendors and the customers (many of whom are congregation members): "Where is your farm?" "What kind of sauce did your mother can?" "That's delicious!" "I've never had that before."

Of course, an onlooker would be mistaken to romanticize markets like these. Sometimes the gap is just too great to overcome. Sometimes a market may appear successful, with many people visiting each vendor. This activity, however, does not always translate into enough sales to be worth the vendors' while. For example, Erika recalls a lamb vendor who stopped participating in the market: "They might sell forty dollars worth of lamb chops, but between gas from Wisconsin and tolls and then to pay me 10 percent . . . Why do they come, you know?"

The income from goods sold is not the only benefit to farmers, however. As established in the goals for the program, the markets also support the Farmer Crisis Fund. Vendors who make more than $150 contribute 10 percent of their earnings to the fund at each market. The Farmer Crisis Fund offers small grants of up to $1,000 to farmers who have emergency costs—medical bills, tractor repair bills, utility bills—as a form of community insurance. In this way, the members of the community take care of one another.[33] These markets are a balancing act. The relationships built between farmers, between farmers and consumers, and within the larger community are important outcomes.

The education of congregations about the real cost of sustainably produced food is an important outcome, too. Even though she frequently witnesses the transformation as faith community members understand why they should pay more for eggs at these markets, Erika admits that worrying about the farmers sometimes keeps her up at night. She feels very keenly the pressure of supporting the vendors' and farmers' livelihoods, a responsibility that is quite heavy for a twenty-three-year-old Lutheran Volunteer.[34] "I felt, always, a little tension in our role," Erika says, "because we have an obligation to the farmers to make [the markets] successful, but we also are about advocating education, so making it really holistic for the congregation in terms of what it means for [them] as a faith community." In other words, through these markets, one hopes, people of faith are discovering the goodness of sustainable agriculture, and the religious responsibility to support these efforts.

Sola Gratia CSA

It is one thing for a church to open its basement to host a farmers market once a year. It is quite another for a church to hire a farmer and turn its property into its very own farm! Yet this is exactly what St. Matthew Evangelical Lutheran Church of Urbana, Illinois, is doing. St. Matt's, as some community members call it, is now home to Sola Gratia Farm, a CSA that serves the Champaign-Urbana area.

Described in brief toward the beginning of this chapter, a CSA (community-supported agriculture) is much like the winter markets program in that it attempts to address a number of diverse needs. It provides local, sustainably farmed food (with known origins) to consumers, it secures a stable market for farmers, it provides farmers with an influx of financial support at the beginning of the growing season, and it strengthens—or, in some cases, establishes—relationships between farmers and the families who eagerly anticipate their weekly boxes of food from them. When a family subscribes to a CSA, they purchase "shares," becoming shareholders in the endeavor. They assume, with the farmer, the risk of a bad season: in the case of drought, fire, floods, blight, tornadoes, heat waves, cold snaps, and so on, shareholders in a CSA say, with their investment, "We are with you." There will be seasons of abundance and seasons of austerity, and the shareholders experience that with the farmer. It is a form of crop insurance, of sorts.[35] Many congregations have volunteered their space as a CSA "drop," where farmers drop off and community members pick up their weekly shares. Few religious communities, however, have started *their own* CSAs, taking the financial responsibility of hiring (and providing benefits to) the farmer, preparing the soil, insuring the operation, and a multitude of other responsibilities that might otherwise be invisible to the congregation.[36] St. Matthew was keenly aware of these responsibilities.

Much like Faith in Place's winter markets program, the idea for Sola Gratia came about in a somewhat serendipitous manner. Brian Sauder, a Mennonite staff member at Faith in Place, is the coordinator for the central Illinois office of the organization. Brian grew up in a rural context with a long-abiding love for nature, and earned a degree in environmental studies at the University of Illinois before completing a theological degree. His office, normally housed in the campus YMCA building on the university campus, was temporarily hosted by St. Matthew's Church. Once, when Clare Butterfield came out to visit him, she took one look at the corn planted on the church acreage and asked, he says, "Brian, have you ever thought about talking to St. Matt's about turning that into a CSA?" Up to that point, the church had, with volunteer farm help, grown corn and soybeans, donating all the profits from their sale to an organization working on hunger issues. For the congregation to think about a more expensive and labor-intensive use of the land would require a period of study and reflection. It also would require taking a not-insignificant risk. But in that brief conversation, and one that followed with the pastor of the congregation, Bob Rasmus, Sola Gratia CSA was born. In the fall of 2010, Brian took a plan to the church council for converting four acres of church land into an organic farm.

Over the next year, the church wrestled with the possibilities and liabilities of the plan. For example, one of the concerns raised by council members was the long history of the congregation's hunger ministries, funded by the corn and soybeans that had been conventionally farmed on church property. In an innovative transformation of that commitment, the council decided that 10 percent of the food produced by the CSA would be tithed to the local food bank. Thus, the church would continue its ministries of feeding the hungry, and in a more direct manner.

The plan was new and risky. St. Matthew's was ready for this creative risk, however, and approved Sola Gratia in the fall of 2011. They hired Farmer Dex, who, with a group of dedicated volunteers, broke ground in the spring of 2012.[37] By the summer of 2012, Sola Gratia had sold seventy-five shares to almost one hundred families and was contributing around two hundred pounds of fresh produce to the Eastern Illinois Food Bank each week.[38] Sola Gratia means "by grace alone." Trusting in God's providence, this congregation is changing the local food system.

SETTING THE TABLE
THEOLOGICAL AND MORAL PERSPECTIVES ON BUILDING
COMMUNITY AND TENDING BONDS OF INTERDEPENDENCE

In the center of each Winter Market, there are several tables and chairs set up just for community fellowship. Church and community members, and sometimes the vendors themselves, sit there and visit during the market, sharing a cup of coffee and perhaps a pastry they have just purchased. Around these tables, the good gifts of God's creation are honored and human relationships deepened and restored.

The sustainable food initiatives supported by Faith in Place have clear goals and, in some ways, measurable outcomes. They respond to real needs in the context of urban life in Chicago and rural life in central Illinois. They go a long way toward closing the gap between farmer and consumer. In fact, Clare is convinced that if more religious communities took up the mission of supporting sustainable food initiatives, their work would transform the state of Illinois, thus literally closing the gap. Both she and Brian cite a study by the Leopold Institute at Iowa State University, which indicates that dedicating just sixty-nine thousand acres of the state's farmland to the production of fruits and vegetables would meet all of the state's fruit and vegetable needs.[39] While this might sound like a lot of land, sixty-nine thousand acres represent a mere three-tenths of 1 percent of all the farmland in Illinois.[40] All of the fruits and vegetables needed to feed six midwestern states could be grown on farmland the size of one county in Iowa.[41] When Clare thinks about those numbers, she grins. "[T]hat's darned encouraging, because maybe . . . how many churches are there? How much land do they own?" If each church in rural Illinois were inspired by St. Matthew's example and contributed four acres to fruit and vegetable production, it is quite possible that the state would be markedly closer to having a thriving local food system.

Faith communities have immense capacities to change the regional food system. Churches in Illinois might very well be the vanguard of a new food context in the state. Even their most modest accomplishments are worthy of celebration. Every new market established for a farmer practicing sustainable agriculture; every new opportunity for a community to taste and trust the sources of its food; every new use of church land in search of a just and faithful way of producing, distributing, and consuming food . . . every one of these is a "little move against destructiveness."[42] These practices embody and give meaning to eucharistic moral commitments: they promote and support sustainable agriculture as a means to care gently for the land, they establish communities of support and financial security for those who work the land, and they even extend aid to the poor and hungry through the Farmer Crisis Fund and the produce tithed to the food bank. Perhaps most poignant, however, are the capacities of these church-supported farming practices to cultivate and nurture a keen sense of the inter-relatedness of humanity and creation.

At the heart of it all are the bonds of interdependence that are strengthened in each exchange, resisting the patterns of alienation that tend to mark the global food system. The mission statement for Sola Gratia Farms is this: "By grace alone may we share our gifts with the hungry, may we be good stewards of the Earth, may we build a community of cooperation and care."[43] With goals similar to those expressed for Faith in Place's winter markets, Sola Gratia is imagining a different way of understanding not only human relationships to the land and the food it produces, but also to the human beings and communities who do the hard work of farming, particularly as they do that work with increasing attention and care for the health of the earth. These practices are a means by which people of faith might recognize that the act of eating makes them agricultural people. This stands in direct contrast with the quality of alienation that so frequently marks a trip to the supermarket. "Eating is an agricultural act," insists Wendell Berry. "Most eaters, however, are no longer aware that this is true. They think of food as an agricultural product, perhaps, but they do not think of themselves as participants in agriculture. They think of themselves as 'consumers.' "[44]

And so this story has come full circle. When tending to the gaps and tensions between the needs of farmers and consumers, people of faith are inevitably confronted by the limitations and commodifying implications of understanding human beings and "consumers." To be a conscious "eater," in contrast, one "must understand that eating takes place inescapably in the world, that it is inescapably an agricultural act, and that how we eat determines, to a considerable extent, how the world is used. This is a simple way of describing a relationship that is inexpressibly complex. To eat responsibly is to understand and enact, so far as one can, this complex relationship."[45] By becoming eaters rather than consumers, people of faith more fully and responsibly inhabit the agricultural act of eating. It is to recognize and, indeed, embody the responsibility of *membership* in an interdependent universe. And by so doing, human "members" of creation slowly repair the broken relationships that perpetuate and exacerbate the gap between the practice of farming and the act of eating.

Of course, the transformation of consumers to members is not easily quantified when looking at practices like the winter markets or the CSA. It may very well be that few of the market shoppers or CSA members would say that their relationship to food has changed. On the other hand, there are bits of evidence to the contrary here and there, and they might give us hope. For example, Erika freely admits that she sometimes worries that congregation members and neighbors might not "get it" when they hear that the humanely and sustainably raised roasting chicken is twelve dollars per pound, compared with the chicken sold for one half, or even one third, that price at the local supermarket. She also, however, recalls one of her favorite markets, a financially very successful market hosted in the diverse Rogers Park neighborhood. Compared to more affluent neighborhoods where shoppers might spend fifty dollars on meats, cheeses, and baked goods, this one had a different feel: "There were people there meeting their neighbors, you know, and it was just a nice, big market, with the music and different kinds of folks. . . . I heard this later, but a lot more fives and tens were being pulled out, you know? Not a lot of twenties. I think people were making one decision: 'I'm going to buy my potatoes here—and I'm going to buy my garlic and my flour and my whatever at (the supermarket)—but I will buy *something* here.' "

The symbolic significance of the decision to purchase at least one item directly from a farmer should not be trivialized. When that farmer explains all the precious characteristics of that particular kind of potato, the best ways to prepare it, and what varieties would be harvested in the next week, she is *re-membering* that market shopper. She is drawing him back into the sacred membership of creation, together with him becoming a living testimony that life "extends in all directions into life-nurturing memberships with soil, plants, animals, people, and ultimately God. To know and appreciate these memberships, *and then to live sympathetically and compassionately into them*, is the crucial task."[46]

To experience an entire farm cycle with a farmer, as shareholders of a CSA do, is another way to "live sympathetically and compassionately" into human membership in creation. The members of Sola Gratia Farm embody their membership by showing up at the farm to aid in the harvesting, sharing with one another recipes for the abundance of turnips they have received this year, and, in the case of one member, even blogging about their experience with the weekly bounty.[47] Perhaps more than anything else, they embody their membership by sharing the harvest with the poorest members of the community by donating hundreds (by the end of the season, even thousands) of pounds of fresh produce to the food bank. In light of the CSA's mission to build a "community of cooperation and care," these are remarkable outcomes for a project in such infant stages.

All who eat food are made better, more "fully alive," as they reestablish the bonds of interdependence with the earth and those who do the work of farming the earth.[48] They are saved from the deep alienation that can result from lives of efficiency and anonymity. At the same time, they work to build a community that resists the deep alienation that threatens farmers, both social and economic. In practices like organizing community-supported agriculture initiatives and hosting farmers markets, religious communities name clearly their dependence on the gifts of the land and the work of the farmers' hands, and bind their own lives and well-being to that of the earth and the farmers. In this way, the risks of sustainable agriculture—and its joys—are shared in community. Like the community that gathers around the table, offers thanks, and shares in the earth's gifts of bread and wine, the diverse practitioners of church-supported farming become members of one another—by grace alone.

CHAPTER FIVE

Growing Food
From Food Insecurity to Food Sovereignty

The staff of the Wood Street Farm is putting up its fourth hoop house. This one is across the street and a little south of the three found at the current farm location in Chicago's Englewood neighborhood. These inexpensive greenhouses, made of plastic and metal piping, allow the workers at Wood Street Farm to start growing plants early in the spring and extend the growing season late into the fall by protecting the plants from the harsh weather of the Windy City. The hoop houses might appear out of place in Englewood, a struggling neighborhood on the West Side of Chicago and home to the largest number of the city's gun violence incidents in 2011.[1] In those greenhouses, however, one finds more than organic collards.

This farm is one of several urban organic agriculture projects sponsored by Growing Home, a nonprofit organization with a mission to "operate, promote, and demonstrate the use of organic agriculture as a vehicle for job training, employment, and community development."[2] The Wood Street Farm is tended by Growing Home's transitional job training program interns, all of whom have barriers to employment such as prison records, homelessness, or substance abuse issues. While some of the food produced is sold at market price at local farmers markets and in a CSA, some of it also is sold at an affordable price to Englewood residents, for whom fresh and nutritious food is not easily accessible. In the midst of so many challenges, the Wood Street Farm is just one indication of the ingenuity of Englewood's community.

It would be rash, however, to assume that the urban farm has solved all of Englewood's quandaries, cautions Seneca Kern, Community Outreach Coordinator for Growing Home. The farm has experienced a series of thefts, community resistance to their use of unoccupied land, and even instances of assault near the property of the farm. The farm must use raised beds because the soil in the lot is so toxic. Without public trashcans or habits of caring for shared space, people sometimes throw their garbage into the garden plots, Seneca shrugs. At the same time, he says, neighborhood residents have begun asking what is going on in those hoop houses and purchasing (at a discount) bags of produce from the farm stand.

In the midst of what has been one of Chicago's largest "food deserts," the Wood Street Farm is trying to renew the community's relationship with food, with the land, and, indeed, with each other. While itself not a faith-based organization, Growing Home (like many religious communities in urban areas) sees the practice of growing food as an avenue to feeding the hungry, supporting the economic and social futures of the community, and rediscovering human dignity and agency.[3]

Urban communities face serious challenges with regard to food justice: food insecurity, issues with food access, community instability, and the disenfranchisement of people. In Chicago and Atlanta, and cities and towns across the United States, religious communities and organizations are beginning to grow their own food. These efforts are examples of the movement toward local food sovereignty, which is " 'the right [for a community] . . . to maintain and develop its own capacity to produce its basic foods, respecting cultural and productive capacity,' as well as the 'right of peoples to define their agricultural and food policy.' "[4] This chapter presents one such practice in detail—the Summer Youth Urban Gardening Program in Chicago—and a few other practices in summary. Finally, the chapter concludes with reflection on the theological and moral significance of practice of growing food, including the call to respond to hunger by seeking justice, rather than mere provision of charitable support; the restoration of human and community dignity; and the joy and even vocational passions discovered in the process.

MAKING A WAY

CONFRONTING IMPEDIMENTS TO FOOD JUSTICE

Growing food in places like Englewood is a remarkable practice of resistance in the face of intense challenges. In many cases, as in that of the Wood Street Farm, the neighborhoods are struggling economically, home to a large number of senior citizens, and in some cases face other difficult issues such as substance abuse and violent crime. The food most easily obtained in communities like these is highly processed, nutritionally lacking, and expensive. Access to reasonably priced fresh fruits and vegetables may be miles away. Attempts by religious communities to address food insecurity sometimes focus on immediate provision of calories, rather than long-term solutions responding to foundational issues of justice in how food is distributed. In light of the abundance of farmland and agricultural production just one hundred miles outside of Chicago and other major U.S cities, the lack of food access is evidence of a failure to share food and ensure its just distribution. It is the political and economic equivalent of excluding the poor from the table in early Christian meal practices. Among the many lenses through which people of conscience and faith might view the issues addressed by the practice of growing food are these four: food insecurity, "food deserts," community instability, and disenfranchisement.[5]

Toward Food Access

Food Insecurity and "Food Deserts"

Every month in the United States, almost 15 percent of households experience food insecurity, in which they are "uncertain of having, or unable to acquire, enough food to meet the needs of all their members because they [have] insufficient money or other resources for food."[6] In households with children, food insecurity is more common, affecting one in every five households.[7] Food insecurity does not necessarily issue in hunger, but hunger is a real and constant threat in food-insecure households. Even among food-secure households, however, some are only "marginally" secure, meaning that they sometimes worry about running out of food before month's end. Since 1995, when food security statistics were first collected, food insecurity has risen by almost 25 percent.[8]

There are many "safety net" programs that offer food supplements to food-insecure families, including government supports like the Supplemental Nutrition Assistance Program (SNAP) and National School Lunch Program (NSLP) and private charity efforts like soup kitchens and food pantries. These support and "emergency feeding" programs have, over time, become necessary additions to the family budget in food-insecure households.[9] The problem with reliance on these programs is twofold: one cannot assume that these sources of food will be regularly available, and reliance on supplemental food assistance can have the effect of eroding the dignity associated with providing for one's family.[10]

Measurements of food security often focus on the family or household as the unit of measurement. While this is an entirely appropriate way of assessing when and how families confront hunger, a macro-level analysis is also necessary to address the structural issues that make food security elusive for so many families. Toward this end, food justice advocates are increasingly promoting *community* food security as the means toward a more just food system. Community food security is "a condition in which all community residents obtain a safe, culturally appropriate, nutritionally sound diet through an economically and environmentally sustainable food system that promotes community self-reliance and social justice."[11] Most immediately, gardens like the one in Englewood provide food for households in their surrounding neighborhoods. Beyond that, however, the practice of growing food contributes to the building of a local, accessible, and sustainable food system that strengthens the whole community.

While poverty is perhaps the most pressing obstacle to food security, its structural aspects include other dimensions of common life, such as transportation, neighborhood crime, and racial demographics.[12] In Englewood, for example, residents report that even though a supermarket is located within walking distance (an inconvenient but not insurmountable one mile), they may struggle to find a means to transport their groceries home, and at times in which they feel safe.[13]

In an attempt to adequately describe this situation of food access, Mari Gallagher and her research firm in 2006 coined the term "food desert": a neighborhood "with no or distant grocery stores but an abundance of fast-food restaurants and other retail outlets offering little or no nutritious food."[14] In Chicago in 2006, she found that almost 633,000 people lived in a "food desert." In 2011 that number had decreased by almost 40 percent, to just under 384,000.[15] Since the original report, Chicago's food access situation has vastly improved. A growing number of neighborhoods are now in a situation of food balance, in which access to grocery stores is equal to that of fast-food restaurants, liquor stores, and convenience stores. At the same time, it continues to be true that in some Chicago neighborhoods, and communities across the country, the most vulnerable members of our communities are affected by a "grocery gap," in which the most readily available food is the least healthy.[16] "Food deserts" persist in urban and rural communities across the country. Researchers and activists alike have sought to determine what is required for a "food desert" to become a flourishing cornucopia of diverse, healthy, and culturally appropriate food.

Toward Food Sovereignty
Community Instability and Disenfranchisement

In response to some of the research on food access, one might assume that the clearest path to food security is the arrival of an affordable supermarket in the neighborhood. Certainly, the presence of a supermarket vastly widens the array of fresh food available in a neighborhood. At the same time, however, the neighborhood continues to be subject to the retail success of the supermarket. The speculative arrival and subsequent closing of a supermarket can severely disrupt community stability. For example, with its volume sales and contracts with food producers and distributors, a supermarket can quickly and efficiently establish a market, sending smaller, locally owned businesses into bankruptcy.[17] When a large retailer sets up shop in a community, it does not necessarily bring with it a felt obligation to be a contributing member of that community, or a sense of ownership with regard to the future of that community. While food access may improve in the short term, community members may well ask whether the presence of a supermarket actually contributes to community stability in the long term.

Assuming that food access—indeed, food security—is solely determined by the presence or absence of corporate retail chains concedes too much power to entities external to a community. If a supercenter opens in a neighborhood and drives down food prices (by cutting labor costs), it may increase access to and affordability of healthy food but simultaneously reduce wages in the community.[18] Relatedly, a large-scale grocery store might open, to great fanfare, in a "food desert" and then, when projected profits do not roll in, close up. The abandoned store shell serves as a reminder to the community of the company's empty promises, as do the never-built stores long since forgotten.[19] As one public health professor put it, "[T]he word 'desert' is also a verb—'to leave someone without help or in a difficult situation and not come back.' . . . The verb 'desert' focuses on action and agency, emphasizing that the lack of access to good food in some areas is not a natural, accidental phenomenon but is instead the result of decisions made at multiple levels by multiple actors."[20] Insofar as the retail giants are exercising their own agency and *sovereignty*, thus exerting authority and power in an area, they sometimes, perhaps even unwittingly, compromise the agency and sovereignty of the people in the community. People are easily disenfranchised in this arrangement.

When the community, on the other hand, improvises and imagines its own responses to food insecurity, they seek not only food security (reliable access to food) but food *sovereignty*. Originally defined by Vía Campesina as "the right of each nation to maintain and develop its own capacity to produce its basic foods, respecting cultural and productive capacity," the concept of food sovereignty can be applied on a smaller scale, too. Food sovereignty prioritizes local production of food for people, in a sustainable way, and works toward building the knowledge and skills to do so.[21] In the context of food sovereignty, the members of the community themselves are leaders in shaping the local food system. They exercise authority in determining the quality, availability, and accessibility of food in the community. Community members who want to grow food are supported in doing so.

When it can produce some of its own food, a community reduces its dependence on outside sources of food, thus moving beyond food security (in which food is provided) toward food sovereignty (in which food is produced). Food sovereignty means both that the community no longer looks solely to the presence of a corporate grocery store to provide for its food needs and that the community does not rely on emergency food ministries of charity for the provision of food. By doing so, the community participates in the movement for food *justice*.[22]

GROWING OUR OWN
PRACTICES TOWARD FOOD SOVEREIGNTY

Religious communities have long histories of feeding the hungry. From food pantries to warm meals to sandwiches delivered on urban streets to the distribution of gift cards to grocery stores, many religious communities have taken seriously the demand to "Give them something to eat."[23] In a family's most desperate moments of poverty and food insecurity, they may turn to congregations and religious organizations for immediate help. In many cases, these religious communities are the "first responders" to hunger, providing not only a meal but also a compassionate ear. They are, in the best sense, faithful ministries of charity.

Some religious communities, however, see that these efforts are limited. They are meant to respond to crises, but do little to address persistent issues of structural injustice. They respond to food insecurity with the provision of food, and when those sources of food are stable and accessible, they contribute to food security. They do not, however, support communities in establishing food sovereignty. Without contradicting the need for emergency food assistance, Christians who want to go deeper see the need for a more structural response: "On the one hand, we are called to play the Good Samaritan on life's roadside, but that will be only an initial act," exhorted Martin Luther King Jr. "One day we must come to see that the whole Jericho Road must be transformed so that men and women will not be constantly beaten and robbed as they make their journey on life's highway. True compassion is more than flinging a coin to a beggar; it is not haphazard and superficial. It comes to see that an edifice which produces beggars needs restructuring."[24] For many churches in communities affected by food insecurity (including among their own members), a more thoroughgoing community-based response to transform the situation is in order.

Practices of growing food seek to transform local structures of food availability in the interest of food sovereignty. Around the country (indeed, the world), in rural and urban communities, in truck beds, discarded tires, church backyards, and abandoned city blocks, people are growing their own food. In so doing, they not only ensure a healthy food supply for their communities but also exercise their own agency and power. In many cases, these projects begin in the hearts and imaginations of people of faith, as they seek to add ministries of justice to their historic ministries of charity. Practices of growing food are popping up in congregations, shelters, food banks, and schools.

YOUTH URBAN GARDENING PROGRAM

It is Harvest Day at Lincoln Memorial Congregational United Church of Christ's garden. Equipped with clippers, gloves, spades, and buckets, the small band of youths and their adult mentors stand in a circle in the midst of the garden to receive their instructions. The younger children are eager, asking, "Can we go in the garden now?" Before they do, however, Pastor Richard James joins the group and offers a prayer, which includes these words:

> Gracious Lord. . . . Thank you for your creative efforts that put everything that is into motion. Father, we thank you for the creativeness that comes in the form of the hands and willing hearts and minds that cleared this piece of land and built these boxes and containers and to use what you have given us to be fruitful. Thank you for all the things that this effort has caused—the relationships, the mentoring, the smiles and joy from the hard work. We ask that you continue to bless this effort. We look forward to a great next year and boxes all the way down to the fence!

The group then gets to work harvesting the last of that summer's produce: strawberries, basil, greens, herbs, tomatoes, and peppers. Pastor James is talking with two of the young women, asking them to pose for a photograph, encouraging them to display the tomato plant between them. Around the edges of the garden, elderly neighbors sit perched on church chairs, watching the youth at work. After about an hour or two, a table placed in the center of the garden is heaped with fresh produce, and the harvest group members gather behind it to document their labor and their accomplishments.

Wylanda Harris, the master gardener for Lincoln Memorial, admits that she was conservative when first laying out the garden plan. New to gardening on this scale herself, she wanted to set achievable goals for the youth responsible for the garden since it was the congregation's first such attempt. By the end of the summer, however, the whole group took a more expansive view. "I think they could grow enough food for their whole neighborhood," Veronica Kyle muses as she surveys the large backyard of the church.[25] Perhaps she imagines "boxes all the way down to the fence," as Pastor James suggested in the opening prayer.

In the summer of 2010, Veronica was working with four congregations on the South Side and West Side of Chicago to develop urban gardens like the one now thriving at Lincoln Memorial.[26] The gardens have two simple objectives: to increase the availability of fresh fruits and vegetables in neighborhoods that have historically lacked access to these foods, and to raise a new generation of young people who know how to grow their own food. Both of these goals are in service of establishing food sovereignty, whereby communities are able to provide for their own food needs in both the immediate and distant future.

The Lincoln Memorial garden is one of probably thousands of church gardens across the country. The practice of growing food in religious spaces is neither new nor uncommon. This particular garden, however, is an innovative practice for several reasons. Lincoln Memorial is a historically African American congregation in the West Woodlawn neighborhood of Chicago. The neighborhood has been home to working-class families, and yet also has witnessed more than its share of violence.[27] Gardens like this one on the South Side and West Side of Chicago are, quite tangibly, instances of new life born in the face of suffering and even death.

West Woodlawn is also in a part of Chicago affected by the "grocery gap," where healthy nutritious food is frequently hard to come by.[28] Veronica Kyle resists the language of "food deserts": "Who told you that you live in a food desert? . . . Who decided that? . . . When people tell you that you're lacking something, you might believe that. The whole idea, what's associated with a food desert in many people's minds is, 'I need a big grocery store in my neighborhood.' . . . No, you don't. You need to have access to healthy food." While the neighborhood clearly lacks access to healthy food at an affordable price, Veronica argues, practices like growing food have the capacity to change that reality, without awaiting the arrival of a supermarket. In fact, waiting for the right kind of retail outlet to arrive in a neighborhood places too much trust in business institutions that have already shown their "predatory" intentions, Veronica argues. After all, particular kinds of retail outlets *have* come to economically stressed neighborhoods: "It's no coincidence that a kid can't walk and get an apple, but they can walk and get a pizza puff or 'flaming hots' from a store. . . . What are [these store owners] investing—nothing. What are they giving back—nothing. [These stores] are not in every community because privileged people have said, No, you can't come." Lincoln Memorial is in a neighborhood marked by this pattern: few retail outlets selling healthy food at affordable prices, and a preponderance of fast-food restaurants and convenience and liquor stories. By growing food in the church's backyard, the Summer Youth Urban Gardening Program has the capacity to change this food landscape. Already, the first harvests of the gardens have been distributed to senior citizens in the church and neighborhood. The youth working the garden eat the produce for lunch, too, sharing with each other recipes for preparing the food. At the end of the summer, they compile a cookbook containing recipes for all the produce and herbs they grew.

Gardens like the one at Lincoln Memorial are innovative practices in that they not only produce food for charitable distribution or offer a window into an embodied creation spirituality (although they do these things, too) but also address serious inequities in food distribution.[29] They are efforts toward food sovereignty, and thus arenas in which practitioners can exercise their own human agency and dignity. Because these gardens also place youth at the center of the practice, they also strive to shape leaders for food sovereignty in the future.

Each of the gardens was planted, tended, and harvested by a small group of youth supervised by a "master gardener." The summer garden program is something like an apprenticeship, in which the youth earn a stipend as they learn and practice gardening, a necessary incentive for youth who need to work in the summer to earn money for themselves and their families. Some of the youth, recruited from the congregation and its surrounding neighborhood, had grandparents or parents who had grown food in their backyards, but most of them had never before tried to grow anything. In fact, Veronica recalls, "Most of them didn't grow, didn't care, and we also had typical young people, very urban: 'Never got my hands dirty. Don't want to. Can't stand bugs, worms.' As a matter of fact, we had a group of girls . . . [who] came to work cute, every day—white jeans and silver sandals. . . . [T]hey thought, 'Well, we thought we're just going to learn *about* it.' So we had to break the news that this is hands-on, and this is 'T-shirt and jeans,' and here are your boots."

Before long, however, the youth embraced the challenge. They learned about soil health, vermiculture, and sustainable agricultural practices. Each young person also was responsible for learning about a particular plant. On harvest day, the youth in attendance welcome the guest volunteers and eagerly tell them about "their" plant, what they learned about it, how they know it is healthy and ripe for harvesting. Veronica describes it as a transformation from suspicion and hesitancy to pride and dignity: "I mean these kids worked in the hottest summer. Show up every day and work that earth. If you walked into the gate, they would give you a tour with so much pride. 'These are our strawberries. These are our onions. And have you ever had this?' " Three young boys, six to eight years of age, also join in the work on harvest day, digging up marigold plants and herbs to take home to their parents. The master gardener, Wylanda, says that these boys and other children from the neighborhood started hanging around the garden as the summer progressed.

In some ways, the effects of these programs are inherently immeasurable: who knows how those children will draw on their experience, decades into the future, in establishing sustainable and accessible local food systems? At the end of the summer, the older youth gardeners wrote reflections about their experiences, offering a small window into the long-term transformative potential of the practice of growing food. Their words poignantly indicate the significance of the program in their lives, already discernible to them:

- "I've learned a lot about planting, and I've had the chance to watch little seeds grow into a big beautiful batch of collards. I've learned to be patient with the growing process."

- "I enjoyed meeting a lot of new friends and this program also helped to keep me out of trouble."

- "I have learned that caring for a garden is more than just planting seeds and watching them grow. I have learned a new lifestyle, one that is much safer than most."[30]

In the end, the Lincoln Memorial garden does address, bit by bit, issues of food security on the South Side of Chicago. More than that, the garden works to establish agency and, indeed, sovereignty in the community as it prefigures a time in which members of the community need not rely on unstable external sources of food. Perhaps its most significant contribution, however, is to the moral formation of these young people, who might become leaders in the movement toward food sovereignty in the future.[31] They express new dimensions of human agency and dignity in their own testimonies to how the garden helped them to cultivate virtues like patience and discover the good of what might be called a "certain kind of life."[32] The same young man who described the garden project as a means to stay out of trouble said this about the experience: "What made me happy was planting something and seeing the process of it growing, like the peanuts. I was amazed to see them actually start growing." The happiness, pride, and joy discovered in the practice of growing food are as essential to human dignity and food sovereignty as the food grown itself. The Lincoln Memorial garden, and others like it, are a means toward food sovereignty and human dignity. They join other practices of growing and distributing food in a variety of settings, all offering hungry people avenues to exercise agency in the production, distribution, and consumption of food.

Other Practices of Food Sovereignty
and Vulnerable Populations

Like in the Summer Youth Urban Gardening Program, other practices of growing and distributing food are emerging in places where human dignity and agency might otherwise be at risk: food banks in major cities establish gardens to supplement the nonperishable donated foods that otherwise characterize the offerings available to the food insecure. A women's shelter in central Illinois begins growing food in boxes and hay bales next to the house. In what used to be a Presbyterian church, community cooperative members gather twice weekly to inventory and distribute food among themselves. In each case, the practices of growing and managing the distribution of food enhance the nutritional quality of food available to vulnerable populations, broaden hunger ministries not only to include charitable contributions of food but also to seek justice and address inequities in food distribution, and bolster the agency of those facing food insecurity. Three of these practices of food sovereignty are described here in brief.

Atlanta Community Food Bank Community Gardens. On 175 vacant lots, abandoned spaces, and apartment green spaces around Atlanta, gardens are popping up. Resourced by the Atlanta Community Food Bank (ACFB), the gardens are tended by neighborhood members, faith communities, and agencies. Almost all of the food grown is distributed among the gardeners and in the local community. ACFB started the community gardens program as a means to extend the organization's mission to "fight hunger by engaging, educating, and empowering the community."[33] Now a secular nonprofit which works with a diverse array of groups, including religious communities, the ACFB was born as an emergency food ministry in the basement of St. Luke's Episcopal Church.[34] Founder and executive director since 1979 Bill Bolling was then serving at St. Luke's as director of community ministries.[35] Whereas the food bank inventory, distributed through ACFB's more than seven hundred partner agencies, is subject to the vicissitudes of charitable giving, the gardens are immediately accessible to community members who are willing to cultivate the land. They are not without assistance in this labor, however. The ACFB supports the community gardens with education, materials, and volunteer labor. One group of youth who worked in ACFB's Hartnett Garden in southwest Atlanta gleaned several hundred pounds of produce for distribution in the neighborhood. By supporting local communities in growing their own food, the ACFB is moving beyond food security to food sovereignty.

Center for Women in Transition Shelter Garden. Tucked in the small patch of lawn next to the transitional home in Champaign, Illinois, is a "pizza garden." Sprouting up out of straw bales are peppers, tomatoes, and savory herbs: all the ingredients for a family-friendly and healthy pizza. Tended by both volunteers and the women and children living in the Center for Women in Transition, the garden was not an easy sell at first. When Brian Sauder of Faith in Place first envisioned and planted the garden in collaboration with the director of the center, he discovered that the center backs up to a toxic waste site. He tested the soil, however, and found it to be safe. Despite this fact, Brian says, "none of the women wanted anything to do with the produce" grown directly in the ground. "It's extremely understandable," he shrugs. The women who live in the center are particularly vulnerable, disenfranchised as a result of abuse, poverty, and alienation. The fact they do not trust even the ground beneath their feet, despairing as this attitude is, should come as no surprise. As a result, the following year the volunteers began working with the children in gardening in raised beds and in straw bales so that fear of soil contamination would not prevent women and children from discovering the dignity-boosting potential of the practice of growing food. For women and children vulnerable to financial insecurity and even violence, the capacity to provide food for themselves, even a small portion of it, can be a remarkable act of self-determination.

Georgia Avenue Food Co-op. Although not itself a practice of directly growing food, the Georgia Avenue Community Ministries' Food Cooperative is another practice toward food sovereignty. Twice a week at the Georgia Avenue Church, one of six co-ops gathers in the church basement. There the co-op members work together to distribute the food received from the Atlanta Community Food Bank. Each member pays a small membership fee (about four dollars each meeting) and receives a box overflowing with food on alternating weeks.[36] The co-ops each have paid coordinators, frequently selected from among their own membership. "It's about 'How do the members, themselves, take ownership?,'" observes director Chad Hale. The emphasis on member ownership is apparent when the coordinators call the weekly meeting to order, a clear example of the ways in which co-ops support member dignity and agency, Chad says: "We've got poor people who are used to being kicked around. We don't want to perpetuate that."

Champaign County Local Foods Policy Council. In central Illinois, Brian Sauder of Faith in Place has been working to establish a local food policy council, which held its first meeting in January 2012. Other groups had made efforts to establish a council in the past, with marginal success. The council, Brian hopes, will be an "intermediary space," where organizers can bring concerns and council members can develop policy recommendations to the appropriate government entity. Local food councils are an organized means by which communities can exercise some degree of agency in the policy arena, where their concerns might otherwise go unheard. As such, they too contribute to food sovereignty.

ABUNDANT TABLE

THEOLOGICAL AND MORAL PERSPECTIVES
ON LOCAL FOOD SOVEREIGNTY

Piles of greens, herbs, and peppers are starting to slide off the edges of the small folding table placed in the center of the Lincoln Memorial garden. Although this particular table has a utilitarian use and is not set for a meal, the image of a feast set out on a table in the center of an urban garden speaks powerfully to the context of food insecurity. In the midst of a neighborhood described by outside "experts" as a "desert," as a place in which food *does not grow*, a table heaped with food tells a different story, one overflowing with eschatological hope. That story is one of a community that works together to provide food for the hungry, that honors and recovers the dignity of growing food, and that discovers the joy of relating compassionately to one another and to God's earth.

The Wood Street Farm in Englewood, the youth urban garden at Lincoln Memorial Church, and the countless gardens tended by congregations, shelters, and neighborhoods across the United States offer living, growing testimony to Jesus' admonition to Peter: "Feed my lambs."[37] While contemporary eucharistic practices that emphasize the symbolic character of the meal might lend themselves to a spiritualized interpretation of the call to feed the hungry, the sheer number of actual meals recounted in the Gospels makes plain the responsibility to ensure the availability of food for the hungry.

Particularly when reflecting theologically upon practices of growing food in communities affected by food insecurity, the stories recounting Jesus' feeding miracles (which appear in all four Gospels) are particularly instructive. Fearing that there will not be enough food, the disciples urge Jesus to send the people home. "How can one feed these people with bread here in the desert?" they protest in one telling of the story.[38] In response, Jesus simply asks them what they have, takes the meager provisions from them, and feeds the people, who number in the thousands. When the disciples share what they have, Jesus makes of their humble offering a feast. The modest garden tended by Wylanda and the teen gardeners at Lincoln Memorial might be a site of similar divine transformation.

Compassionate people of faith might wonder whether, if their own congregations are not located in neighborhoods affected by food insecurity, they should start a garden to grow food for the hungry.[39] A person or congregation, however, interested in addressing some of the systemic economic issues of food distribution and consumption may want to go deeper than immediate provision of food. The challenge lies in becoming partners rather than problem solvers: "When I'm around church people, I always check. . . . Have they substituted the vision of service for the only thing that will make people whole—community? Are they service peddlers or community builders?" John McKnight provocatively asks. "Peddling services is unchristian—even if you're hell-bent on helping people. Peddling services instead of building communities is the one way you can be sure not to help."[40]

At the Harvest Day celebration at Lincoln Memorial, the *youth* gardeners were the most-informed experts on any given plant in the garden. The community members themselves had determined what would be grown, when it would be harvested, and how it would be distributed. Of course, they asked for and received technical help when necessary. On the whole, however, members of other congregations who wanted to participate in the Lincoln Memorial garden became the gardeners' *partners* in working toward food sovereignty, rather than their service providers in charitable contributions toward food security. Indeed, several of the volunteers were not from the West Woodlawn neighborhood. Some of them came from neighborhoods where fresh (even organic) food was ubiquitous. And yet they were not "peddling services": they waited for instructions and wisdom to be offered from the community members who were the experts on that community, its members, and the food they had been growing there. Together they are transforming the Jericho Road, one garden at a time.

The complexities of weighing ministries of charity and justice present challenges to every religious community in a broad range of contexts. Even the earliest Christians struggled to understand and respond to the demands of economic and social justice. In the communities described in the book of Acts, the earliest Christians wondered whether and to what degree they should share their possessions. Despite the call to share possessions, some among them continued to go hungry.[41] Similarly, Paul recounts the ways in which attendants at the earliest eucharistic meals continued to treat the poor as objects of charity, giving to them the leftover or poorest quality of food.[42] The eschatological thrust of the Eucharist, however, is a shared meal of abundance in which each participant not only eats but contributes to the meal, placing her gifts upon a table already weighed down in the midst of a garden, with enough food for all.

In practices of growing food, and in the movement toward food sovereignty, religious communities and people of faith set the table, prepare the meal, and invite the guests. When volunteers come to visit the garden, to work for an hour or two, the community members are the hosts, extending hospitality to the guests in the garden. The community gardeners are the ones who know the soil, the plants, and the recipients of the food they are growing. Particularly in otherwise food-insecure communities like Chicago's 20th Ward, urban gardeners exercise their agency and authority in planning, implementing, and harvesting their own food. Moving from receiving food charity to participating in food justice means "ensuring that the benefits and risks of where, what, and how food is grown and produced, transported and distributed, and accessed and eaten are shared fairly."[43] The practice of growing food is a means to nurture human agency—the capacity to make decisions, act accordingly, and reflect upon one's experience—and an entrée to active and meaningful participation in the movement toward food justice. Along the way, dignity is honored and restored as well. Whereas urban youths and their families might otherwise be quite alienated from the earth and the means of food production, these gardens restore that relationship, bit by bit.

When Veronica Kyle visited any one of the Summer Youth Urban gardens, she was struck by the pride the youth took in their work: "Putting something in the ground one day, then two, three, four, five days down the road, ten days later, seeing this little sprout stick out. For some of them, it was like, 'Wow!' And then to grow, to nurture it and taste it. 'This is what a tomato tastes like from the ground. This is okra.' I would go and visit and they would go, 'Mrs. Kyle, you don't know? This is basil. Rub it in your hand. Smell it.'" The same teenagers who were none too impressed by the prospect of digging in the dirt discover that, in fact, there is much satisfaction and, indeed, joy to be found in the practice of growing food: "Now they went from 'Ugh!' to 'Taste and see.' The creator is good, that's how I looked at it. It was like taste this and see that the Lord is good. It was that kind of wonderful revelation that I'm nurturing something and I'm doing something good."

In the backyards of churches and community centers, people are doing something good. In their conscientious tending of the earth, discoveries of the dignity of growing their own food, and feeding the most vulnerable members of their communities, youth and adults growing food are a living testimony to God's creative activity in the midst of struggle. Manna arrives in the desert.[44] "See, I am doing a new thing. Do you not perceive it?"[45]

CHAPTER SIX

Transformative Travel
Education, Encountering the Other, and Political Advocacy

Cuentepec is a small pueblo not sixty kilometers from Cuernavaca, Mexico; but it is, in some ways, another world.[1] Cuernavaca is a resort community for wealthy Mexicans, boasting lush vegetation and temperate climates. Dubbed the "City of Eternal Spring," it is home to modern condominiums, high-end shops, museums, and a festive town square:[2] a temperate and lush respite from the crushing population in the urban center of Mexico City, the second-largest urban area in the western hemisphere.[3] A van ride to Cuentepec can take more than an hour, the last half traversing a country road dotted with rustic adobe homes and small farms. In the pueblo of Cuentepec itself, Felipa and other indigenous women cook over wood-burning stoves in small, enclosed stone kitchens, providing meals for their families and neighbors. Modern technology has been slow to come to Cuentepec: sewers were introduced only in 2000, and even now only half the households have them, according to Maria Louisa, a local social worker.

Felipa and other women in the community use at least three varieties of corn to make tortilla, sopes, and tamales from scratch. They patiently humor guests who want to learn how to make tortilla: stripping the corn from the cobs, preparing the *nixtamal* (soaked and cooked corn prepared with an alkaline solution), grinding the corn by hand on a *metate* (large stone) with a *mano* (rolling-pin-shaped tool), mixing the dough, rolling out the tortillas, and cooking them atop the wood-fired *comal* (stove).[4] The lumpy, unevenly shaped tortillas are devoured as fast as they come off the stone, topped with nothing more than a roasted tomato-and-garlic salsa and *crema*. As they sample their efforts, Felipa's guests marvel at the tortillas' simplicity yet depth of flavor, and how the deep red corn produces such a different flavor than the blue-black corn.

Sitting around a large table with Felipa and her husband, Pedro, in their backyard, one senses that life has been satisfying, even if difficult, in Cuentepec. Pedro is a corn farmer. He grows varieties of corn not seen in the United States: rich blue-black, white, deep gold, and vibrant red. During the growing season, he takes corn to sell in the market in Cuernavaca. He takes the husks, too, selling them for tamales. As for many farmers in rural Mexico, however, Pedro's backbreaking labor of farming is not profitable enough to sustain the family through the year. In the winter months, Pedro heads back into the city to find work to supplement his income. Felipa and other women in the community have also established an artisan cooperative with Maria Louisa, making needlework, clothing, and aprons to sell in markets and to visitors to Cuentepec.

Farmers like Pedro in rural areas of Mexico practice methods of sustainable agriculture not because it is in vogue, but because the indigenous farming traditions run very deep in these communities. Despite being encouraged to use chemical fertilizers and herbicides, many of these farmers do not take that path. Even these very remote communities are experiencing the effects of global agriculture, however. The advent of genetically modified seeds, for example, has increased the productivity and resistance of corn and soybeans, and ensures a larger harvest for the farmer who can afford to purchase these seeds. The use of these seeds in the United States, combined with commodity subsidy payments and the removal of trade tariffs in Mexico, has meant that huge quantities of cheap U.S. corn are flooding the Mexican market.

Speaking in the indigenous Nahuatl language, Pedro confirms that he has faced more difficulty in the market, although he does not immediately attribute that difficulty to global economic shifts.

When asked whether he worries about transgenic seeds, he shrugs it off. He has heard about them, he says, but he prefers to use and save seeds from the varied corn species his ancestors farmed. To a group from the United States learning about the effects of global trade on rural agriculture, Pedro appears to be standing on a precipice that he does not yet see.

Encounters like these are the bread and butter of organizations like the Chicago Religious Leadership Network for Latin America (CRLN), which hosts several such *Encuentros* delegations to the region each year. During these educational tours, Christians from the United States see with their own eyes and hear with their own ears the struggles faced by farmers, migrants, rural families, and the urban poor in Mexico, Guatemala, and Cuba. The experience of witnessing these realities firsthand prompts for many of the pilgrims a process of discernment upon their return to the United States: "For many, . . . delegation visits are conversion experiences; transforming the way we see the world and our place and power in it. We find ourselves wrestling with how we are called to respond, collectively and individually, to such realities."[5] For some, the conversion experience of learning about the political dimensions of poverty, agricultural pressures, and hunger demands a particular response: political advocacy.

Practices of education and advocacy seek to make visible the frequently invisible web of the global food system: its economic and environmental dimensions, the farmers and laborers in distant and unknown places, and the policy environment that exacerbates some of the challenges posed by the global food system. Educational tours and other opportunities for engaged learning, like CRLN's *Encuentros* programs, invite participants into personal relationships with the most vulnerable members of the global food system, expose participants to structural issues in global agriculture, and challenge participants to commit to both personal and political actions in response to what they have encountered. Practices of education and advocacy thus have the capacity to deepen participants' understandings of interdependence, moral agency, and the responsibility to "expand the table," ensuring a space for farmers and laborers around the world.

SIN MAÍZ, NO HAY PAÍS
FARMERS, GLOBAL AGRICULTURE, AND TRADE

Above the entrance to the bustling San Angel market in southern Mexico City, visitors are greeted by a spectacular bas relief mural depicting the history of Mexico. Each panel represents a distinct theme or era, from indigenous agricultural cultures to contemporary struggles in a globalized economy. Several panels recall popular movements in Mexico. One of them features people holding several protest signs: "Art. 27,"[6] "Tacos de Etanol," and "No a la ley Monsanto."[7] These images are representative of the Mexican movement for food sovereignty, in which they are protesting land grabs, the conversion of corn crops from food to ethanol production, and the incursion of genetically modified seeds into the Mexican market. Each represents a site of resistance to the cultural, political, economic, and social dimensions of the global food system in Mexico. Each represents a facet of the popular movement whose slogan is "Sin Maíz, No Hay País." Translated, the crisis is stark: "Without Corn, There Is No Country."[8]

Prior to the Mexican Revolution in the early part of the twentieth century, most of the farmland in the country was controlled by a very small percentage of landowners. One of the primary grievances at the heart of the revolution was a call for land reform, particularly among peasants (campesinos) and two of their political heroes, Pancho Villa and Emilio Zapata.[9] As the revolution was winding down, the Mexican Constitution was drafted, including Article 27, which privileged the public interest over private ownership in the use of land, a commitment which might include measures such as dividing up large estates and developing small cooperatives and agricultural centers. As land was redistributed, the government provided ejidos (publicly held communal lands) for campesinos to farm. With the implementation of the North American Free Trade Agreement (NAFTA), however, the constitution was amended to allow for more flexibility in selling these lands. Ejidos were no longer protected, and much of that land was sold to multinational corporations.[10] These rapid changes in agriculture have wrought havoc on the land and lives of corn farmers. They have also affected daily life for many Mexicans.

In Mexico the average family of four eats approximately one kilogram of tortillas each day. Freshly made tortillas are packed with nutrients and form the core of the Mexican diet. Mexicans receive as much as 40 percent of their daily protein intake from tortillas, as well as a dose of antioxidants and niacin.[11] When tortilla prices spike, tripling or quadrupling as they did in 2007, the ramifications for poor families are severe, forcing minimum-wage laborers to spend a full third or more of their daily wages on this single food product.[12] The spike in 2007 was the source of a major protest in Mexico City.[13] Corn is the foundation of the Mexican diet, and has been the foundation of Mexican agriculture as well. Prior to the implementation of NAFTA, corn production accounted for 60 percent of land under cultivation, and 40 percent of agricultural workers.[14] Now corn farmers in Mexico struggle to make enough in the marketplace to support their families, as they are forced to compete with subsidized corn dumped in the market by U.S.-held corporations.[15] Multinational corporations like Grupo Gruma (owner of the Maseca brand), which controls as much as 80 percent of the Mexican tortilla flour market, buy massive quantities of the cheap corn and store it to sell later at a higher price. Their speculative purchasing and hoarding is creating an artificial restriction in the supply of corn, driving up prices for consumers while depressing prices for producers.[16]

Far beyond its role as a nutritional and agricultural staple, corn is foundational to Mexican culture: indeed, it is at the cultural and indigenous spiritual core of the country's identity. Thousands of varieties of corn are cultivated in Mexico, the country credited with domesticating the crop.[17] Both central Mexican and Mayan (southern Mexico) indigenous traditions consider corn to be sacred.[18] They trace the origins of Mexican civilization to the discovery and domestication of corn, an achievement frequently attributed to the deity Quetzalcoatl.[19] Human life depends upon corn for its very survival.[20] According to Mayan sacred tradition as recorded in the *Popol Vuh*, human beings were formed from ground corn and water: "Food [corn] entered their flesh, along with water to give them strength. Thus was created the fatness of their arms. . . . And so there were four who were made, and mere food was their flesh."[21] Corn, as the substance of human flesh, the origin of society, and the fundamental source of life, demands the protection of both spiritual and human beings.[22] *Sin maíz, no hay país.*

Yet U.S. Americans know very little about Mexico, its agriculture, and its cultural history. As one participant in a delegation from the United States put it, "Mexico is so close to the United States, and yet so far away." To address this knowledge gap, strengthen the bonds between Christians in the United States and Mexico, and raise consciousness about the global food system's effects around the world, faith-based education and advocacy organizations are hosting groups who want to lessen the distance so keenly felt.

ENCUENTROS
ENCOUNTERS, EDUCATION, AND ADVOCACY

For three years, CRLN has organized January trips to central Mexico to explore the theme of "Tortillas and Trade."[23] The program was envisioned and facilitated by the coordinator for CRLN's *Encuentros* program, a young woman fresh from two years of mission service in Costa Rica. Erica Spilde had watched the implementation of the Central American Free Trade Agreement (CAFTA)—and the strong resistance to it among religious and social justice organizations in Costa Rica—while she was serving there from 2005 to 2007.[24] Since part of her work in Costa Rica involved educating visiting U.S. Americans about issues of social injustice, she quickly learned that while many Central Americans made a point to learn about the restrictions and effects of the trade agreement, visitors from the United States frequently arrived with little or no knowledge about the implications of CAFTA. She chose Mexico as the destination for the Tortillas and Trade travel seminar because Mexico's history with free trade agreements was longer[25] and because the country might seem more "accessible" to participants: "I really wanted us to have a trip that people could go on to learn about these issues that was less intimidating and also didn't require really advanced knowledge—that was kind of a '101.'"

The goal is simple: to examine the impact of global trade on the well-being of everyday Mexicans through the lens of food, agriculture, and hunger issues. For potential delegates unacquainted with trade policy, the focus on food might provide a more familiar lens, Erica says: "We're going to try to keep it really focused on trade and hunger issues because that's an accessible way for people of faith—and it's less political. Trade is very political, but if you look at it from a hunger standpoint, it's less 'political.'" Some of the participants join these delegations because they are interested in learning more about Mexico. Some are passionate about the issues of hunger and poverty, and some are concerned about the proliferation of "free trade agreements" in Central and South America. The delegates bring a diverse set of experiences and perspectives, with vocations as varied as social worker, baker, pastor, student, nurse, and educator. Many of them bring experience working in food pantries and other hunger ministries in their own communities, and some have worked in ministries reaching out into Latino communities. At the same time, they hear about suffering in Mexico, see the increased rates of immigration over the last twenty years, and wish that they knew more. For many of them, Erica says, there is a general sense that "we're being very poor neighbors, . . . a common sense of 'this needs to change,' and a sense of urgency about that. I think there's a sense of not being quite sure how to do it."

Grounded Learning
Educational Practices for U.S. Christians in Mexico

In response to both the hopes for the program and the diverse experiences brought by participants, the Tortillas and Trade program employs an experientially based pedagogical model, whereby participants are placed in direct relationship with artisans, laborers, activists, indigenous persons, professors, farmers, religious leaders, and the poor. They learn by being in relationship with the people of Mexico, by placing their bodies in the places and spaces Mexicans inhabit, and by confronting the structural barriers to human and ecological flourishing that Mexicans face. And they eat. A lot. They share meals with each other, and with their hosts, both rich and poor. In each of these meals, they take into their bodies the culture, the flavor, the history, and the struggles of the people whom they encounter. Educational programs like the *Encuentros* delegations are based in an understanding that learning happens by doing. Upon returning to the United States, the participants reflect on their experience, and each of them identifies one or two actions they will take in solidarity with the people of Mexico. The experience is an example of "traveling for transformation," which seeks a "complete reshaping of the participants' view of themselves and of their world. This radical new orientation is to result in a reordering of values and new ways of acting out those values in individual behavior and in political and social action for change."[26]

CRLN works with partner agencies in Mexico to facilitate these "transformative travel" experiences. One of their partners is the Cuernavaca Center for Intercultural Dialogue on Development (affectionately called the CCIDD). The CCIDD is an ecumenical retreat center whose mission is "to provide opportunities for churches and other groups from the U.S. and Canada to encounter the presence of God in the struggle for justice in the Americas, and to empower them to work for social transformation."[27] In some cases, the education happens didactically: guests come to the CCIDD and share their experiences, or offer a lecture on relevant political, economic, or cultural themes. The primary pedagogical model embraced by the CCIDD and CRLN, however, is experientially based.

Drawing on the theory and practice of Paulo Freire, educational practices like these are designed to raise consciousness by inviting learners to identify and pose problems directly as a result of their experience[28]: *Why* has the price of tortillas risen so dramatically? *Why* are farmers moving to Mexico City and taking menial jobs? *Why* has the Mexican government removed financial supports for corn farmers, while corn farmers in the United States still receive government subsidies? *Why*, in the squatter settlement of Cuernavaca's La Estacíon, are there trucks delivering soft drinks, while most of the patched-together homes do not have clean water? These questions arise with some urgency when U.S. Americans, through a series of educational practices, experience the challenges confronting everyday Mexicans, in many cases with exponential intensity since the passage of NAFTA in 1994. Along the way, they learn firsthand about the financial struggle to feed a family; movements of resistance among *campesinos* (peasant farmers); and the ancient, yet vulnerable, culinary artisanship of indigenous women.

"We couldn't afford it": an exercise in household economics. Almost every group that visits the CCIDD participates in the "Cuernavaca Quest," an exercise designed to introduce the participants to the reality of the city and the economic disparities

among its residents through a self-guided socioeconomic tour. In the morning, small groups receive fifty-five pesos (roughly $4.50 USD), about the amount a low-wage laborer might earn in a day.[29] With those fifty-five pesos, the group must purchase a selection of items that a Mexican shopper might need for a family of four for one day: a liter of cooking oil, a kilogram of corn tortillas, a kilogram of tomatoes, a single roll of toilet paper, and a kilogram of beans. Most, but not all, groups are able to manage the task, but just barely. Participants are immediately confronted with the challenge of feeding a family of four on the paltry income of a low-wage worker, let alone the even more austere budgets of the growing numbers of the chronically underemployed. They also quickly realize that low-wage workers can hardly spend hours, as they have, trying to locate the best prices for the necessary staples by shopping in multiple locations, including the corporate-owned *Comercial Mexicana* (called the "Mega") and the local *mercado*, or people's market.

One of the more disheartening discoveries takes the group back to the economic, cultural, and nutritional importance of corn in Mexican life. The most drastic price differential noted by shoppers is in the price of tortillas. While tortilla prices have skyrocketed in Mexico, the Mega has managed to keep prices relatively low by purchasing the cheap corn produced in the United States in bulk, at the lowest prices. At the Mega, alongside U.S. American products like Wonder Bread and Cherokee brand clothing, one can purchase a kilogram of tortillas for seven and a half pesos,[30] but would pay exactly twice that at a locally owned tortilleria, or as much as twenty pesos for hand-pressed tortillas at the *mercado*. One participant notes, "I felt really bad. I wanted to buy the tortillas from the women at the *mercado*, but we couldn't afford it." As is so often the case not only in Mexico but around the world, a shopper's poverty means that she may not be able to afford the tortillas made from Mexican corn and crafted by local artisans and thus support the local and regional economy.

Another startling discovery is the relative cost of daily items in U.S. dollars. For example, one group completing the exercise discovered that one kilogram of dried beans costs about $1.32 USD in Mexico, while the same quantity might cost $2.86 USD in the United States. While the price differential might seem to favor Mexicans, consider the number of hours a minimum-wage worker would have to work in order to purchase a kilogram of beans: in the United States (at $7.25 USD per hour), he would have to work for about twenty-four minutes, while in Mexico (at about $0.53 USD per hour), he would have to work for almost two-and-a-half hours, or about six times longer than his U.S. counterpart.[31] With regard to meat, the difference in relative price is even greater: a worker in the United States would earn enough to purchase a pound of meat in about twenty-five minutes, while the Mexican worker would need to work for five and a half hours, or about thirteen times longer than his U.S. counterpart.[32]

The Cuernavaca quest makes an indelible impression on participants. After the exercise, participants sometimes feel overwhelmed and somewhat helpless in response to the daily struggles of Mexicans, which are exacerbated by the complicated situation of economics and trade in Mexico. This exercise, which can be quite alienating to U.S. Christians trying to navigate it on their own, is always paired with other practices that put them in direct relationship with Mexicans who welcome them into their homes and share their stories.

Food sovereignty: tasting a movement. Delegations often meet with Javier Galván and the staff of the National Union of Autonomous Regional Peasant Organizations (UNORCA), a coalition of *campesinos* supporting rural food producers, crowding around the conference table in their cramped offices. As Javier begins describing the challenges faced by rural farmers in the post-NAFTA era, small tastes of the coffee produced by these same farmers are passed around the table. *Campesinos* would benefit markedly in a context of food sovereignty, Javier says, because they could farm in ecologically and socially sustainable ways, producing enough food for their local communities. The luscious, smooth coffee that the guests are sipping represents the *campesinos'* agricultural craft, which is threatened by the emphasis on growing food only for export.[33] As the group prepares to leave, Javier places on each of their wrists bracelets made of coffee beans, a physical reminder of the complexities of trade and the yearning for sovereignty and abundance among the *campesinos*.

Making tortillas: receiving hospitality. When a group visits the rural pueblo of Cuentepec, they do not receive reports of the most recent statistics regarding corn production and prices, poverty in the community, or food availability (although these are readily accessible from the in-country host organization). Instead, they kneel down on a mat behind a tiny cottage, shuck a dried ear of corn, and then take turns vigorously raking it across a tool made up of bound dried corncobs. As the kernels pop easily of the cob, raining down onto the bamboo mat, one young woman marvels, "Whoa!" Similar exclamations arise upon the strain of grinding the corn by hand and when, under host Felipa's careful tending, the first tortilla miraculously puffs up on the *comal*. Over lunch, which includes the tortillas the group has just made, Pédro and Felipa rehearse some of the changes in corn farming, and the potential threat these changes pose to their way of life. The urgency of their story, representative of many *campesinos*, comes to life amid the corn's varied and rich hues; its flavors, distinct and wild; and the embodied experience of making a tortilla from scratch.

"Confess. Transform. A life ever changed": commitments to action. Upon the conclusion of each of the *Encuentros* delegations, participants are invited to craft six-word memoirs representing singular experiences or overall impressions of their experiences on the journey.[34] Among those written after Tortillas and Trade programs are these: "Fifty pesos. Not enough. So hard." "Mexican corn farmers. NAFTA. Maquila workers." And "Confess. Transform. A life ever changed." The poetic exercise of creating these word images represents one more integral practice of the Tortillas and Trade educational model. As they write these six-word memoirs, share photographs, and retell stories, participants in the *Encuentros* programs reflect on their journey and its educational significance in their lives. This space, set aside for reflection, is quickly populated by the sensory images that shaped the participants' shared experience. They recall meeting *campesinos* and other indigenous workers, holding in their hands the precious varieties of corn grown around Mexico, tasting the fruits of corn and coffee farmers, and struggling to purchase basic food supplies on a day's wages, among many other practices.

The learning is not limited, however, to the personal and even spiritual transformation of which participants invariably speak. The groups brainstorm specific and often small actions to which they might commit as a response to what they learned through the program. One woman commits to reading *La Jornada*, an independent Mexican newspaper, weekly.[35] Three of them commit to economic practices like intentionally purchasing fairly traded coffee and chocolate and supporting local farmers at home. All of the members of one group commit to advocacy practices like contacting congressional representatives regarding both the Farm Bill and renegotiation of NAFTA. After a few months, most participants admit that ongoing commitment to these actions (each participant commits to one or two of them) proves surprisingly difficult.

These practices of discerning ongoing opportunities for commitment, no matter how difficult, are constitutive of the education and advocacy continuum at the heart of educational travel programs like these. The CCIDD explicitly states as a goal for visitors to the center that they might "become empowered to work for social transformation on a personal and collective level."[36] Similarly, CRLN hopes that program participants will "return home educated and motivated to share in the work for peace, justice and human rights."[37]

Other Practices of Education and Advocacy

As in the *Encuentros* program, education and advocacy practices are frequently woven together in conferences and organizing meetings, reflecting the assumption that to be a good advocate, one must be well-informed (and, conversely, that education necessarily issues in practices of advocacy). For example, during a 2012 conference entitled "Food + Justice = Democracy" organized by the Institute for Agriculture and Trade Policy, participants heard many speakers on the topics of land and food, representing a wide range of cultural traditions. Each day, however, included a "Peoples Movement Assembly" process, whereby organizers hoped the participants would form a social movement in the interest of seeking a just food system.[38] At the end of the conference, a declaration of principles (and correlative actions) was drafted, which included concern for labor, land, food sovereignty, community development, climate change, and immigration, among other themes.[39] From a more explicitly religious point of view, each spring mainline Protestant advocacy groups host the "Ecumenical Advocacy Days" in the nation's capital. In 2013 the theme for the event was food justice, and participants spent two or three days in seminars, worship, and policy briefings. These days serve as a theological and theoretical foundation and training for lobbying visits to congressional offices.[40] Other educational practices leave the advocacy response up to participants, making the connection between the two more implicit. After conferences like "Food, Glorious Food: The Eucharist and Your Foodshed" (part of the Ghost Ranch Education and Retreat Center's Earth-Honoring Faith Series coordinated by Christian ethicist Larry Rasmussen) and the Land Institute's Prairie Festival, many participants return to their communities with renewed commitment and deepened theological, philosophical, and scientific perspectives.

All of these educational practices, like the Tortillas and Trade program, awaken participants to new dimensions of the global food system and invite participants to invest themselves anew in the struggle for economic, environmental, and social justice. The strength of the model embodied in CRLN's Tortillas and Trade program, however, is its attention to *both* the intensely personal dimensions of the global food system and the social context of those personal stories within the systemic and structural challenges that so profoundly affect health, familial life, agriculture, economic stability, and environmental well-being. By highlighting interpersonal, embodied engagement, the program seeks to open the way for transformation, connecting these educational experiences with participants' vocational and spiritual selves.

EXPANDING THE TABLE
THEOLOGICAL AND MORAL REFLECTIONS ON ENGAGED LEARNING AND ADVOCACY

As each Tortillas and Trade group departs Cuernavaca by bus, the participants are often surprised to see Sister Kathy and other staff members still waiting alongside the terminal, waving until the bus has driven out of sight. Participants often feel quite emotional: "Maggie, Sister Kathy, and Wayne all united at the gate until the bus pulled away. Tears filled my eyes as I waved a final goodbye. I have been in the presence of angels these past few days, and I thank God for the opportunity given me. I look forward to what the future holds."[41] The level of emotional engagement, after just four or five days at the CCIDD, is striking. When a U.S. American

Christian is brought to tears, after such a short visit in Mexico, it serves as a testimony to the transformative potential of immersion experiences.

Sojourners at the CCIDD grasp for words to describe the profound and transformative experience of being guests at the tables of their Mexican brothers and sisters. Tables—and meals shared around them—figure prominently for participants in the Tortillas and Trade program. Whether the table is in the center of the UNORCA offices, in the backyard of Pedro and Felipa's home in Cuentepec, or on the idyllic patio of the CCIDD, it serves as the space for hospitality, sharing, celebration, reflection, contestation, and self-examination. All of these tasks are of the sort Letty Russell names as components of "kitchen table theology."[42] The kitchen table, as a site for theological and moral reflection, expands and reshapes the eucharistic table to include all aspects of life, contributing to a spirituality of connection with self, others, and God.[43] It also disrupts notions of host and guest, work and worship, and roles and relationships.

To be welcomed to a kitchen table is to enter into the everyday with the host. By inviting her guests to the kitchen table, the host disrupts formalities. She invites the guests to tie on an apron, wash dishes, hear family stories, and laugh with one another. A kitchen table is simultaneously a place of intimate and vulnerable hospitality, in that guests are welcomed into the life and shared work of a home, and a place of negotiation and justice, in that those seated at the table have voice, agency, and responsibility.

Being Re-membered
Hospitality, Sharing, and Gratitude

Guests from the United States sometimes have difficulty when visiting contexts that struggle with global poverty, hunger, and other systemic issues related to economic globalization. When confronted with the relative economic disparity, the instinct to "help" is powerful. "What do you need?" guests might ask. The impulse to address immediate needs can be very strong and yet prevents program participants from really encountering the communities they visit: "I think the service aspect . . . can also alleviate [discomfort], like we're going there to help and to fix, and it just creates a really difficult power dynamic," observes *Enceuntros* coordinator

Erica. "People walk away without having a full experience of recognizing the strength of that community and what that community has to offer as well." In order to honor the dignity and agency of the communities they are encountering, Christians from the United States must resist the paternalistic urge to offer solutions rather than seek authentic relationships with their brothers and sisters. They must, in short, become *guests*.[44] In some ways, hospitality is not defined by the roles of host and guest but is found in the relationship between persons who have made an intentional entry into the unpredictable play of hospitality.[45]

Conversations on hospitality in the United States, particularly as it relates to global relationships, frequently turn on the question of immigration and border hospitality, whether or not the United States will *welcome* migrants. The power-holding host, the one who extends hospitality, offers a gift to the guest, always retaining the privilege of revoking the welcome. Imbalances of power remain, and the guest is subject to the whims and goodwill of the "benevolent host."[46] Absolutely hospitality, in contrast, disrupts the power imbalance, demanding that one be confronted by and respond to the "other" standing before her.[47] Whereas U.S. Christians might (even unwittingly) be accustomed to standing in the place of the privileged and powerful host in global relationship building, the kind of transformative travel described here challenges them to step out of that role. In so doing, the participants in an *Encuentros* program acknowledge the limits of what one can know about the other: "[T]he other is what I myself am not. The other is this not because of the other's character, or physiognomy, or psychology, but because of the other's very alterity."[48] In other words, disrupting the power imbalances between guest and host requires setting aside the assumption that one "knows" the other, or that one knows "what is best."

The simple yet elusive capacity to be a guest, to receive hospitality and welcome, among those whom they might have perceived to be in need of intervention is a deeply challenging lesson for economically privileged Christians from the United States. The impulse of benevolence—meaning, literally, the disposition to do good—is very strong, particularly when confronted with one's own complicity in global structures that so severely harm vulnerable persons and communities. While "transformative travel" invites and, indeed, expects participants to "do good" once they have observed firsthand the systemic economic oppression resulting from trade policy and farm subsidies, the first and often hardest task is to become a guest. Becoming a guest reverses dynamics of power and privilege to which U.S. Americans might be accustomed. Becoming a guest requires receiving rather than giving, listening rather than speaking, and waiting rather than doing.

Becoming a guest also means being received, welcomed, and re-membered, all of which are postures Christians assume when they approach the eucharistic table. One of the invitations to the Eucharist used in the Iona community recounts Jesus' own experience of being a guest, before being a host:

> He was always the guest.
> . . . Upsetting polite company,
> befriending isolated people,
> welcoming the stranger,
> he was always the guest.
>
> But here,
> at this table,
> he is the host.
>
> So come, you who hunger and thirst
> for a deeper faith,
> for a better life,
> for a fairer world.
>
> Jesus Christ,
> who has sat at our tables,
> now invites us to be guests at his.[49]

Before becoming the host, Jesus made himself vulnerable by sharing meals with a diverse array of people, building relationships with them and becoming a member of their families and communities. When Christians gather as guests around the eucharistic table, welcomed by the host Jesus, they receive their identities as members of the body of Christ.

Being a guest at the table is a radical, vulnerable position, and one that might be challenging for Christians who want to "do good." Furthermore, being the vulnerable guest invariably reveals to the participant that despite her desire to do good, she in fact is complicit in structures that harm her hosts. And yet, those who host *also* make themselves vulnerable by welcoming guests into their homes and around their kitchen tables.[50] Their welcome is a sacred gift of hospitality. This is certainly true of the Christian families and communities in places like Cuernavaca, who welcome groups from the United States who might not be prepared to receive their welcome. Hospitality opens the host to risk, when they receive guests (who might very well be hostile) without condition.[51]

Receiving this gift of being re-membered into the world communion, for Christians with economic privilege, opens the way to transformative experience. As one trip participant put it, "The morning was a great experience, and a real eye-opener for us, I think. There was a great contrast between the beauty of the setting and the reality of garbage strewn down the side of the ravine, the power of the communal life and identity and the challenges they face. In so many ways we're worlds apart, yet I felt very much welcomed as a friend, sister, and co-conspirator—in the literal meaning of the word—sharing breath and spirit."[52] Having shared meals, been radically welcomed, heard stories, seen suffering, and encountered powerful communities of resistance in places like central Mexico, participants in transformative travel and their hosts become members of one another.[53] They have expanded the table. "Sharing breath and spirit," guest and host are no longer alienated from one another, but brothers and sisters, entrusted with the difficult work of tending interdependence.

Being Neighbors
Justice and Interdependence in a Globalized Economy

The work of tending interdependence is difficult in part because it so often begins with being confronted with one's own privilege and complicity in structures that harm persons, communities, and the earth. Humans are everywhere "entangled in the curse."[54] With each experience in Cuernavaca, participants in the Tortillas and Trade program are confronted with the complexity of the global food system—and its labor, environmental, economic, and social challenges—as well as their complicity in this system. When a group visits with Benito and Ramuelda in the squatter's settlement of La Estacíon, they are warmly welcomed into the family's self-constructed cinder-block home (other homes are made from aluminum sheeting or old train cars). The couple recounts the stress they have experienced over the past year, while Benito worked undocumented in agriculture in the United States. Steady work, particularly agricultural work since NAFTA, is so hard to come by in Mexico that a few months working undocumented seemed the best financial option, despite its risks. The family continues to struggle to afford cooking gas, food, clothing, and school fees for the children. After meeting with the family, the group names all the emotions they felt during the visit: from sadness and frustration, to respect and love, to anger and shame. This range of emotions is testimony to the complexities of an interdependent world, in which one person's flourishing and suffering is bound up in the life of another.[55] In the affective and embodied encounters with Christians in Mexico (and other places), participants in the Tortillas and Trade program are existentially confronted with their own obligations: "In the face-to-face encounter with the other, the face of the Other (le visage d'Autrui) enacts a structure of responsibility more primary than consciousness, more binding than mutuality, more engaging than agency, more stern than the imperative appeal of juridicality, and more immediate than the vulnerability of bare skin."[56] In the encounter with the other, human responsibility is immediate and without qualification, demanding not particular actions but the whole self.

"Which of these was a neighbor?" Jesus asks the lawyer in Luke's Gospel.[57] When the lawyer approaches Jesus, he wants to know to whom he should feel obligated: "Who is my neighbor?" He is asking the wrong question, however. The question for Christians is not about conscribed obligations or the boundaries of hospitality. Instead, it is about the character required to be a good neighbor to those in need. In a globalized economy, even people and communities who are geographically very far away become neighbors. Seemingly insignificant consumer choices, domestic food policies, immigration policies, and multinational corporations all affect—for good or for ill—the flourishing of persons, communities, and the earth around the world. Being a good neighbor, in this context, requires seeing injustice, confessing complicity, and seeking to establish partnerships marked by mutuality and solidarity.[58]

Central American theologians pleaded with U.S. Christians in 1988, "Even though distant from you geographically, we are very close to you. So close as a matter of fact, so as to be the reverse side of your own situation. We are your neighbors. Do not turn a deaf ear to Central America's cry. Do not walk by the other side."[59] In the case of Mexico, however, the distance between neighbors is not so great. A flight from Chicago to Mexico City is a mere four hours long. Populations have surged, and violence has increased, in cities along the border as *campesinos*, no longer able to farm in their own communities, seek relatively higher-paying manufacturing jobs. As those jobs have dried up, *campesinos* have begun flowing across the border, looking for agricultural work in the United States because they can no longer farm in Mexico.[60] One of the effects of the Tortillas and Trade program is that participants can no longer act as if they do not know, do not see, the myriad ways in which the global food system is adversely affecting their neighbors, the people of Mexico. They now know, in sharp detail, the exact contours of how they are complicit in "being very poor neighbors."

And so the work of tending interdependence requires confession. Christians from the United States are confronted with their own complicity when they see that the cheap food that is so widely available in the United States depends on global markets that drive down labor costs and food prices in other parts of the world. When they hear, firsthand, that the emphasis on agriculture for export makes it increasingly difficult for *campesinos* to farm for their families and local communities, they are confronted with the fact that their daily coffee habit might be contributing to harm in Mexico. When they realize that the influx of cheap corn threatens not only Mexican corn farmers but the very cultural and spiritual foundation of Mexican identity, they are motivated to look anew at U.S. food and farm policy. Just as a prayer of confession is necessary preparation for receiving the Eucharist meal, confession is necessary preparation for seeking a just global banquet, too.

Finally, though, being a neighbor requires a desire and intentional practices to seek authentic partnerships with persons and communities who are caught in the machine of the global food system. "In my understanding of solidarity and compassion, it's not in any way about what I do or what I give others," Ada María

Isasi-Díaz argues. "It's the interconnections we create with each other, how we support each other."[61] As each group's time at the CCIDD draws to an end, the staff hosts a closing worship service with them, in which they reflect upon their time in Mexico, what they will most remember, and what they hope to do in solidarity with Mexicans once they return home. It is a moment of challenge and commitment, but it also is a moment of mutual support. Many participants name this evening of sharing food and Eucharist as a poignant moment in their trip, and find it difficult to say goodnight: "It was beautiful. We worshiped with CCIDD staff, . . . lit several candles to pray for specific individuals we had met in Mexico. The Eucharist followed. Our service concluded with a 'sending' done by the women of CCIDD, which included a blessing, clay necklace, and hug."[62] In the process of becoming neighbors, perhaps U.S. Christians are themselves saved. God is in the midst of this work, transforming lives and relationships.

The participant in the Tortillas and Trade program who wrote "Confess. Transform. A life ever changed" named poignantly the theological and moral complexities evoked by transformative travel. They are neighbors, the U.S. Christians, even as they are complicit in political structures that harm vulnerable communities in Mexico. They are guests, too, dependent upon the hospitality and welcome of those whose experience they scarcely know. As for Sister Kathy and the rest of the staff of the CCIDD, they are the hosts. That little band standing there, waving as the bus pulls away, practices radical hospitality. It is a final gesture of support, a poignant reminder that it is the U.S. Christians, the "fixers," who are in need of prayer.

CHAPTER SEVEN

Vocational Sustainability
Agriculture and Ingenuity on the College Farm

Stroking the belly of one of the three unnamed farm cats, a young woman who works on Warren Wilson College's farm is describing to the assistant farm manager her concerns about Blanche, who seems not quite herself. Blanche is of one of the farm's swine. Soon another crew member enters the farm shop, reporting the sow's mild temperature fluctuations and disinterest in feeding time. Quickly, the workers—clad in cutoff jeans, boots, overalls, and drying layers of mud—determine a modest course of action (continued monitoring), with only marginal direction from their supervisor. They know what they are doing: "These guys are good now," observes farm manager Chase Hubbard. "When they've done this summer experience, towards the end, it's so satisfying to watch them on their own as a team make decisions. . . . These guys get it, and it's way more satisfying to be involved in the process, too." Situated in the rolling Appalachian Mountains ten miles from Asheville, North Carolina, the farms and gardens of Warren Wilson College offer a glimpse into new (yet old) agricultural practices, new models of local food systems, and new vocational imagination among young adults.

It might seem an unlikely way of doing higher education. Boots are lined up along the wall, flannel shirts and jackets hang from hooks, and dusty books—on goat husbandry, seeds, and erosion—are piled on the shelves next to the rustic door. The scene in the farm shop stands in stark contrast to what one might imagine when conjuring a college classroom, and the expanse of pastures, alongside the smells and sounds of a working farm, a far stretch from the usual images associated with a "liberal arts college." And yet, the kind of education gained in spaces like these has the capacity to form leaders equipped with the imagination and improvisational skills necessary to help build a more just and sustainable food system. Some of the Warren Wilson alumni are already leaders of just this sort, pursuing vocations in conservation, farming, nonprofit work, environmental education and advocacy, community organizing, and service in local government.

Colleges and universities—as well as elementary and secondary schools and institutions of theological education—around the United States are reclaiming the practices of small and midscale farming. In some cases there are curricular programs focusing on alternative agriculture, while in others the efforts are led by students who carve out space for gardens in nooks and crannies around campus.[1] In each of these educational institutions, students are introduced to a different way of relating to the land, to sustainable and ingenious lifestyles, and to the possibility of growing food for themselves, their families, and their communities. In some cases the theological and spiritual dimensions of these practices are made explicit, but in many cases they remain implicit, working underneath the practicalities and details of tending the soil, feeding the swine, and harvesting the herbs.

Warren Wilson's unique educational model seeks to address many of the challenges of the global food system, including the environmental effects of industrial farming practices, the anonymity and alienation that characterize contemporary food systems, and the dearth of young adults considering the vocation of farming. The practice of sustainable agriculture, particularly as a component of a liberal arts education, contributes to the formation of persons and, through them, whole communities who are crafting sustainable food systems. Indeed, through these practices, they are crafting sustainable lives as well—in a sense, developing vocational sustainability. Without assuming any particular theological perspective among the students engaged in these practices, a grounded practical theology of food is served by mining their work and experience for the spiritual and theological wisdom embedded therein. These practices challenge, deepen, and enrich eucharistic perspectives on the global food system, insofar as they inculcate deepened commitment to tend the earth, honor the work necessary to place food on the table, and cultivate a capacity for improvisation and creativity.

GROUNDED
RESPONDING TO THE ENVIRONMENTAL AND HUMAN COSTS OF THE GLOBAL FOOD SYSTEM

The environmental consequences of the contemporary system of food production have been well documented. The demands of industrialized agriculture issue in destruction of habitats, air and water pollution, soil erosion, drastic reductions in biodiversity, and mistreatment of animals. Advocates for industrialized farming argue that these effects are best managed by technological means and that our current agricultural methods are necessary to produce an adequate quantity of food that consumers are able to purchase at an affordable price. The driving down of food costs, however, and the attendant demands (placed on the shoulders of individual farmers) of efficiency and quantity have borne human and social costs as well: farming has become, for many, no longer an economically or even emotionally sustainable vocation. Implicit, and sometimes quite explicit, in the Warren Wilson model is a critique of the environmental and human costs of the global food system.

Environmental Costs
Losing Soil, Biodiversity, and Human and
Animal Health

The soil provides the first and most basic assessment of environmental health. When the soil is malnourished or unstable as a result of agricultural practices, the whole system is at risk. Current agricultural methods (particularly monocropping) drain nitrogen from the soil, requiring the use of fertilizers. After years of decline, soil erosion has again begun to surge, and in some places topsoil has been disappearing between ten and fifty times faster than it is forming.[2] When audiences challenge his critical reading of intensive farming practices, theologian (and son of a farmer) Norman Wirzba responds with a simple question: "I ask them, how is your soil? Is your soil healthy?"[3]

Fertile soil forms the foundation of the "biotic pyramid," and the last century's changes in agriculture have failed to treat the soil as integrally related to other life forms and processes, assuming that soil health and fertility can be addressed technologically.[4] Agro-science interventions to restore soil fertility, Aldo Leopold feared, view the human worker of the land as a conqueror, rather than as a "biotic citizen."[5] These conflicting interpretations of the human being's role in the ecosystem are mirrored in interpretations of Genesis in which the human being is alternately conceived as the one with dominion and power to subdue the earth and as a member of creation, charged with the task of tending (even serving) the earth.[6] The latter is clear even in the very words of Genesis 2, in which the human being (ʾādām) comes to life out of the arable soil (ʾădāmâ).[7] Humanity's failure to maintain its interdependence with the soil has contributed to the slow deterioration of the soil and a disruption of Leopold's "biotic pyramid," requiring ever more invasive interventions to maintain its capacity to produce.[8]

Leopold's conception of the biotic pyramid was not only founded on healthy soil but also required a level of biodiversity severely at risk in contemporary agriculture. While "traditional" farms might be home to grains, vegetables, spices, animals, and trees, the industrialized farm has lost most of that diversity, focusing on only one or two crops, or the mass breeding and feeding of one kind of animal. Furthermore, the use of pesticides, herbicides, chemical fertilizers, and aggressive irrigation systems disrupts natural ecosystems.[9]

Finally, however, one must consider the relationship between these environmental costs and the lives of animals, including humans. Dairy cattle, chickens, and hogs are frequently kept in concentrated animal feeding operations (CAFOs) and subjected to any number of the following conditions: perennial standing on concrete floors in their own feces, lack of access to daylight or the outdoors, alterations to their bodies (docking of tails, clipping of beaks and toenails) without pain relief, severe overcrowding to the point of aggression, and epidemic disease outbreaks among the animals.[10] Reports of the conditions in the most extreme of the animal confinement practices reveal an existence far removed from even the most basic criteria of animal welfare. Awareness of these realities gives many people of conscience pause: "[W]e protect 'companion animals' like hamsters while largely ignoring what amounts to the torture of chickens and cows and pigs. In short, if I keep a pig as a pet, I can't kick it. If I keep a pig I intend to sell for food, I can pretty much torture it," observes Mark Bittman, pointing out that popular conceptions of animal cruelty frequently exclude farm animals.[11]

In addition to concerns about industrialized farming practices, effects on farm animal welfare, studies are raising important questions about human health. A recent study, for example, found a staggering array of chemicals and pharmaceuticals present in chicken feathers, including antidepressants, hormones, caffeine, and numerous antibiotics.[12] To these concerns about pharmaceuticals in the food supply one can add the public health impact of the air and water pollution sometimes caused by large quantities of animal waste produced by CAFOs.[13] Poor communities are disproportionately vulnerable to these risks, since CAFOs are more likely to be located near their homes.[14] All of these studies are bracing and can leave even the most concerned citizen despairing: "Frankly, after reading these studies, I'm so depressed about what has happened to farming that I wonder: Could a Prozac-laced chicken nugget help?" laments opinion columnist Nicholas Kristof.[15]

In short, these intensive, technologically supported methods of animal farming are levying unsustainable costs on all parts of the ecosystem, particularly in relationship to public health, the environment, and animal well-being. They require an "unacceptable level of risk" and result in "unnecessary harm."[16] Given these sobering reports, one might wonder whether there are any viable alternatives if agriculture in the United States cannot be sustained in its current trajectory.[17] A reorientation of this magnitude requires a sea change, transformations in public consciousness that are rooted deeply in how human beings understand their relationship to the land. It requires a resurrection of Aldo Leopold's "land ethic," and a way of life in service of restoring ecological sustainability.

Advocates of a sustainable agricultural future argue that the answer to this question is "yes," and that the work begins with reimagining and re-membering the farmer at the heart of the food system. In farm programs like the one at Warren Wilson, young adults are invited to bring their own understandings of a "land ethic"; their intentions to live in a more sustainable way, deeply conscious of interdependence; and their creativity and capacity for improvisation to bear in a new ecological context. On the Warren Wilson farm, students discover their own capacities and commitments to relate to the land, the food it yields, the animals with whom humans share it, and the friends with whom they share that sacred task. The vocational (and avocational) commitment that students bring to the college farm marks a significant reimagining of the dignity of a life lived with deep connections to the dirt.

Human and Social Costs
Losing Young Farmers and Community Futures

While the return of young adults to farming vocations now carries a certain degree of cultural capital, and notable minorities of young adults are choosing the agricultural life, this is a rather recent development.[18] For two or three generations, not only have young adults turned away from the farming lifestyle, but some proponents of industrialized farming have lauded this departure from the hard labor of farming as a positive development in the industrialization of agriculture. Over the past fifty years, farmers (and all who work the land), as well as their communities, have borne many of the costs of industrialized agriculture: costs to their health, their economic stability, and their vocational integrity.[19] At the heart of the matter is a failure to preserve the viability and dignity of the farming lifestyle. Vocational sustainability—or a way of life that is economically, ecologically, and socially sustainable—is virtually absent.

When John Davis envisioned the "efficiencies" that could be gained by turning a larger proportion of the agriculture sector over to agribusiness, he knew that some farmers would simply not be able to compete.[20] Certainly, between the time Davis explicated the agribusiness model and the turn of the twenty-first century the number of farmers has dramatically decreased, while the average age of the American farmer has dramatically increased. In the last forty years, Agriculture Secretary Tom Vilsack testified to the Senate Agriculture Committee, the United States has lost one million farmers.[21] In 1974 the average age of the American farmer was forty-five. In 2007 the average age was fifty-eight.[22] Between 2002 and 2007, the number of farmers under the age of twenty-five decreased by 30 percent.[23] Secretary Vilsack is rightly concerned about the future of rural life in the United States if young adults no longer consider the life of farming to be a vocation with meaning, dignity, and sustainability.

One factor that compromises the fulfillment and dignity available to the farmer is the anonymity and alienation that characterize the contemporary food system. With many farmers growing produce and raising livestock for corporate food producers, and with distant corporate owners reaping many of the profits from farm production, the ideal of the farming family growing food for its community is at great risk.[24] The reliance on transient migrant labor adds another group of nameless, faceless contributors to the food system. Furthermore, the bucolic farm depicted on food labels is a far cry from today's "conventional" farm, a place that few consumers ever see up close.[25] In a final dimension of anonymity and alienation, some of the technological interventions in farming distance the farmer not only from the community and the consumers of the food he produces, but from the very land itself. When pressed to farm with ever more aggressive methods, rather than responding to needs of the land, the farmer looks more like Leopold's "conqueror" than "biotic citizen," and a far cry from belonging to creation.[26]

When one first steps into the farm shop at Warren Wilson, it is clear that the agricultural lifestyle being crafted by the students, staff, faculty, and even alumni is quite different. Although the college farm is not allergic to technological interventions, its primary story is that of a community living as a member and tender of the ecosystem. Next to the refrigerator bearing a notice about the milk stored therein is a wall of photographs depicting the student workers, the cows, the pigs, a cartoon or two, and assorted news clippings: not unlike the kinds of memorabilia one might find stuck to a family refrigerator. Members of the Farm Crew are building a life together, relating to one another, the animals, and the earth with attention, authenticity, and creativity.

THE FARM CREW
Sustainable Agriculture and Working
the College Farm

Inside the farm shop, the assortment of mismatched chairs, left-behind jackets, nameless farm cats, haphazard bulletin boards, doors left ajar, and equipment parts distributed around the space bespeak a place that is "lived in." The items comprise the residue of the people (and their stories) who come and go through this place, some of them long since moved into new communities and new work after college graduation. Some of them, disinclined to leave the life they have built here, have not moved all that far away, starting organic farms, breweries, and small businesses in the western North Carolina area. As organically as the Warren Wilson College Farm operates, however, its presence and identity are not by happenstance. Warren Wilson's innovative and historic work program, its environmental commitments, its farms and gardens, and its deep roots in Appalachian agriculture provide an integrative educational context in which sustainable agriculture is discovered and nurtured and the farming vocation is restored and reimagined with dignity.

Working the Farm

"[Y]ou kind of crest this hill and . . . come down into this valley and off to the right, there's this big white barn that says 'WWC Herefords,' and there are cows in the fields! . . . I was like, 'This is the campus? This is not like any place I have ever seen.' I can still, to this day, remember the experience of seeing those mountains and seeing those fields for the first time. So, yeah, there was obviously something that drew me to Warren Wilson," recalls J. Clarkson, development director for the MANNA Food Bank in Asheville, North Carolina, about his first visit to Warren Wilson some twenty years ago. Indeed, the pastoral setting of the school sets it apart from many other colleges and universities. The pastures and barns at two of the three main approaches to the campus signal to the visitor that he has arrived to a unique place and community.

Warren Wilson is one of seven designated "work colleges" in the United States. Students' education is shaped by the "triad," a commitment expressed in the college's mission statement: "to provide a distinctive . . . undergraduate education [that] combines academics, work, and service in a learning community committed to environmental responsibility, cross-cultural understanding, and the common good."[27] Each student works an on-campus job for fifteen hours per week, in addition to completing one hundred hours of service to the community and carrying a regular academic course load.[28] The work program has clear material effects: a student's total costs of attendance are subsidized by about $3,500 per year.[29] At the same time, however, the college has maintained, since its origins in the late 1800s, that the work requirement (alongside service and academics) is an integral component of "holistic, experiential education."[30]

The work program has had three broad purposes: to lower the cost of attendance; to build, maintain, and operate the campus; and to contribute to the broader formation of the student.[31] Through its many incarnations, the school has held fast to these commitments. As school historians put it, "In the early days, it had helped farm boys become better farmers. But now it brought together young people from different races, social groups, and nationalities, many of whom had been raised in relative prosperity, to learn job skills, responsibility, and cooperation for the good of the community. Even with the new baccalaureate program, a Warren Wilson education involved more than book learning."[32] As the student population has increasingly come from more economically privileged backgrounds, the third purpose—the formation of the student—has emerged as the primary philosophical framework for interpreting the benefits of the work program. In fact, as one administrator recalls, every once in a while parents might request that, in exchange for paying more toward tuition, their child be excused from the work requirement in order to focus on her studies. Such requests are denied, reflecting the centrality of the program in the educational model: "The mission of the Work Program is to provide students with productive work that creates opportunities for the Warren Wilson College community to acknowledge, examine, and celebrate the ethics and value of work in the educational process."[33] Students may choose from more than one hundred work crew assignments, learning such varied crafts and skills as automobile and bicycle maintenance, fiber arts, blacksmithing, religious leadership, administration, and, of course, farming and gardening.

Spotting one of the thirty or so members of the Farm Crew around campus is no challenge, says one professor: "It is an identity. . . . [B]ecause they have to dress for work, you can always tell: 'Oh yeah, that's somebody on theFarm Crew.' It's funny." The farm and garden crew assignments are highly desirable. To increase the likelihood of scoring a work assignment on the Farm Crew, eager students frequently volunteer time on the farm in addition to their regular work assignments elsewhere on campus, like the Landscaping Crew, Dining Services Crew, and Recycling Crew. One student recalls how she first had to volunteer to string lights on the farm in order to earn her coveted spot on the Farm Crew. "I think it is a big draw," observes Environmental Studies Professor Mallory McDuff. "But the irony of it is that many of them don't get to work on the farm until they've been here for two years, just because it is kind of a hierarchy. . . . [I]t's kind of like our fraternities and sororities, . . . the higher tier. These work crews that are outdoors and, ironically, manual labor are an attraction to the students."

The farm and garden may have particular appeal because they bring together the school's two signature commitments: the work program and sustainability. For many years now, the farm has employed practices of sustainable agriculture, which they define as "farming in a style that is environmentally sound and economically viable, provides valuable and satisfying work to us, and is based on the humane and careful husbandry of our cattle and swine."[34] These practices include soil and water conservation strategies—crop rotation, grazing management, composting, and habitat maintenance—and humane treatment of farm animals.[35]

The farm is a laboratory for sustainable agriculture, and yet also, as an ecosystem, is understood as a living organism itself. To treat it only as a laboratory, even a laboratory of sustainable agriculture, risks an instrumental approach to the land—a store of resources for human use and manipulation, which is its own form of commodification. As a living ecosystem, however, the land exerts claims upon the Farm Crew. In a letter to Farm Crew members at the beginning of the fall semester, Farm Manager Chase Hubbard makes this appeal: "Working on this farm is a great privilege for all of us. Farming this rich, Swannanoa Valley is something we are all drawn to, a passion we share in common. My hope is that the farm, with all her diversity—soils, wildlife, livestock, forests, river, etc.—will captivate you, like so many students before."[36] "She"—the farm—is a living being, and the students working on the Farm Crew are members of it, with passions and responsibilities in relationship to it.

Warren Wilson's Historical Roots
in Appalachian Agriculture

The agricultural identity of the school, which began as a natural consequence of the student population, has persisted through all of the phases of Warren Wilson College's history. The college began as a collection of Appalachian mission schools, started by the Presbyterian Board of Home Missions to address the educational and social needs of young women and men in the region.[37] The Asheville Home and Industrial School (est. 1887), the Dorland-Bell School (est. 1887), and the Mossop School (est. 1909) set out to educate local girls in the agricultural and coal-mining communities of western North Carolina and eastern Tennessee. The Asheville Normal and Collegiate Institute (est. 1892) prepared teachers for these and other schools.[38] Having experienced an education of the "head, hand and heart,"[39] the girls at the mission schools asked for a similar institution for their brothers, and the Asheville Farm School was founded in 1894. From the very beginning, the number of "boys" (actually adolescents and young men) eager to attend the Farm School exceeded its capacities, and the school turned applicants away every year. The Farm School offered young men opportunities in basic education and agricultural education through its work program. Much like the mission of the girls' schools, the Farm School's educational model emphasized, as one graduate put it, "not only book larnin' but habits of industry and . . . righteousness in its proper relationship to life."[40] All of these mission schools shared the holistic triad curriculum that characterizes Warren Wilson College to this day: academics, work, and Christian instruction and service (alternately described as morality).[41]

Despite economic uncertainty, the Farm School continued to evolve in the early part of the twentieth century. In the early 1930s, Superintendent Henry S. Randolph, influenced by John Dewey's theories of progressive education, led the school in envisioning a new, more integrated approach to the threefold educational emphasis. The motto, in the mid-1930s, was "learning to do by doing and learning to live by living."[42] The education of head, heart, and hand continued, with students increasingly charting their own course through the institution.[43] As regional infrastructure—and thereby access to schools—improved and similar institutions emerged throughout the region, and as denominational mission support waned, the leaders of the school continually reinvented the school, strengthening its ties to its roots. In addition to appreciating and building upon the agricultural identities of its students, the school would provide students with a "postsecondary program that would 'fit young people to earn a living in the mountains' and provide them with an 'understanding of the essentials of right social and civic living.' "[44]

By the time of the Second World War, the school was receiving fewer applications to the high school, and it turned its focus to postsecondary education. It also became coeducational, and increasingly drew students from overseas.[45] In 1942 the Asheville Normal Teacher's College was closed and merged with the burgeoning postsecondary program at the Farm School, and the Dorland-Bell and Mossop schools closed. The "comprehensive plan" of the mission board resulted in the establishment of the Warren H. Wilson Vocational Junior College.[46] Twenty years later, as more students enrolled in the "college preparatory" program (rather than pursuing terminal degrees), Warren Wilson's future was once again recast, and in 1965 the college welcomed its first class of four-year degree students.

Throughout these evolutions, the farm has remained a symbol and grounding for the school, honoring the school's rural and agricultural roots. As such, choosing "Warren Wilson" as the name for the vocational and, later, liberal arts college was a fitting decision. Warren H. Wilson was a Presbyterian minister and professor of sociology who had dedicated his life to questions of church, labor, and rural life.[47] Working for the Presbyterian Board of Home Missions as superintendent of the Department of Church and Country Life, Wilson advocated for churches to adopt sustainability programs (in the broadest sense of the word), including soil conservation and recreational ministries. He also understood the vocation of farming to be nothing short of a sacred calling:

> The holy land is the tilled land. The true place in which to worship God is the orchard and the garden: for these we cooperate with God

and so glorify and enjoy Him. For the round of life that passes through our bodies and makes them a temple of the Holy Spirit passes through the orchard trees, the garden plants, the cattle in their stall and the sheep in the fold. If they were not there, we could not glorify God, for we could not live. So their bodies, too, are temples or vestibules of the divine presence in the world.[48]

Naming the school after Wilson was a testimony to his commitment to not only the well-being of the land, people, and religious communities in rural America but also God's embodied presence among them.

On Religion (or Not)

Learning and Farming in a Church-Related

Liberal Arts College

In the earliest days of the school's history, Warren Wilson students not only worked the farm and took academic courses but also were required to attend worship, participate in Bible study, and engage in other explicitly Christian practices.[49] In the 1960s, however, with increasing religious diversity among students and waning interest in religious institutions, slowly the school's religious identity receded into the background.[50] Although the college is still related to the Presbyterian Church (USA), student perspectives on religion vary widely. In some cases, Christians in particular report feeling a little alienated on campus. This climate is observable to students and faculty alike: at a reading from her book on religious environmentalism in a local book shop, Mallory McDuff says, "I was talking about that integration (between faith and the environment) and one of my students was in the audience and she actually piped up and said, 'It's been really great to have Mallory talk about faith in the classroom. . . . I've seen other students relax around the issue and be more comfortable talking about how they were brought up,' which is interesting, particularly at this campus."

This hesitancy regarding religion—particularly Christianity—may be partly attributable to the cultural context from which many of the college's students have come, Mallory hypothesizes. About 20 percent of the students come from North Carolina, and many others come from nearby states like Virginia, Georgia, and Florida, in which evangelical Christianity is pervasive.[51] Once they get to Warren Wilson, she says, "it's more hip to be Buddhist than to be Christian." One need not dig very far, however, before uncovering the spirituality of land that undergirds the ethos at Warren Wilson. For example, surveying the pigs foraging one of the several wooded areas on Hickory Nut Gap Farm, farmer and Warren Wilson alumnus Jamie Ager is not particularly prone to theologizing. Hickory Nut Gap Farm, however, has deep roots in rural ecotheology, dating back to when Jamie's great-grandfather, Presbyterian minister James McClure, first settled in the area. McClure, the son of the president of McCormick Theological Seminary, preached in local churches, but mostly worked as a farmer and organizer for the regional Farmers Federation.[52] He also inaugurated a "Lord's Acre" program among local farmers during the Depression, whereby farmers would contribute agricultural products to the church: "Every time the Lord's hen and chickens come strutting through the yard they preach a little about the Lord."[53] Although Jamie describes his own perspective as "not particularly religious," he describes his own philosophical and moral framework for farming, in which everything "works together" in an interdependent ecosystem. The pigs foraging one plot of land help prepare it for the next planting. His perspective—and the arrangement of the farm—is embodying the kind of "land ethic" envisioned by Aldo Leopold. Students joining the Farm Crew are encouraged to embrace such a land ethic: "You will never regret investing yourself fully in your work here. . . . We want and need you to take ownership of this farm. Treat it and its resources as if they were your inheritance, but remember, despite having this ethic, we do not own this farm nor any of it's [sic] tools or other resources. Please reflect on what being a steward here means, for the land and other resources, and what your legacy will be."[54]

Of course, some students make their way through the Warren Wilson program with ever-deepening and self-conscious faith commitments, and the experience of the work program and college farm is integrated into their theological perspectives. Abigail Bissette, who went on to pursue a graduate degree in social work, published an essay in her denominational magazine entitled "Unexpected Encounters with Faith and Piglets": "I, like many at WWC, came because I fell in love with the baby pigs at the student-operated farm. I was also drawn to the college's promise of hard work, academic excellence and deep care for others and the world. Somewhat ironically, I am leaving Warren Wilson with a greater sense of what it is like to be in communion with Christians than what it is like to be in communion with baby pigs."[55]

Nathan Ballentine, once moderator of the national youth leadership network in the Presbyterian Church (USA), now works in urban agriculture and food justice in Tallahassee, Florida. Known as the "Man in Overalls," Nathan sees a deep connection between his Christian faith and his experience as a member of the Farm Crew, albeit in an innovative way: "Yeah, what I saw at Warren Wilson was folks living really faithfully, just to use that language. They were living their ideals and . . . doing their darndest to make the kind of world that is articulated as the Kingdom of God, and that was a whole lot more enriching than dissecting doctrine."

Even students and alumni who do not claim a theological lens or religious identity, however, offer a moral vision of the dignity of work and the tending of the land and the interdependence with which it is sustained. Perhaps most importantly, the Farm Crew offers a vision of vocation deeply necessary in today's world, particularly in a global food system that is both mammoth and—in some ways—exceedingly unstable. Warren Wilson may, indeed, be preparing the moral leaders who will be equipped to engage creatively and responsibly in that context: "Warren Wilson was far too human ever to be a utopia," reflect college historians, "but it was a community that was not content with just accepting the human experience as it is."[56]

BUILDING THE TABLE
TENDING THE EARTH, HONORING WORK, AND BECOMING *BRICOLEURS*

Despite eschewing explicitly theological frameworks, the Warren Wilson farm, and the students who are working it, have a great deal to contribute to theological and moral perspectives on food and agriculture. Without forcing a theological perspective upon the students that they would not claim for themselves, people of faith and religious communities who are committed to caring for the earth, honoring work, and cultivating interdependence have a great deal to learn from the Farm Crew. Embedded in the practices of work and sustainable farming is an ecospirituality that honors land (including the human communities living upon it), work, and the capacities for creativity and improvisation.

The grounded ecospirituality emerging in the college farm perhaps is rooted in the rural theology and philosophy that pervades the region and so deeply informed namesake Warren Wilson's own theology. When humans farm, when they connect to the land, they *become* members of it, sharing the same divine breath of life. In this shared life, God's interdependent creation, our lives depend on other lives. A deep and embodied realization of this interdependence has the capacity to evoke reverence for soil, plant, and animal, and for God's provision for all living things. It also, however, makes plain human responsibility to tend these vulnerable bonds of interdependence, honoring the "round of life that passes through our bodies" and through God's body, the earth.[57] On the Farm Crew and at the college, students are keenly aware of their obligation to the places from which they have come, and the places in which they find themselves: "That was something that Warren Wilson did to a lot of people, too," Nathan Ballentine recalls. "Inoculate them with a sense of place."

The members of Warren Wilson's Farm Crew are encouraged to understand themselves as stewards and tenders of the land. They also, however, are reminded that the land does not belong to them—instead, they belong to it and are thereby "captivated by her."[58] When they succeed in inhabiting this way of being in relationship to the land, they embody Leopold's land ethic, understanding the land as a "community": "All ethics so far evolved rest upon a single premise: that the individual is a member of a community of interdependent parts. His instincts prompt him to compete for his place in that community, but his ethics prompt him also to co-operate. . . . The land ethic simply enlarges the boundaries of the community to include soils, waters, plants, and animals, or collectively: the land."[59] Insofar as members of the Farm Crew understand themselves as belonging to the land, they understand that the land, which Christians might call God's body, exerts moral claims upon them.[60] The students described at the beginning of this chapter, who so eagerly collaborated to evaluate and care for Blanche the pig, accepted and responded to the moral claims exerted by the farm and all of its members: human, animal, plant, soil.

Leopold's land ethic presents people of conscience with a moral and philosophical framework in which they might reimagine their place as members of the land. Certainly, this perspective shapes some of the alumni's ways of thinking about ecology and agriculture. The land ethic also resonates with Christian eco-theology, however: "What if, with Christianity, we accepted the claim that the Word is made flesh and dwells with us; with feminism, that the natural world is in some sense sacred; with ecology, that the planet is a living organism that is our home and source of nurture?" asks Sallie McFague. "What if we dared to think of our planet and indeed the entire universe as the body of God?"[61] The members of the Farm Crew daily place their own bodies in service of God's sacred body, the land.

The college farm is also restoring dignity to the vocation of farming. For his senior thesis, J. Clarkson took up Thomas Jefferson's ideal of the "yeoman farmer": "I got very into Thomas Jefferson and his writing. He has a quote that people who cultivate the earth are the chosen people of God, if ever he had a chosen people."[62] As more young adults like Nathan Ballentine, Jamie Ager, and other Warren Wilson alumni choose "the life of farming,"[63] they invest the vocation with dignity and honor and invigorate it with their energy, innovation, and imagination. They also are enlivening the local food context in Asheville, starting community-supported agriculture initiatives (CSAs), establishing local food policy councils, and preserving the historically diverse agricultural landscape in the region.[64] Quite literally, they are reinventing farm "culture" in both rural and urban contexts, retrieving the original sense of the world: "in its earlier Middle English usage the word 'culture' referred to a piece of land. More specifically, it referred to a *cultivated* piece of land (the Latin *cultura* means 'cultivation of soil'), suggesting that the sign of a cultured person was to understand and know how to work with gardening realities like soil and plant and animal life."[65]

The Farm Crew is a fertile ground for honoring the earth and the vocation of farming. It is not, however, a nostalgic return to an era past. Not only is turning back the clock impossible, but to do so also would require a severe degree of moral blindness to the economic, social, and environmental injustices that plague the global food system at this time in history. Instead, the Farm Crew is best understood as an incubator for reconceiving agriculture in the face of these tremendous challenges. The Farm Crew, and places like it, are particularly suited to this work because they can nurture and benefit from the unique strengths of their members: young adults. The waves of young adults who have come after the baby boomers are a resourceful and creative group, a class of "tinkerers," argues Robert Wuthnow. Borrowing a page from Claude Lévi-Strauss, he concludes that today's young adults are particularly adept in the art of *bricolage*. A *bricoleur*, in preindustrial societies, was a handyperson who assembled something new out of scraps and what might seem like junk. The tinkerer, like the *bricoleur*, is one of a society's most resourceful and creative members in a context of uncertainty: "The challenge is thus to encourage people to draw responsibly from the full range of resources at their disposal and to work at putting together their lives in ways that are collectively as well as personally beneficial."[66]

These capacities—and, indeed, virtues—for practicing the art of *bricolage* are essential for young adults considering the sacred vocation of farming. Through creative visions like collaborative or incubator farming, urban agriculture, and bivocational lifestyles, alumni of the Farm Crew are carving out a new way of pursuing the life of farming. Ballentine, for example, has crafted a creative vocational trajectory by creating small produce gardens on commission for families (his "job") and organizing communities for a just local food system (with some grant support). All of this is not to say, of course, that young adults considering a calling to the land should be abandoned to fend for themselves in the unpredictable and vulnerable world of sustainable agriculture. They need economic and technical support. It *is* to say that they should be supported and honored for what they are: visionaries, and the vanguard of a new movement in ecology and earth-bound faith. They can serve as moral leaders for their communities, modeling sustainability, interdependence, and good work and inviting others to join them by growing food in their own "temples and vestibules of divine presence": lawns, schoolyards, and church spaces.[67] "Gardening work creates in us an indispensible 'imaginary' that enables us to think, feel, and act in the world with greater awareness for life's complexity and depth," Norman Wirzba writes. "Gardens are the concentrated and focused places where people discover and learn about life's creativity and inter-dependence. Insofar as we are good gardeners we will commit to working with God's creativity in ways that strengthen human and nonhuman life together."[68] The farm shop is the staging area for a riotous kind of creativity. Closely mentored by the farm manager and yet turned loose to improvise in response to the living, breathing farm in which they live, the Farm Crew is an embodied witness against alienation.

Unearthing Beauty
Everyday Visionaries and Hope for the Food System

DIRTY HANDS
RELIGIOUS ACTIVISM AND THE FOOD MOVEMENT

"Is this a movement?" President Barack Obama is reported to have asked Michael Pollan.[1] The president likely wanted to know whether the activists seeking a more just food system were organized, shared a common vision, and agreed upon goals and tactics for changing patterns of food production, distribution, and consumption. Taken together, all of these practices—church-supported farming, growing food, transformative travel, and vocational sustainability—do constitute a social movement, in which religious participants collaborate with other people of conscience to address common injustices, struggles, and opportunities with regard to the global food system. One might justifiably ask, Is the movement succeeding? To be sure, when people of faith participate in these practices, they have in mind concrete goals and specific, appropriate strategies for meeting those goals. They see a well-defined problem of urban hunger, economic oppression, agricultural poverty, environmental degradation, or devalued laborers, and set out to ameliorate that problem. In many cases, they make measurable, if meager, progress.

157

At the same time, however, their efforts are frequently constrained by significant barriers. First, as outlined above, the global food system is unfathomably complex. Even more, that complexity is complicated by stubborn patterns of injustice. These injustices are more than symptoms of a broken system: to use Christian theological language, they are bound up in sin. In other words, the brokenness of the food system is a consequence of humans and social groups being "entangled in the curse," each complicit in systems that perpetuate hunger, economic disparity, violence to the earth, and alienation from the land, God, and each other.[2] These injustices frequently can be attributed to human greed, indifference, and exploitation. They also are exacerbated, however, by even unwitting complicity in the system: consumer demand (or need) for cheap food depresses labor wages, for example, and policies ostensibly designed to support farmers encourage environmentally destructive farming practices. Structural sin present in the global food system is not solely attributable to bad actors, although they surely exist. We all are culpable. We all are caught.

When confronting the structural sin present in the global food system, it might be tempting to look for a curative theological response. "If we just took our eucharistic theology more seriously," well-meaning Christians might wonder, "would we be in this mess?" Although the perpetual return to the table at the center of Christian traditions is essential to a faithful response to the global food system, it is not sufficient. Healing the food system is not solely a matter of addressing intellectual or even theological gaps, but of repairing real, material relationships in the world. It requires, quite literally, getting one's hands dirty—planting, cooking, harvesting, feeding—and a willingness to persevere even in the midst of a broken food system.

"LITTLE MOVES"
THE REAL CONTRIBUTIONS OF EVERYDAY VISIONARIES

In light of the ongoing challenges of the global food system—despite them, even—people of faith are setting a table of resistance, a table of abundance, in the midst of struggle. Growing vegetables on Chicago's South Side, supporting farms scattered across rural Illinois and North Carolina, sharing food in Mexican kitchens and church basements, people of faith are working to transform the global food system. They are hopeful, but not naïve. Earnest in their analyses of local and global issues, they seek to identify the little plot of earth that they can cultivate and in which they can make a difference. Indeed, they are making a difference. Practices of church-supported farming, growing food, transformative travel, and vocational sustainability are bearing real effects in local food systems, agriculture, ecosystems, and even political and economic structures. This is good food!

All of these practices are "little moves against destructiveness."[3] They are modest in scope: supporting a dozen farmers and artisans by opening a farmers market, converting four acres of farm land from corn and soybean production to organic produce, growing enough produce in the church backyard to feed the senior members of the congregation, starting up community food security organizations or farmers cooperatives, or calling a legislator. They also are quite fragile and transient, subject to the vicissitudes of changing leadership, political structures, economic fluctuations, and volunteer commitment. These practices are implicated in the same web that constrains all human decisions and actions regarding food: balancing concerns about food cost and nutritional value with moral commitments regarding labor practices and environmental effects. Yet, despite their modest scope, their fragility, and these constraints, these practices are really something, small miracles that testify to health in the face of so much life-denying destructiveness. The very lives and commitments of practitioners are a powerful witness to an alternative path. In them, change is born.

Along the way, then, a deeper kind of transformation is taking place. In contrast to measurable changes in the nutritional values of available food, food miles, soil erosion data, or trends in labor and wages, this kind of transformation is rarely visible or quantifiable. Through the vision and imagination cultivated in these food practices, the seeds for a thriving food system are taking root. The participants in these efforts are modest about their effects, hesitant to make grand claims about their capacity to change the system. They sometimes describe with facility, however, how they have *been changed* as a result of their engagement in these practices:

> As we are on our way home we are called to ask ourselves: What do we do with all of this knowledge and these experiences? How do we

share it with others? How can we continue our lives without forgetting? We start tomorrow back at work or school with the tasks of our everyday lives to face. But we continue to act and to celebrate by reading, teaching, supporting international legislation like a renegotiation of NAFTA, and supporting fair trade. We continue to remember by supporting our local farmers markets and sharing home cooked meals with friends and family. These past eight days in Mexico have changed my perspective.[4]

Julie, a participant in an *Encuentros* trip to Mexico, expressed these deep questions and hopes in her final group diary entry, written on the airplane back to Chicago. The four women in her traveling group are not likely to reverse harmful U.S. farm and trade policies. They are likely, however, to live differently as a result of their experiences on the trip, including how they participate in the political process that determines these policies. Likewise, some of the adolescents who worked in the Chicago youth urban gardening project described how the work not only produced food for their neighbors, but *changed their lives*. For many religious activists, this is no surprise. While they might begin with measurable goals and carefully planned strategies, they often report finding that although they had set out to change the situation, it was they who were changed in the process. In the pursuit of social transformation, they themselves are being transformed.[5]

In other words, an assessment of the contributions made to the quest for good food by the practices of church-supported farming, growing food, transformative travel, and vocational sustainability must take into account these deeper dimensions of personal and social transformation. Perhaps, embodied in the lives of the practitioners, these fragile, halting, and humble practices provide windows into an alternative future. In the process of crafting a more just food system, they also craft lives of meaning and purpose that contribute to a new collective imagination.[6] In this, perhaps these religious practices are far more valuable to communities and societies than one might gather on first glance. As sources of moral vision and imagination, religious activists like Veronica Kyle, Nathan Ballentine, and other everyday people of faith working for justice in the food system serve a function in society much like that of protestors, as described by James Jasper: "Entire lives can be artful creations, as protestors try to fit their convictions into their daily routines. They epitomize Socrates' call for 'the examined life.' Protestors often find new ways of living, new modes of applying moral visions in everyday life. . . . Protest offers many virtues to its practitioners, giving meaning to their lives. Their moral sensitivity, often painful but also deeply satisfying, is precious to them as well as being their greatest gift to the rest of us."[7] It is no exaggeration to describe these religious activists for food justice as everyday visionaries.

At their heart, then, these instances of fragile goodness and interdependence serve as windows of grace, demonstrating care for the poor, dignity for the laborer, reverence for all forms of life, and a way of life deeply related to others, the earth, and God. When members of the Sola Gratia CSA show up not only to pick up their shares of produce but to work in the fields, they testify with their bodies to the sacred work of tending the earth, and honor the expertise of Farmer Dex. They also joyfully share in the gift of collaborative work, building relationships with one another and with the farm. When teenagers on the South Side of Chicago welcome a visitor to their church garden, explaining with pride the best way to nurture a strawberry plant, they testify to God's provision and abundance even in a place others have called a "desert." They establish a relationship with the soil and discover the dignity inherent in the practice of growing food. When a small group of U.S. Americans accompany their host in Cuernavaca, Mexico, on a short walk to the tortilleria down the street, they encounter an increasingly rare practice of artisanship and observe a relationship of ongoing mutual respect between producer and consumer. And when young adults on a rural college farm work together to tend to a sick sow, whom they know by name, they resourcefully practice an improvisational kind of agricultural creativity. They also honor life in all its complexity.

In their little moves against destructiveness, people of faith discover and reveal God's presence in the everyday. They express their wonder in response to God's provision and the earth's beauty. But they also stand as a witness to the sin and brokenness that characterize the food system, and that make truly good food a near impossibility. Finally, they fortify the bonds of interdependence that join people together in communities;[8] in Christ's body, the church; and in human relationships with God's body, the earth.[9]

In these seemingly small things, they are visionaries.

UNEARTHING BEAUTY
HOPE FOR GOOD FOOD

When accompanying these visionaries as they go about their work, one is struck by the ease with which they smile, laugh, and interact with the people around them. They recount with lighthearted, self-deprecating humor their missteps and the characters they have met along the way. Despite the serious, indeed life-and-death character of their work, their lives testify to the joy discovered in sharing meals, working in collaboration, touching the earth, learning ancient crafts, and nurturing life from seed. Herein lies our greatest hope for a flourishing food system. The grounded practical theology of food constructed in these pages demands attention to this joy: "Sometimes we practice hope by doing everything we can to unearth a moment of beauty and then to defend it vigorously from all that threatens to push it back underground."[10] The agricultural image of "unearthing beauty" captures the theological movement propelling everyday visionaries as they faithfully respond to the global food system. It is a theological composting of sorts. Turning over one bit of earth, debris, and waste at a time, these food practices invite intimate knowledge of the scope and depth of the problem, and yet also the potential to discover new life buried within its layers.

With clear eyes and callused hands, these everyday visionaries yet observe the beauty and goodness that reside in the deep perception of interdependence. In the midst of the food system's woundedness and harm, they connect with a deeper source of health and thriving. This kind of hope is distinguished from a more naïve optimism, in that the relationship between action and social change is not a matter of strategic calculus, but faithful perseverance in the face of immense obstacles. Students of feminist theologian Letty Russell recount the lively parties thrown in Russell's home at the conclusion of each semester of social analysis, during which they have confronted head-on the oppressive systems that threaten life at every turn: "Here they join together in eating, singing silly songs, and creating skits filled with humor and hope. . . . As Letty always reminds her students in the midst of the party, what they are experiencing is just a brief glimpse of God's gift of shalom to all creation. The joyous meal offers a preview of the New Creation that God, in Jesus Christ, has promised to all. Her parties are thus a small but powerful enactment of the 'liberating eschaton' that stretches before all humanity."[11]

Glimpses. Small but powerful enactments. Like the celebratory meal in Letty Russell's home, the food practices described in these pages illustrate in sharp relief the creative tension between the global food system and biblical images of abundant feasts. This creative tension is always present for hopeful Christians: "In this hope the soul does not soar above our vale of tears to some imagined heavenly bliss, nor does it sever itself from the earth. . . . It does not calm the unquiet heart, but is itself this unquiet heart in man. Those who hope in Christ can no longer put up with reality as it is, but begin to suffer under it, to contradict it."[12] Where hope is unearthed in the global food system, it necessarily evokes a sense of dissonance, which Jürgen Moltmann describes as the "unquiet heart." The tension in the unquiet heart, however, is something not to be avoided, but embraced as an opening for change, as Martin Luther King Jr. exhorted: "I must confess that I am not afraid of the word, tension . . . there is a type of constructive tension that is necessary for growth."[13]

The unquiet heart honored and nurtured in the practices that constitute a grounded practical theology of food is a source of profound imagination and creativity. In fact, imagination is a crucial capacity for engaging the creative tension present in these practices. Although sometimes confused with fantasy, imagination is grounded in the everyday struggle: "the role of imagination is not to resolve, not to point the way, not to improve. It is to awaken, to disclose the ordinarily unseen, unheard, and unexpected."[14] Imagination makes it possible for everyday visionaries to persevere, even thrive, within the global food system. In part, food practices cultivate eschatological imagination *because* they dwell in the mundane, nurturing attentiveness to the most ordinary stuff of the material world: dirt, water, sweat. People of faith who are capable of this kind of imagination invite all of us into deeper, more faithful dimensions of creativity: "Though it is possible for people to passively inhabit land, they are at their cultured best when they work with it, learn from and modify it, turning a particular plot into a place that satisfies human hunger, desire, and need for art."[15]

Finally, these practices model a way of life that is pursued *as if* flourishing were the norm: as if God's gifts of good food, labor with dignity, luscious soil, honored animals, and social relationships of mutual respect and compassion were fully realized in our time. To some, these everyday visionaries might seem a little crazy: making a garden in what has been called a "desert," starting a working farm in the churchyard, forsaking the full-time job with benefits in order to start a community sustainable food initiative, to travel across borders to confront one's own complicity in a broken system. At the very least, it seems "maladjusted," to borrow Martin Luther King Jr.'s language. Societies, however, need "creatively maladjusted" people: "[T]here are some things in our society, some things in our world, to which we should never be adjusted. There are some things concerning which we must always be maladjusted if we are to be people of good will. . . . And through such creative maladjustment, we may be able to emerge from the bleak and desolate midnight of man's inhumanity to man, into the bright and glittering daybreak of freedom and justice. . . . I have not lost hope."[16]

Hope for good food demands a degree of creative maladjustment. It requires living into an alternative reality, planting and tending hearty little seedlings of agricultural beauty in the desolate places. In so doing, we "look for God's unexpected reversals, . . . live in anticipation of the coming of the New Creation, . . . [and live] a Christian life oriented absolutely in love and service toward God's design for the future."[17]

Here's to the creative, imaginative, persevering everyday visionaries. May God bless their work, and ours to come.

Notes

1   Although I am calling this a grounded practical theology, it is true that practical theology as a discipline generally prioritizes this kind of attention to everyday life. See especially Bonnie Miller-McLemore's exposition of the four meanings of practical theology. Bonnie J. Miller-McLemore, *Christian Theology in Practice: Discovering a Discipline* (Grand Rapids: Eerdmans, 2012), 106–10.

2   In placing ethnographic data and narratives in conversation with social analysis and theological reflection, the method of this book is similar to what Rebecca Chopp describes as "mutually critical correlation." In other words, an interdisciplinary method that is truly mutually critical insists on allowing social analysis to propose theological questions, and invites practices to push back on theological traditions. See Rebecca Chopp, "Practical Theology and Liberation," in *Formation and Reflection: The Promise of Practical Theology*, ed. Lewis S. Mudge and James N. Poling (Minneapolis: Augsburg Fortress, 2009).

3   Some practices not addressed in depth in this book, but which are clearly relevant, are (1) religious involvement in the labor justice movement, (2) church programs addressing obesity and nutrition, and (3) animal rights and moral vegetarianism. All of these appear in the context of discussions of the dignity of work, globalization, food access, and sustainable agriculture. Where possible, I try to point to resources that develop these concepts and practices more exhaustively. The latter—animal rights and moral vegetarianism—warrants more discussion: in 2010, I co-taught a course on Food and Globalization, in which one of our field trips was to a "conventional" dairy farm in rural Michigan. In that farm, the dairy

cows were strictly confined in small enclosures, side by side, and stood on concrete all day. They would be put out in the sun, on the grass, when they were calving or injured. As we walked back to the van, a student and I discovered that we shared the same sense that the cows staring back at us were sentient beings—that they were experiencing and sensing what was happening to them—and that this life was no kind of life for any animal. (Indeed, dairy cows in conventional farms are bred and milked at a pace that shortens their life spans by several years, in contrast to dairy cows in organic farms.) See Charles Benbrook, *A Deeper Shade of Green: Lessons from Grass-Based Organic Dairy Farms* (Washington, D.C.: Organic Center, 2012), 6. At the very least, industrial agriculture raises serious issues for Christians concerned about animal dignity and quality of life. For some Christians, this concern leads to the practice of vegetarianism or veganism.

In this book, I treat animal welfare and vegetarianism in broad strokes and under the broader rubric of an ecotheological perspective. One of the core theological principles underlying my argument is that human relationships to food are characterized by a radical degree of alienation. The proper response, then, is to seek an ecospirituality that is characterized by deep cognizance of shared vulnerability and the interdependence of humans, other animals, and other life forms. In this attention to vulnerability and interdependence, I share a moral position with Andrew Linzey: "the weak and vulnerable make a special claim upon us." Andrew Linzey, *Creatures of the Same God: Explorations in Animal Theology* (Brooklyn, N.Y.: Lantern Books, 2009), xiii. For Linzey, this means that animals require attention in the specific, while I retain a systemic view, considering animals (including humans) as part of a whole. Linzey finds this approach inadequate, and particularly finds that it lets those of us who identify with the ecotheological perspective "off the hook," so to speak, with regard to the question of whether it is ever acceptable for humans to kill (more vulnerable) animals in order to eat, when it is not necessary. Linzey, *Creatures of the Same God*, 29–44. When we fail to wrestle with this particular question, Linzey argues, we reveal a deep "speciesism," in that human interests are arbitrarily favored over those of other living beings, even when we could choose otherwise. Andrew Linzey, "Is Christianity Irredeemably Speciesist?" in *Animals on the Agenda: Questions about Animals for Theology and Ethics*, ed. Andrew Linzey and Dorothy Yamamoto (Chicago: University of Illinois Press, 1998), xi–xx.

Although some readers may find the treatment of animals—in the specific—to be inadequate, I do not agree that an ecotheological perspective is necessarily a speciesist approach. In fact, it acknowledges the permeable boundaries between species. As one interview subject put it, "Why do we discriminate between the tiny microbes that are destroyed when we eat vegetables and the larger, fuzzier things that we use to sustain ourselves?" While I do think there are relative distinctions to be drawn between sentient beings and other forms of life, the challenge is an important one: how *do* we distinguish between life forms and take appropriate moral responsibility for our relative power, in most cases, over other life forms? Here, theological reflections on animals have an important point:

in its efforts to resist the charge of anthropocentrism, and to emphasize interdependence, ecotheology may sometimes issue in a peculiar abdication of responsibility with regard to humanity's transcendence in relationship to the life of animals. Daniel K. Miller, *Animal Ethics and Theology: The Lens of the Good Samaritan* (New York: Routledge, 2012), 137–41.

Finally, in reference to Linzey's concern that the "weak and the vulnerable make a special claim upon us," I return to the voices of the human beings that are disproportionately vulnerable in our food system: the poor. So frequently, arguments about food, diet, and ecology exclude them and their concerns about food security, just wages, and nutrition. While it is a gross and manipulative distortion to pit concerns about animal welfare against concerns for vulnerable humans (certainly factory farms victimize them both!), the delicate balance I am trying to maintain in this book between social justice and ecological well-being makes it difficult to treat animal welfare and vegetarianism with much specificity. The sustainability movement has suffered from a degree of moral superiority that alienates the poor. (See, e.g., Mark Bittman's controversial argument from the *New York Times*: "Taking the long route to putting food on the table may not be easy, but for almost all Americans it remains a choice, and if you can drive to McDonald's you can drive to Safeway. It's cooking that's the real challenge. [The real challenge is not 'I'm too busy to cook.' In 2010 the average American, regardless of weekly earnings, watched no less than an hour and a half of television per day. The time is there.]" Bittman's larger argument, about the need for cultural change with regard to how U.S. Americans view the practice of cooking, is an important one. But along the way he makes some rather dismissive comments. Mark Bittman, "Is Junk Food Really Cheaper?" *New York Times*, September 24, 2011.) The animal rights movement, too, suffers from a degree of moral superiority. Andrew Linzey himself notes that this is both off-putting to those outside the movement and disingenuous. A better approach, he argues, is a " 'progressive disengagement from injury to animals'—a strategy that involves each of us going as far as we can toward realizing the goal of living a cruelty-free and violence-free life. But we must realize that not all people are able to move at the same pace, and that many of us are deeply attached in one form or another to the benefits of animal exploitation." Linzey, *Creatures of the Same God*, xv. Most of the practitioners described in these pages embody, in varying degrees, this progressive disengagement.

I will touch on this tension between animal rights and ecological perspectives in many places. All of the practices described in these pages, if they do not address animal welfare directly, at least have room for doing so. The tension is important, and bears real material consequences. For now, however, I leave this ideological argument unresolved, allowing its ambiguities and tensions to seep into the other arguments I pursue more explicitly.

4   Mallory McDuff, *Natural Saints: How People of Faith Are Working to Save God's Earth* (New York: Oxford University Press, 2010).

5   For more on these trends and challenges, see Jacey Fortin, "After Meat

Workers Die of Covid-19, Families Fight for Compensation," *New York Times*, October 6, 2020; Renée Johnson and Jim Monke, *What Is the Farm Bill?* CRS Report for Congress, September 26, 2019 (Washington, D.C.: Congressional Research Service), 7; Glenn Thrush and Thomas Kaplan, "G.O.P. Faction Sinks Vast Bill On Farm Policy," *New York Times*, May 19, 2018; Yamil Berard, "'Push Comes to Shove Moment' for Rural Hospitals in Georgia," *Atlanta Journal-Constitution*, September 24, 2020; Todd Post, "Baltimore's Black Churches Take on Food Apartheid," *Bread for the World*, last modified February 5, 2020, accessed October 14, 2020, https://www.bread.org/blog/baltimores-black-churches-take-food-apartheid.

INTRODUCTION

1   For a discussion of the social and performative meanings of eating, see L. Shannon Jung, *Food for Life: The Spirituality and Ethics of Eating* (Minneapolis: Augsburg Fortress, 2004), 46–53. For a historical view of the cultural and religious significance of eating, see Charles L. Harper and Bryan F. Le Beau, *Food, Society, and Environment* (Upper Saddle River, N.J.: Prentice Hall, 2003), 31–61.

2   Gabriel Axel, *Babette's Feast* (Orion Classics, 1987); George Tillman Jr., *Soul Food* (Twentieth Century Fox, 1997).

3   In 1980 food critic Gael Greene used the term "foodies" to describe the "devotees" of chef Dominique Nahmias' Parisian restaurant Le Restaurant d'Olympe. At the time, Nahmias was an exemplar of shifts in culinary philosophy that favored "regional tradition" over complicated techniques. Gael Greene, "What's Nouvelle? La Cuisine Bourgeoise," *New York*, June 2, 1980. Similarly, Ann Barr and Paul Levy (seemingly apart from Greene's use of the word) used the term to describe "people who, because of age, sex, income and social class, simply did not fit into the category 'gourmet,' which we insisted had become 'a rude word.'" Paul Levy, "What Is a Foodie?" *The Guardian: Word of Mouth Blog*, June 14, 2007.

4   Levy, "What Is a Foodie?" Notably, the subtitle of Barr and Levy's book, *The Official Foodie Handbook*, is *Be Modern—Worship Food*. Paul Levy and Ann Barr, *The Official Foodie Handbook: Be Modern—Worship Food* (New York: Arbor House, 1985).

5   In an episode of IFC's *Portlandia*, an earnest couple in a farm-to-table restaurant is so concerned about the origins of the chicken on the menu that, after seeing the chicken's "papers," they ask their server to hold their table while they pay a quick visit to inspect the farm in question, a mere thirty miles away. In a commercial for Geico Insurance, a similarly earnest couple quizzes a vendor about the produce, "Does your cauliflower have a big carbon footprint?" See Eliot Glazer, "See Gallagher (Yes, That Gallagher) in a Geico Commercial," *Vulture*, 2012, http://www.vulture.com/2012/07/gallagher-in-a-geico-commercial.html (accessed November 20, 2012); *Portlandia*, season 1, episode 1.

6   Psalm 104:14-15.

7   See chapter 3.

8   President Obama, in a meeting with Michael Pollan, reportedly asked

about the social traction of the issues related to food production: "Is this a movement?" Robert Gottlieb and Anupama Joshi, *Food Justice, Food, Health, and the Environment* (Cambridge, Mass.: MIT Press, 2010), 79.

9   *Putting Meat on the Table: Industrial Farm Animal Production in America* (Pew Commission on Industrial Farm Animal Production and Johns Hopkins Bloomberg School of Health, 2006), 5.

10   Luke 24:30-31.

11   See, e.g., Deuteronomy 27:19; Leviticus 19:9-10; Malachi 3:5; Acts 6.

12   See, e.g., Genesis 2:15; Leviticus 25:1-7; Isaiah 28:24.

13   Miller-McLemore, *Christian Theology in Practice*, 103.

14   Both of these movements—sustainable agriculture and community food security—have also been challenged by the animal rights and moral vegetarianism movement. See Patricia Allen, *Together at the Table: Sustainability and Sustenance in the American Agrifood System* (University Park: Pennsylvania State University Press, 2004), 139–40.

15   Marion Nestle prefers the term "food industry," offering an exhaustive list of all the sectors involved in this trillion-dollar industry, including those involved in the "production and consumption of food and beverages: producers and processors of food crops and animals (agribusiness); companies that make and sell fertilizer, pesticides, seeds, and feed; those that provide machinery, labor, real estate, and financial services to farmers; and others that transport, store, distribute, export, process, and market foods after they leave the farm. It also includes the food service sector—food carts, vending machines, restaurants, bars, fast-food outlets, schools, hospitals, prisons, and workplaces—and associated suppliers of equipment and serving materials." Marion Nestle, *Food Politics: How the Food Industry Influences Nutrition and Health* (Berkeley: University of California Press, 2002), 11.

16   Nestle, *Food Politics*, 26.

17   Healthy, fresh foods, when available in convenience stores, often are sold at a markedly higher price point than in small groceries or supermarkets. See, e.g., Angela D. Liese, Kristina E. Weis, Delores Pluto, Emily Smith, and Andrew Lawson, "Food Store Types, Availability, and Cost of Foods in a Rural Environment," *Journal of the American Dietetic Association* 107, no. 11 (2007): 1919. In that particular study, tomatoes were not markedly more expensive in the convenience store, but other healthy food items, like eggs and apples, were.

18   Sarah Jaffe, "McJobs Should Pay, Too: Inside Fast-Food Workers' Historic Protest for Living Wages," *Atlantic*, November 29, 2012, http://www .theatlantic.com/business/archive/2012/11/mcjobs-should-pay-too-inside -fast-food-workers-historic-protest-for-living-wages/265714/# (accessed December 2, 2012).

19   Gottlieb and Joshi, *Food Justice*, 6.

20   Sharon Welch has argued that the middle class is actually particularly susceptible to discouragement and despair, and that this is partially an effect of their privilege: they have achieved some success, and when new barriers present themselves, their commitment wanes. Sharon D. Welch, *A Feminist Ethic of Risk*, rev. ed. (Minneapolis: Fortress, 2000), 41.

21   Welch, *A Feminist Ethic of Risk*, 103.

22   Psalm 23:5a.

CHAPTER 1

1 Michael Pollan, "Farmer in Chief," *New York Times Magazine*, October 12, 2008, http://www.nytimes.com/2008/10/12/magazine/12policy-t .html (accessed June 7, 2012).

2 The "global food system" refers to the transnational patterns of food production, distribution, and consumption.

3 Eric Schlosser, "Still a Fast-Food Nation: Eric Schlosser Reflects on 10 Years Later," *Daily Beast*, March 12, 2012, http://www.thedailybeast .com/articles/2012/03/12/still-a-fast-food-nation-eric-schlosser-reflects -on-10-years-later.html (accessed December 1, 2012).

4 Taggart Siegel, *The Real Dirt on Farmer John* (CAVU Pictures, 2005).

5 See Curtis E. Beus and Riley E. Dunlap, "Conventional versus Alternative Agriculture: The Paradigmatic Roots of the Debate," *Rural Sociology 55*, no. 4 (1990): 602.

6 Cash crops are more profitable because they are eligible for commodity subsidy payments.

7 Tom Vilsack, Testimony at U.S. Senate Committee on Agriculture, Nutrition, and Forestry, Farm Bill Oversight Hearing, June 30, 2010.

8 Harper and Le Beau cite anthropologist Mark Grey, who says, "No one wants to state the truth—that food processing in American today would collapse were it not for immigrant labor." Harper and Le Beau, *Food, Society, and Environment*, 128. See also Raj Patel, *Stuffed and Starved: The Hidden Battle for the World Food System* (Brooklyn, N.Y.: Melville House, 2008), 60–62.

9 Fred W. Friendly, *Harvest of Shame* (CBS News, 1960). See also Gottlieb and Joshi, *Food Justice*, 18–19.

10 Gottlieb and Joshi, *Food Justice*, 18.

11 Gottlieb and Joshi, *Food Justice*, 19.

12 Gottlieb and Joshi, *Food Justice*, 20–21.

13 Eric Holt-Giménez, Zoe Brent, and Annie Shattuck, *Food Workers— Food Justice: Linking Food, Labor and Immigrant Rights* (Oakland, Calif.: Food First/Institute for Food and Development Policy, 2010).

14 Food Security in the U.S., Definitions of Food Security, USDA Economic Research Service, http://www.ers.usda.gov/topics/food-nutrition -assistance/food-security-in-the-us/definitions-of-food-security.aspx#. UVJTWFtC7Ws.

15 Holt-Giménez, Brent, and Shattuck, *Food Workers—Food Justice*.

16 Yvonne Yen Liu and Dominique Apollon note that "[f]ood processing has one of the highest rates of injury incurred in the workplace in 2008. Much of the work involves repetitive, physically demanding work and use of dangerous tools and machinery to cut, slice or grind. However, much of the workforce lacks access to adequate care, one that is linguistically and culturally competent, to treat their workplace injuries. Nor do they receive adequate training from their employers to operate machinery in a safe manner." Yvonne Yen Liu and Dominique Apollon, *The Color of Food* (New York: Applied Research Center, 2011), 14. See also Harper and Le Beau, *Food, Society, and Environment*, 128.

17 Liu and Apollon, *The Color of Food*, 3.

18 Liu and Apollon, *The Color of Food*, 9–12.

19 John H. Davis, "From Agriculture to Agribusiness," *Harvard Business Review* 34, no. 1 (1956): 110.

20 Davis, "From Agriculture to Agribusiness," 109.

21 Davis, "From Agriculture to Agribusiness," 109.

22 A graph illustrating "Agribusiness in Action" in Davis' *Harvard Business Review* essay confirms the hourglass analogy. See Davis, "From Agriculture to Agribusiness," 108. See also Harper and Le Beau, *Food, Society, and Environment*; Patel, *Stuffed and Starved*, 11–13.

23 William Neuman, "Cargill Recalls Ground Turkey Linked to Outbreak," *New York Times*, August 3, 2011.

24 As 2012 presidential candidate Mitt Romney put it, "Corporations are people, my friend." See Philip Rucker, "Mitt Romney Says 'Corporations Are People' at Iowa State Fair," *Washington Post*, August 11, 2011, http://www.washingtonpost.com/politics/mitt-romney-says-corporations-are-people/2011/08/11/gIQABwZ38I_story.html (accessed October 1, 2012). The concept of corporate personhood, dating back to the early nineteenth century, is generating a great deal of scholarship at the moment, and is too complex to be within the purview of this book. For an editorial that traces a bit of the history of the subject, see "The Rights of Corporations," *New York Times*, September 22, 2009. For an analysis of the relationship between corporate personhood and corporate responsibility, see Rita Manning, "Corporate Responsibility and Corporate Personhood," *Journal of Business Ethics* 3, no. 1 (1984).

25 Karl Marx is perhaps the most well-known critic of the alienation that threatens the relationship between a laborer (here, a farmer) and the very thing her labor produces in a capitalist system. In what might be described as extreme forms of corporate capitalism, the farmer is alienated not only from the food she grows, but even from the very process of growing it (means of production). Her labor itself even becomes a commodity for the employers—the stakeholders of the corporation for which she farms. Karl Marx, "Estranged Labour," in *The Marx-Engels Reader*, ed. Robert C. Tucker (New York: W. W. Norton, 1978).

26 "Market success," in the food system, requires that food be understood as a commodity: something bought and sold at a profit.

27 *Food Marketing to Children and Youth: Threat or Opportunity?* (New York: Institute of Medicine of the National Academies, 2005).

28 Marion Nestle, "Surprise! Food Companies Still Market to Children," *Atlantic*, August 26, 2011.

29 Recent research indicates that, even with the rise in global food prices, Americans still spend less than 10 percent of their disposable income on food. In contrast, in the early 1950s, Americans spent more than 20 percent of their disposable income on food. See Food CPI and Expenditures, USDA Economic Research Service, table 7, http://www.ers.usda.gov/data-products/food-expenditures.aspx. With growing wealth disparity, however, it is important to note that low-income families in the United States continue to spend approximately 20 percent of their income on food. (In other countries, the proportion is as high as 43 percent.) See "The Amount Spent on Food Rises with Income while the Proportion Falls," in *An Illustrated Guide to Research Findings from USDA's Economic Research Service* (Washington, D.C.: USDA Economic Research Service, 2009).

30 Food Security in the U.S., Key Statistics and Graphics, USDA Economic Research Service, http://www.ers.usda.gov/topics/food-nutrition-assistance/food-security-in-the-us/key-statistics-graphics.aspx#.UVJWRVtC7Ws.

31 In 2008, 12,727,450 households participated in SNAP. In 2010, 18,618,436 households participated. See "Supplemental Nutrition Assistance Program (Monthly Data—National Level)" (Alexandria, Va.: Supplemental Nutrition Assistance Program [USDA Food and Nutrition Service], 2011). Of course, receiving SNAP benefits increases food security. The rise in the number of households filing for these benefits, however, is one signal of increased food insecurity in the United States. This increase is partly due to expanded eligibility for the program in 2009's American Recovery and Reinvestment Act. See Mark Nord and Mark Prell, "Food Security of SNAP Recipients Improved Following the 2009 Stimulus Package," *Amber Waves* (June 2011), http://www.ers.usda.gov/amber-waves/2011-june/food-security-of-snap.aspx#.US2R8BlmbDk.

32 To some, "food deserts" is a pejorative term, in that it defines a community according to what it lacks. In any case, the term here is used descriptively, and in conversation with theoretical literature. Mari Gallagher writes, "Residents of food deserts—large geographic areas with no or distant grocery stores—face nutritional challenges evident in diet-related community health outcomes. Those outcomes worsen when the food desert has high concentrations of nearby fast food alternatives." Gallagher, *Good Food: Examining the Impact of Food Deserts on Public Health in Chicago* (Chicago: Mari Gallagher Research and Consulting Group and LaSalle Bank, 2006). Robert Gottlieb and Anupama Joshi also note that the location of grocery outlets also assumes the use of an automobile to access the stores, since stores are regularly built near freeway exits, with ample parking, and yet at a great distance from public transportation. See Gottlieb and Joshi, *Food Justice*, 46.

33 Robert Kenner, *Food, Inc.* (Magnolia Pictures, 2008). There is some current debate about whether fast food and junk food are really cheaper than simple home-cooked meals, one of the claims in *Food, Inc.* This debate turns primarily upon how one measures the time required to prepare/acquire the meal in question. See Bittman; Tom Philpott, "Is Cooking Really Cheaper Than Fast Food?," *Mother Jones*, October 4, 2011.

34 These are some of the advantages described by advocates for biotechnology. See "Questions and Answers about Food Biotechnology," International Food Information Council Foundation http://www.foodinsight.org/Resources/Detail.aspx?topic=Questions_and_Answers_About_Food_Biotechnology (accessed January 13, 2013).

35 There are many economic and political issues associated with genetically modified crops, including the holding of patents on these modified life-forms. The prevalence of genetically modified corn in the United States has delivered a severe economic blow to Mexican agriculture, for example.

36 Since the use of genetically modified organisms in food is a relatively recent development, research on the effects of these methods is still nascent. See, e.g., Andrew Pollack, "Foes of Modified Corn Find Support in a Study," *New York Times*, September 20, 2012. Given the absence of data on the long-term effects of consuming genetically modified ingredients, consumer

pressure for disclosure of these ingredients is mounting. In 2012, e.g., a proposition in California requiring labeling of genetically modified foods was defeated by a margin of about six percentage points. Opponents to the measure, including large corporations using these technologies, spent about $45 million dollars to defeat it. See "State Ballot Measures—Statewide Results," California Secretary of State http://vote.sos.ca.gov/returns/ballot-measures/ (accessed December 1, 2012); Alexandra Sifferlin, "California Fails to Pass Genetically Modified Foods Labeling Initiative," Time.com, November 8, 2012, http://www.cnn.com/2012/11/08/health/california-gm-foods/index.html.

37 Ken Stier, "How Frankenfood Prevailed," *Time Magazine*, June 28, 2010.

38 Marion Nestle, *What to Eat* (New York: North Point Press, 2006), 324.

39 Alice Park, "All Sugars Aren't the Same: Glucose Is Better, Study Says," *Time Magazine*, April 21, 2009.

40 Kathleen A. Page, Owen Chan, Jagriti Arora, Renata Belfort-DeAguiar, James Dzuira, Brian Roehmholdt, Gary W. Cline, Sarita Naik, Rajita Sinha, R. Todd Constable, and Robert S. Sherwin, "Effects of Fructose vs Glucose on Regional Cerebral Blood Flow in Brain Regions Involved with Appetite and Reward Pathways," *Journal of the American Medical Association* 309, no. 1 (2013): 63–70, http://jama.jamanetwork.com/article.aspx?articleid=1555133.

41 National School Lunch Program: Participation and Lunches Served, http://www.fns.usda.gov/pd/slsummar.htm.

42 *Commodity Foods and the Nutritional Quality of the National School Lunch Program: Historical Role, Current Operations, and Future Potential* (Washington, D.C.: Food Research and Action Center, 2008), 6–7.

43 *Commodity Foods*, 25.

44 State Fact Sheets: United States, USDA Economic Research Service, http://www.ers.usda.gov/data-products/state-fact-sheets/state-data.aspx?StateFIPS=00#.UVJYeltC7Ws.

45 U.S. and World Population Clocks, U.S. Census Bureau, http://www.census.gov/main/www/popclock.html.

46 Food Security in the U.S., Community Food Security, USDA Economic Research Service, http://www.ers.usda.gov/topics/food-nutrition-assistance/food-security-in-the-us/community-food-security.aspx#.UVJYWFtC7Ws.

47 In 2007 a community food assessment in central and south Los Angeles found that in the three neighborhoods studied, less than 2 percent of the food outlets in the areas studied were "full-service supermarkets." While consumers could purchase food at convenience and specialty stores (such as bakeries or carnecerías), these outlets frequently did not have items recommended by the USDA "Thrifty Food Plan." When they did carry these items, they were more expensive than identical items in a supermarket. See *Food Access in Central and South Los Angeles: Mapping Injustice, Agenda for Action* (Los Angeles: Center for Food and Justice, Urban and Environmental Policy Initiative, Occidental College, 2007).

48 Gottlieb and Joshi, *Food Justice*, 48.

49 Wendell Berry, "The Body and the Earth," in *The Art of the Commonplace: The Agrarian Essays of Wendell Berry*, ed. Norman Wirzba (Berkeley, Calif.: Counterpoint Press, 2002), 93.

50 In the United States, the farm crisis of the 1980s was accompanied by an outbreak of suicides. Raj Patel has described similar crises in India, Sri Lanka, China, Australia, and the United Kingdom. Patel, *Stuffed and Starved*, 26.

51 Just before he died, Lee shouted, "The WTO kills farmers." His daughter interpreted his death in this way: "He didn't die to become a hero or to draw attention to himself. He died to show the plight of Korean farmers—something he knew from personal experience." Patel, *Stuffed and Starved*, 35–36.

52 Patel, *Stuffed and Starved*, 27–29.

53 Tom Vilsack, "Briefing on the Status of Rural America," United States Department of Agriculture, 2010.

54 Tom Vilsack, "Agriculture Secretary Vilsack Makes Case for Stronger Rural America," news release, United States Department of Agriculture, 2010.

55 Vilsack, Testimony.

56 See, e.g., Gottlieb and Joshi's account of the impact of cheap garlic imported from China in a local California garlic-producing region. Gottlieb and Joshi, *Food Justice*, 100–101. Agriculture subsidies established in the Farm Bill contribute significantly to this dynamic.

57 See, e.g., Gottlieb and Joshi, *Food Justice*, 59–60, 109–14.

58 The cultural effects of the globalization of food are well documented. See George Ritzer, *The McDonaldization of Society 6*, 6th ed. (Thousand Oaks, Calif.: Pine Forge Press, 2011). Gottlieb and Joshi write, "Yet the appeal of fast food is precisely its ability to mimic changes that were initially developed as part of a changing U.S. food system, which in turn has strongly influenced a global food system that does not recognize borders. French fast-food chronicler Rick Fantasia argues that by the time McDonald's entered the French market in the 1980s, its basic policy had become 'not to adapt to foreign cultures, but to change the cultures to fit McDonald's.'" Gottlieb and Joshi, *Food Justice*, 113–14.

59 Christine Ahn and Albie Miles, *Free Trade Kills Korean Farmers* (Oakland, Calif.: Food First/Institute for Food Development and Policy, 2011).

60 Gottlieb and Joshi, *Food Justice*, 116. For more information on the Vía Campesina movement, see "La Via Campesina: International Peasant Movement," http://viacampesina.org/en/. The concept of "food sovereignty" can also be applied on a local scale.

61 Wendell Berry, "It All Turns on Affection" (2012 Jefferson Lecture, National Endowment for the Humanities, April 23, 2012 [emphasis in original]).

62 Aldo Leopold argued that a proper "land ethic" is characterized by understanding oneself as a member or citizen, rather than conqueror, of the land: "All ethics so far evolved rest upon a single premise: that the individual is a member of a community of interdependent parts. His instincts prompt him to compete for his place in that community, but his ethics prompt him also to co-operate. . . . The land ethic simply enlarges the boundaries of the community to include soils, waters, plants, and animals, or collectively: the land." Leopold, "The Land Ethic," in *A Sand County Almanac* (New York: Oxford University Press, 2001), 171.

63 Although the treatment of animals receives some explicit attention in this

project, it is important to note that the broader invocation of "land," "earth," and "ecosystem" is meant to include and imply all life forms—from microscopic organisms living in the soil, to plants, to animals, including humans. In part, this admittedly ambiguous approach derives from a focus on the theme of interdependence, emphasizing humanity's role as *members* of creation. Although some scholars have critiqued eco-theological perspectives for not attending explicitly to the suffering of animals, feminist commitments to interdependence and the "mending of creation" leave room for considering the plights of all vulnerable life forms and resists simplistic idealizing of "nature." Linzey, *Creatures of the Same God*, 29–44; Kwok Pui-lan, "Mending of Creation: Women, Nature, and Eschatological Hope," in *Liberating Eschatology: Essays in Honor of Letty M. Russell*, ed. Margaret A. Farley and Serene Jones (Louisville, Ky.: Westminster John Knox, 1999), 144–55.

64 Davis, "From Agriculture to Agribusiness."

65 Pollan, "Farmer in Chief."

66 Norman Wirzba, *Food and Faith: A Theology of Eating* (New York: Cambridge University Press, 2011), 14.

67 Although this discussion is necessarily brief and selective, entire books and major reports have been dedicated to the environmental effects of modern agriculture. See, for example, *Farming for the Future: A Sustainable Agriculture Agenda for the 2012 Food and Farm Bill* (Washington, D.C.: National Sustainable Agriculture Coalition, 2012); *Putting Meat on the Table*; Harper and Le Beau, *Food, Society, and Environment*.

68 Wirzba, *Food and Faith*, 22.

69 Davis, "From Agriculture to Agribusiness," 111.

70 Food, Conservation, and Energy Act of 2008, H.R. 6124, 110th Congress (2008). The Food, Conservation, and Energy Act is frequently called, in shorthand, the Farm Bill, despite the fact that it includes many other food policy programs, such as the Supplemental Nutrition Assistance Program (SNAP). The Farm Bill is discussed in chapter 2.

71 Rotating between corn and soybeans is better for the land than farming only corn, all the time, but still makes soil vulnerable to fertility issues and erosion. See William Neuman, "High Prices Sow Seeds of Erosion," *New York Times*, April 12, 2011.

72 Kenner, *Food, Inc.* Peter Singer made the argument that animals are no longer "raised," but produced in factory farms. Peter Singer, *Animal Liberation* (San Francisco: HarperCollins, 2001).

73 The welfare of animals is a serious concern in the quest for good food.

74 Gottlieb and Joshi, *Food Justice*, 28.

75 Frank App, "The Industrialization of Agriculture," *Annals of the American Academy of Political and Social Science* 142, Farm Relief (1929): 228–34; Harold F. Breimyer, "The Three Economies of Agriculture," *Journal of Farm Economics* 44, no. 3 (1962): 681, 690. See also V. James Rhodes, "Industrialization of Agriculture: Discussion," *American Journal of Agricultural Economics* 75, no. 5 (1993): 1137.

76 For accounts of the Green Revolution in India, Africa, and Cuba, see Patel, *Stuffed and Starved*, 119–63; Vandana Shiva, *The Violence of the Green Revolution* (New York: Zed Books, 1991).

77 Shiva, *The Violence of the Green Revolution*, 11. Instead of peace and prosperity, Shiva argues, the excessive scientific manipulations that have characterized this approach to agriculture in India have resulted in a reduction in biodiversity, compromises to soil fertility, water conflicts, and economic and political exploitation.

78 Curtis Beus and Riley Dunlap argue that much of the debate between advocates of alternative (organic, sustainable, and biodynamic) agriculture and proponents of conventional agriculture turns not on numbers, but on competing paradigms. Beus and Dunlap, "Conventional versus Alternative Agriculture," 593–94. In a similar vein, in response to a recent study comparing the yields of conventional farming to organic farming, Ari Levaux writes, "To assume that the best farming practice is the one that produces the highest yield is like observing that a Lamborghini outraces a bicycle, and thus should be the world's only vehicle." Ari Levaux, "The War between Organic and Conventional Farming Misses the Point," *Atlantic*, May 14, 2012.

79 Davis, "From Agriculture to Agribusiness," 107; Gottlieb and Joshi, *Food Justice*, 28–29.

80 Michael Pollan recounts Berry's astute observation in his 2008 open letter to the soon-to-be president-elect. Pollan, "Farmer in Chief."

81 The last century has seen a marked decrease in crop diversity. A 1983 study by the Rural Advancement Foundation estimated that about 93 percent of major crop varieties had gone extinct. E.g., in 1903 seed companies sold 307 varieties of corn, but by 1983, only twelve varieties were held in the U.S. National Seed Storage Laboratory. See the graphic entitled "Our Dwindling Food Variety," in Charles Siebert, "Food Ark," *National Geographic*, June 2011. See also Brian G. Henning, "Standing in Livestock's 'Long Shadow': The Ethics of Eating Meat on a Small Planet," *Ethics and the Environment* 16, no. 2 (2011): 72–73.

82 Neuman, "High Prices Sow Seeds of Erosion."

83 Davis, "From Agriculture to Agribusiness," 114. When Davis made this argument in 1956, corporate-sized farms accounted for only 1 percent of all farms, and 6 percent of all farm output. In 2007 those numbers looked quite different: very large farms (farms producing goods totaling more than $1 million in sales) accounted for 6 percent of all farms in the United States, but 59 percent of all farm output. See 2007 Census of Agriculture, Farm Numbers, USDA–National Agricultural Statistics Service, http://agcensus.usda.gov/Publications/2007/Online_Highlights/Fact_Sheets/Farm_Numbers/farm_numbers.pdf .

84 Demeter International is the nonprofit organization that educates farmers on biodynamic principles and certifies biodynamic farms. Many sustainable and organic farms may use similar practices, but have not sought certification as a biodynamic farm, a trademarked classification. For Demeter's standards for a biodynamic farm, see Demeter Association, Inc., "Biodynamic® Farm Standard," Philomath, Ore., 2012.

85 The Environmental Protection Agency (EPA), primary regulator for waste management in CAFOs, defines an Animal Feeding Operation (AFO) as a small-area lot or facility in which animals are "stabled or confined and fed or maintained for a total of 45 days or more in any 12-month

period." The EPA reports that there are approximately four hundred and fifty thousand AFOs in the United States. "Animal Feeding Operations," Environmental Protection Agency, http://cfpub.epa.gov/npdes/faqs.cfm?program_id=7. Of those operations, only about 15 percent are considered CAFOs, defined according to a minimum number of animals and its methods for dealing with animal waste. "What Is a CAFO?" Environmental Protection Agency, http://www.epa.gov/region7/water/cafo/.

86 "What Is a CAFO?"

87 In the summer of 1995, three lagoon collapses were reported in North Carolina, sending an estimated 35 million gallons of waste into the water supply. See "Duplin Spill Lets Poultry Waste Out," *Charlotte Observer*, July 5, 1995; Gottlieb and Joshi, *Food Justice*, 30–34. Contamination is not the only threat to the water supply: intensive agriculture (both crops and livestock) requires a great deal of water, using as much as 70 percent of the global freshwater supply. Henning, "Standing in Livestock's 'Long Shadow,'" 70.

88 JoAnn Burkholder, Bob Libra, Peter Weyer, Susan Heathcote, Dana Kolpin, Peter S. Thorne, and Michael Wichman, "Impacts of Waste from Concentrated Animal Feeding Operations on Water Quality," *Environmental Health Perspectives* 115, no. 2 (2007): 308. In fact, the Food and Agriculture Organization of the United Nations (FAO) reported that half of all antibiotics produced in the world are administered to livestock. See Henning, "Standing in Livestock's 'Long Shadow,'" 66.

89 Gottlieb and Joshi, *Food Justice*, 31, 33.

90 There has been some debate as to whether the livestock industry or our patterns of transportation have the most significant environmental effects. See Lisa Abend, "Meat-Eating vs. Driving: Another Climate Change Error?," *Time Magazine*, March 27, 2010, http://www.time.com/time/health/article/0,8599,1975630,00.html; Richard Black, "UN Body to Look at Meat and Climate Link," BBC News, http://news.bbc.co.uk/2/hi/8583308.stm. In any case, both of these aspects of our lifestyle, particularly in the United States, have environmental implications. The 2006 FAO report estimated that the livestock industry accounts for approximately 18 percent of greenhouse gas emissions. See Henning Steinfeld, Pierre Gerber, Tom Wassenaar, Vincent Castel, Mauricio Rosales, Cees de Haan, *Livestock's Long Shadow: Environmental Issues and Options* (Rome: Food and Agriculture Organization of the United Nations, 2006). Even the most vociferous critics of the FAO report, however, have not disputed the fact that livestock production is responsible for 18 percent of emissions. See Henning, "Standing in Livestock's 'Long Shadow,'" 88 n. 22.

91 Pollan, "Farmer in Chief." Pollan argues that in 1940 our food system "produced 2.3 calories of food energy for every calorie of fossil-fuel energy it used into one that now takes 10 calories of fossil-fuel energy to produce a single calorie of modern supermarket food."

92 Rich Pirog, Timothy Van Pelt, Kamyar Enshayan, and Ellen Cook, *Food, Fuel, and Freeways* (Ames: Leopold Center for Sustainable Agriculture, Iowa State University, 2001), 9.

93 Pirog et al., *Food, Fuel, and Freeways*, 9. The Leopold Center at Iowa State University reports that the weight of agriculture imports into the

United States, for example, increased by 26 percent between 1995 and 1999. The North American Free Trade Agreement came into force in 1994.

94 Wirzba, *Food and Faith*, 23.

95 Harper and Le Beau, *Food, Society, and Environment*, 91.

CHAPTER 2

1 Food CPI and Expenditures.

2 "The Amount Spent on Food."

3 Jung, *Food for Life*, 81.

4 David Wallinga, "Agricultural Policy and Childhood Obesity: A Food Systems and Public Health Commentary," *Health Affairs* 29, no. 3 (2010): 406.

5 One of the reasons fast food is so cheap, Gottlieb and Joshi argue, is that the wages paid to workers in the fast-food industry are so low. Gottlieb and Joshi, *Food Justice*, 54. See also Liu and Apollon, *The Color of Food*.

6 Gottlieb and Joshi, *Food Justice*, 51–54. The obesity epidemic is a problem in all populations in the United States (to the tune of about $147 billion per year in health-care costs), but particularly in children, among whom obesity is growing three times as fast as among adults. Gottlieb and Joshi, *Food Justice*, 65; Wallinga, "Agricultural Policy and Childhood Obesity," 409. Laura Carlsen notes how the United States is now also exporting obesity to Mexico, exacerbated by the North American Free Trade Agreement (NAFTA). Laura Carlsen, "NAFTA Is Starving Mexico," Foreign Policy in Focus, October 20, 2011, http://www.fpif.org/articles/nafta_is_starving_mexico.

7 Wallinga, "Agricultural Policy and Childhood Obesity," 407.

8 Wallinga, "Agricultural Policy and Childhood Obesity," 405–6.

9 Food, Conservation, and Energy Act of 2008. At the time of this writing, the 2012 Farm Bill was being debated in the United States Senate. Since the Farm Bill is renegotiated every five years, interested readers would do well to ascertain the status of Farm Bill negotiations. Several nonprofit research and advocacy organizations (including the Institute for Agriculture and Trade Policy and the National Sustainable Agriculture Coalition) maintain current analyses of the bill's status. See Institute for Agriculture and Trade Policy, http://www.iatp.org/ (accessed June 12, 2012); National Sustainable Agriculture Coalition, http://sustainableagriculture.net/ (accessed June 12, 2012).

10 Gottlieb and Joshi, *Food Justice*, 80–83.

11 At the time of this writing, the cost of the 2012 Farm Bill under negotiation has not yet been determined. The cost of the 2008 Farm Bill was $289 billion. See Edwin Young, Victor Oliveira, and Roger Claassen, "2008 Farm Act: Where Will the Money Go?" *Amber Waves* (November 2008), http://webarchives.cdlib.org/sw1vh5dg3r/http://ers.usda.gov/AmberWaves/November08/DataFeature/ (accessed June 15, 2012).

12 Gottlieb and Joshi, *Food Justice*, 83–86.

13 Bill Lilliston, *What's at Stake in the 2012 Farm Bill?* (Minneapolis: Institute for Agriculture and Trade Policy, 2012).

14 Readers will note, below, that the single largest expense in the 2008 Farm

Bill is the Nutritional Assistance Title, allocated almost $200 billion over five years. The commodity and crop insurance titles, while a relatively smaller proportion of Farm Bill spending, have a marked impact on what kind of crops are grown and in what quantities, and on the price of food in the United States. Combined with trade policy, explored below, these supports have global implications.

15 "Review of U.S. Farm Programs," Agree, http://foodandagpolicy.org/policy/review-us-farm-programs (accessed June 16, 2012).

16 Food, Conservation, and Energy Act of 2008.

17 The 2012 Farm Bill, under discussion at the time of this writing, would eliminate direct payments and strengthen crop insurance programs. See "Chairwoman's Summary of the 2012 Farm Bill," U.S. Senate Committee on Agriculture, Nutrition and Forestry, http://www.ag.senate.gov/news room/press/release/2012-farm-bill-committee-print (accessed June 27, 2012). The National Sustainable Agriculture Coalition and the Institute for Agriculture and Trade Policy both have expressed reservations about this change. While they favor reductions in direct payments for commodity crops, they argue that unlimited support for crop insurance for conventional agricultural practice is irresponsible without encouraging farmers to "adapt to and mitigate climate change." Instead, they advocate for real risk management in the face of climate change, sought through diversified farming operations. See *Farming for the Future*, 10–11; Julia Olmstead and Jim Kleinschmit, *A Risky Proposition: Crop Insurance in the Face of Climate Change* (Minneapolis: Institute for Agriculture and Trade Policy, 2012).

18 Food, Conservation, and Energy Act of 2008, Sec. 1001.1004.

19 In food policy, other kinds of crops—fruits and most vegetables—are called "specialty crops." While the Farm Bill does provide for financial assistance for research and some initiatives in "horticulture and organics," this support is minimal in comparison to the commodities programs. Food, Conservation, and Energy Act of 2008, Secs. 7311, 10001–10404.

20 *Farming for the Future.*

21 "Review of U.S. Farm Programs."

22 Nigel Key and Michael J. Roberts, *Commodity Payments, Farm Business Survival, and Farm Size Growth* (Washington, D.C.: USDA Economic Research Service, 2007), iii.

23 Davis had warned, "Should we fail to develop agribusiness answers to present problems, then by default we will have decided to go the route of big government programs for supporting prices that do not come within the scope of agribusiness." Somehow we have managed to develop both agribusiness control in the food system *and* major governmental commodities spending, neither of which make any measurable contribution to the economic situation of the small and midscale farmer. Davis, "From Agriculture to Agribusiness," 115.

24 NSAC proposes that a redefinition of "active management" should "require the payment recipient to either farm at least half-time or provide at least half the labor and management on his/her share of the operation." *Farming for the Future*, 9.

25 Daniel Imhoff, "Overhauling the Farm Bill: The Real Beneficiaries of Subsidies," *Atlantic*, March 21, 2012, http://www.theatlantic.com/health/

archive/2012/03/overhauling-the-farm-bill-the-real-beneficiaries-of
-subsidies/254422/ (accessed June 17, 2012).

26 Brian Walsh, "Getting Real about the High Price of Cheap Food," *Time Magazine*, August 21, 2009, http://www.time.com/time/magazine/article/ 0,9171,1917726,00.html (accessed June 26, 2012). There is some dis-agreement over the degree to which farm policy is actually a "cheap food" policy, however. See Bruce A. Babcock, "Cheap Food and Farm Subsidies: Policy Impacts of a Mythical Connection," *Iowa Ag Review Online* 12, no. 2 (2006), http://www.card.iastate.edu/iowa_ag_review/spring_06/ article1.aspx (accessed June 27, 2012); Robert Paarlberg, "The Incon-venient Truth about Cheap Food and Obesity: It's Not Farm Subsidies," GOOD (2011), http://www.good.is/post/the-inconvenient-truth-about -cheap-food-and-obesity-it-s-not-farm-subsidies/ (accessed June 27, 2012).

27 Corn, Background, USDA Economic Research Service. http://www .ers.usda.gov/topics/crops/corn/background.aspx#.UVMNsVtC7Wt (accessed March 25, 2013).

28 Corn, Background. Together, ethanol and feed production account for approximately 90 percent of the corn grown in the United States.

29 Young, Oliveira, and Claassen, "2008 Farm Act."

30 Michele Simon and Siena Chrisman, *Enough to Eat: Food Assistance and the Farm Bill* (Minneapolis: Institute for Agriculture and Trade Policy, 2012).

31 Simon and Chrisman, *Enough to Eat.*

32 At the time of this writing, the U.S. Senate was debating an amendment to the Farm Bill that would have capped SNAP spending at $45 billion per year and turned that funding over to states in the form of block grants. That amendment was defeated, but for legislators who consider nutritional assistance to be an "entitlement program," efforts to cut that program will continue. See "Senate Rejects Amendment to Cut Food Stamps Pro-gram, Replace It With Block Grants to States," *Washington Post*, http:// www.washingtonpost.com/business/senate-rejects-amendment-to-cut -food-stamp-program-replace-it-with-block-grants-to-states/2012/06/13/ gJQANIHDaV_story.html (accessed June 14, 2012).

33 "Newt and the 'Food-Stamp President,'" *Economist*, January 2, 2012, http://www.economist.com/blogs/democracyinamerica/2012/0/newt -gingrichw; "PolitiFact," *Tampa Bay Times*, January 17, 2012, http:// www.politifact.com/truth-o-meter/statements/2012/jan/17/newt -gingrich/newt-gingrich-says-more-people-have-been-put-food-/ (accessed June 15, 2012). Gingrich also racialized this claim, saying if he were invited to address the NAACP, he would tell them, "the Afri-can American community should demand paychecks and not be satis-fied with food stamps." See Lucy Madison, "Gingrich Singles Out Blacks in Food Stamp Remark," CBS News, http://www.cbsnews.com/8301 -503544_162-57353438-503544/gingrich-singles-out-blacks-in-food -stamp-remark/ (accessed June 15, 2012). African Americans actually make up only 22 percent of SNAP benefit recipients. See Esa Eslami, Kai Filion, and Mark Strayer, *Characteristics of Supplemental Nutri-tion Assistance Program Households: Fiscal Year 2010* (Alexandria, Va.: USDA Food and Nutrition Service, Office of Research and Analysis, 2011), 57. It is true that, between 2008 and 2010, the USDA reported a

46 percent increase in the number of households receiving SNAP benefits. See Supplemental Nutrition Assistance: Average Monthly Participation (Households), USDA Food and Nutrition Service, http://www.fns.usda .gov/pd/16SNAPpartHH.htm. Gingrich did not acknowledge that this was due, in part, to the expansion of eligibility requirements during the economic recession. Since 2007 SNAP enrollment has increased almost 70 percent. See Simon and Chrisman, *Enough to Eat*.

34 Gottlieb and Joshi, *Food Justice*, 84.

35 Between 2010 and 2011, SNAP spending at farmers markets increased by 55 percent. See Simon and Chrisman, *Enough to Eat*.

36 *Double Value Coupon Program: 2011 Outcomes* (Bridgeport, Conn.: Wholesome Wave Foundation, 2012).

37 Sarah Wheaton, "N.A.A.C.P. Backtracks on Official Accused of Bias," *New York Times*, July 21, 2010. Sherrod was describing an event from 1986, when she was working for a nonprofit organization.

38 Bob Herbert, "Thrown to the Wolves," *New York Times*, July 24, 2010.

39 Marcus K. Garner and Christian Boone, "USDA Reconsiders Firing of Ga. Official over Speech on Race," *Atlanta Journal-Constitution*, July 21, 2010.

40 See, e.g., Tadlock Cowan and Jody Feder, *The Pigford Cases: USDA Settlement of Discrimination Suits by Black Farmers* (Washington, D.C.: Congressional Research Service, 2011). In fact, when defending his original decision to request Sherrod's resignation, Secretary of Agriculture Tom Vilsack said that his stand on this case was, at least in part, informed by the USDA's history of bias in awarding grants and loans. Once the full story was clear, Vilsack offered Sherrod a new job, which she declined. Sheryl Gay Stolberg, Shaila Dewan, and Brian Stelter, "With Apology, Fired Official Is Offered a New Job," *New York Times*, July 22, 2010.

41 Laura Ackerman, Don Bustos, and Mark Muller, *Disadvantaged Farmers: Addressing Inequalities in Federal Programs for Farmers of Color* (Minneapolis: Institute for Agriculture and Trade Policy, 2012).

42 bell hooks describes this loss poignantly: "This separation from nature and the concomitant fear it produced, fear of nature and fear of whiteness, was the trauma shaping black life. . . . Living in modern society, without a sense of history, it has been easy for folks to forget that black people were first and foremost a people of the land, farmers. . . . When we talk about healing that psyche, we must also speak about restoring our connection to the natural world." bell hooks, *Belonging: A Culture of Place* (New York: Routledge, 2009), 10, 36, 39.

43 Vilsack, Testimony.

44 Isolde Raftery, "In New Food Culture, a Young Generation of Farmers Emerges," *New York Times*, March 6, 2011.

45 Ackerman, Bustos, and Muller, *Disadvantaged Farmers*.

46 Food, Conservation, and Energy Act of 2008, Sec. 14013.

47 "Groups Tell Senate to Support Beginning and Socially Disadvantaged Farmers," National Sustainable Agriculture Coalition, http://sustainable agriculture.net/blog/bfrdp2501-sign-on-letter/ (accessed June 14, 2012).

48 Renée Johnson, *The 2008 Farm Bill: Major Provisions and Legislative Action* (Washington, D.C.: Congressional Research Service, 2008), 9.

49 *Farming for the Future*, 28.

50 "Farm and Commodity Policy: Glossary," USDA Economic Research Service (accessed June 16, 2012).

51 JoAnn Berkenkamp and Bill Wenzel, *Everyone at the Table: Local Foods and the Farm Bill* (Minneapolis: Institute for Agriculture and Trade Policy, 2012).

52 Food, Conservation, and Energy Act of 2008, Title X.

53 *Farming for the Future*, 69–71.

54 Food, Conservation, and Energy Act of 2008, Title II, Subtitles B–E.

55 Food, Conservation, and Energy Act of 2008, Title II, Subtitle F.

56 *Farming for the Future*, 6.

57 For a summary of the history of the global spice trade, see Felipe Fernández-Armesto, *Near a Thousand Tables: A History of Food* (New York: Free Press, 2002), 148–62.

58 "Free Trade Agreements," Office of the United States Trade Representative http://www.ustr.gov/trade-agreements/free-trade-agreements (accessed June 29, 2012). At the time of this writing, an additional agreement has been signed (but not entered into force) with Panama, and an Asia-Pacific regional agreement was under negotiation, which would bring the number of countries to more than twenty.

59 Harper and Le Beau, *Food, Society, and Environment*, 123.

60 Harper and Le Beau, *Food, Society, and Environment*, 121.

61 Harper and Le Beau, *Food, Society, and Environment*, 121–22.

62 Some of the personal contours of the relationship between Christians in the United States and food production, distribution, and consumption in Mexico after NAFTA are explored below in chapter 6.

63 Philip T. von Mehren and Eduardo Ruiz Vega, "The Interrelationship between NAFTA and Mexican Law (Excerpt from Curtis, Mallet-Prevost, Colt and Mosle, International Report, 1996)," Institute for Agriculture and Trade Policy, http://iatp.org/documents/interrelationship-between-nafta-and-mexican-law-the (accessed July 8, 2012).

64 Gottlieb and Joshi, *Food Justice*, 108.

65 Although this section focuses on the global effects of free trade agreements (particularly as they intersect with U.S. farm policy), it is important to note that most farmers in the United States have not thrived as expected under trade liberalization, either.

66 Carlsen, "NAFTA Is Starving Mexico."

67 Manuel Roig-Franzia, "A Culinary and Cultural Staple in Crisis," *Washington Post*, January 26, 2007, http://www.washingtonpost.com/wp-dyn/content/article/2007/01/26/AR2007012601896.html. Analysts attribute the rise in tortilla prices to a variety of factors: market control concentrated in the hands of a few large agribusiness firms, the globalization of the corn market, and the major corn market disruption caused by the development and increasing popularity of ethanol. See also Carlsen, "NAFTA Is Starving Mexico"; Patel, *Stuffed and Starved*, 52–54.

68 Roig-Franzia, "A Culinary and Cultural Staple in Crisis." In 2007 then-president Felipe Calderón announced the Tortilla Price Stabilization Pact, which would cap the price of tortillas to stem the wild fluctuations in price. Responses to this measure have been mixed, with free-trade advocates criticizing it as an intervention and food security advocates finding the cap to still be too high for poor families.

69 Carlsen, "NAFTA Is Starving Mexico"; Gottlieb and Joshi, *Food Justice*, 109.

70 K. Hansen-Kuhn, Sophia Murphy, and David Wallinga, *Exporting Obesity: How U.S. Farm and Trade Policy Is Transforming the Mexican Food Environment* (Minneapolis: Institute for Agriculture and Trade Policy, 2012).

71 Rafael Romo, "Mexico's Other Enemy: Obesity Rates Triple in Last Three Decades," CNN.com, January 4, 2011, http://articles.cnn.com/2011 -01-04/world/mexico.obesity_1_obesity-rates-obese-people-junk-food? _s=PM:WORLD (accessed July 7, 2012).

72 "Fat Mexico: Sins of the Fleshly," *Economist*, December 16, 2004, http:// www.economist.com/node/3507918?Story_ID=3507918 (accessed July 6, 2012).

73 Gottlieb and Joshi, *Food Justice*, 87.

74 Gottlieb and Joshi, *Food Justice*, 87.

75 *Commodity Foods*, 16.

76 *Commodity Foods*, 18–21.

77 Gottlieb and Joshi, *Food Justice*, 88. The story, while jarring, is not a far stretch from what former Speaker of the House Newt Gingrich suggested in a December 2011 presidential campaign appearance in Iowa: "You have a very poor neighborhood. You have kids who are required under law to go to school. They have no money. They have no habit of work. What if you paid them part-time in the afternoon to sit in the clerical office and greet people when they come in? What if you paid them to work as the assistant librarian? . . . What if they became assistant janitors, and their job was to mop the floor and clean the bathroom?" Jonathan Easley, "Gingrich: Poor Kids Have Bad Work Habits 'Unless It's Illegal,' " The Hill, December 1, 2011, http://thehill.com/video/campaign/196663 -gingrich-poor-children-have-bad-work-habits-unless-its-illegal. Combined with Gingrich's comments on SNAP benefits (see above n. 33) it is clear that from Gingrich's point of view (and that of those who agree with him), public assistance programs are at odds with developing a strong work ethic. This argument is, at best, tenuous: to qualify for free or reduced-cost school lunch, a family of four may have an income of up to $41,328; and 40 percent of households receiving SNAP have at least some source of income (aside from public assistance). See *National School Lunch Program Fact Sheet* (Washington, D.C.: USDA Food and Nutrition Service, 2011); Eslami, Filion, and Strayer, *Characteristics*.

78 "Program Synopsis: Community Food Projects," USDA National Institute of Food and Agriculture, http://www.nifa.usda.gov/funding/cfp/ cfp_synopsis.html (accessed July 6, 2012).

79 "Farm to School Grant Program," USDA Food and Nutrition Service, http://www.fns.usda.gov/cnd/f2s/f2_grant_program.htm (accessed July 6, 2012); "Grants: Community Food Projects Competitive Grants Program," USDA National Institute of Food and Agriculture, http://www .csrees.usda.gov/fo/communityfoodprojects.cfm (accessed July 6, 2012).

80 "National Farm to School Network: Nourishing Kids and Community," http://www.farmtoschool.org/aboutus.php.

81 For a description of these developments in the United States, see Harper and Le Beau, *Food, Society, and Environment*, 59–70.

82 Harper and Le Beau, *Food, Society, and Environment*, 71–72.

83 E.g., Harper and LeBeau note, "the median size of *E. coli* and other disease outbreaks nearly doubled . . . between 1973 and 1987, the same period that rapid packing concentration happened." Harper and Le Beau, *Food, Society, and Environment*, 125.

84 William Neuman, "Raw Milk Cheesemakers Fret over Possible New Rules," *New York Times*, February 4, 2011. In a telling conversation revealing some of the concerns of artisan cheesemakers, see this story and comments posted at *Culture* magazine: Kate Arding, "Sally Jackson Closes Down: With New Regulation, How Can Small Cheesemakers Stay in Business?" *Kate's Blog*, Culture: The Word on Cheese, 2010, December 22, 2010, http://www.culturecheesemag.com/blog/kate_sally_jackson_closes.

85 "Cottage Food Law States," Cottage Food Laws, http://cottagefoodlaws.com/state-regulations/cottage-food-law-states/ (accessed July 6, 2012).

86 Foods considered possibly dangerous (like dairy products) are generally excluded from cottage food laws. For current examples of cottage food regulations, see the state law recently implemented in Illinois and the ongoing negotiations of state agricultural regulations in Georgia. See Cottage Food Regulations (40-7-19), Georgia Department of Agriculture Food Safety Division (2012); Food Handling Regulation Enforcement Act: Cottage Food Operation (Public Act 097-0393), Illinois General Assembly (2012).

87 Alethea Harper, Annie Shattuck, Eric Holt-Giménez, Alison Alkon, and Francis Lambrick, *Food Policy Councils: Lessons Learned* (Oakland, Calif.: Food First/Institute for Food and Development Policy, 2009), 14.

88 Gottlieb and Joshi, *Food Justice*, 201–6.

89 Harper, Shattuck, Holt-Giménez, Alkon, and Lambrick, *Food Policy Councils*, 16.

90 Allen, *Together at the Table*, 21–28.

CHAPTER 3

1 Nuri made this statement when he offered a public tour of the Truly Living Well farms to members of the American Academy of Religion in November 2010.

2 "Truly Living Well Center for Natural Urban Agriculture," http://trulylivingwell.com/ (accessed January 3, 2013).

3 Jung, *Food for Life*, 43.

4 Jung's argument is not this simple: he argues that human relationships to food, both individual and collective, are disordered, and thus obscure the capacity to encounter God in the food system. It is possible to read Jung, however, as seeing the problem of a disordered food system as a primarily spiritual problem, with little to say about how Christians might engage the material economic and political dimensions of the system.

5 For a summary of (and response to) these arguments in public discourse, see Barbara R. Rossing, "River of Life in God's New Jerusalem: An Eschatological Vision for Earth's Future," in *Christianity and Ecology*, ed. Dieter T. Hessel and Rosemary Radford Ruether (Cambridge, Mass.: Harvard University Center for the Study of World Religions, 2000).

6   For a popular article recounting some of the most extreme versions of this perspective, see Glenn Scherer, "Christian-Right Views Are Swaying Politicians and Threatening the Environment," *Grist Magazine* (2004).

7   Anna Case-Winters, *Reconstructing a Christian Theology of Nature: Down to Earth*, ed. Robert Trigg and J. Wentzel van Huyssteen, Ashgate, Science and Religion Series (Burlington, Vt.: Ashgate, 2007), 22–23; Lynn White, "The Historical Roots of Our Ecologic Crisis," *Science*, March 10, 1967.

8   That is to say that both theological anthropology (who we are) and eschatology (our hope for a new world) *also* are sources of strength for a grounded theology and ethics of food, as developed below.

9   "Eucharist," in *Baptism, Eucharist and Ministry: Faith and Order Paper 111* (Geneva: World Council of Churches, 1982), III.29, II.D.19, and II.E.24. These are just three of seemingly countless meanings of the Eucharist, many of which are explored in this ecumenical document created by the Faith and Order Commission of the World Council of Churches.

10   1 Corinthians 11:22.

11   1 Corinthians 11:28, 33. Richard B. Hays argues that this is not a problem of "bad manners," but an indictment of the community's failure to address social inequality. See Richard B. Hays, *First Corinthians*, Interpretation, A Bible Commentary for Teaching and Preaching (Louisville, Ky.: Westminster John Knox, 1997), 197.

12   Letty M. Russell, *Church in the Round: Feminist Interpretation of the Church* (Louisville, Ky.: Westminster John Knox, 1993), 12. The concepts of round table, kitchen table, and welcome table provide the structure for Russell's feminist ecclesiology.

13   1 Corinthians 10. See Hays, *First Corinthians*, 200.

14   The argument here is not that such personal dimensions of the Eucharist are in error. To the contrary: the deep personal meaning of the Eucharist is clear in *Baptism, Eucharist, and Ministry* (*BEM*), a text from the World Council of Churches. The first two meanings proposed by *BEM* are thanksgiving to God and memorial of Christ's sacrifice, inviting worshippers to introspection and prayer. At the same time, however, through the power of the Holy Spirit, the Eucharist is also a communion of the faithful, and anticipates the coming of the kingdom of God, in all of its social implications. See "Eucharist," II.A-E.

15   Wirzba, *Food and Faith*, 150.

16   Jung, *Food for Life*, 43.

17   "Eucharist," II.D.20.

18   "Eucharist," II.D.20.

19   "Music: 'I'm Gonna Sit at the Welcome Table,'" PBS Online, http://www.pbs.org/wgbh/amex/eyesontheprize/story/04_nonviolence.html#music (accessed November 13, 2012).

20   See also Russell, *Church in the Round*, 149.

21   Romans 12:4-5.

22   The moral implications of membership in creation are discussed in more detail below.

23   Jung, *Food for Life*, 47.

24   Wirzba, *Food and Faith*, 34.

25   Jung, *Food for Life*, 43.

26 Acts 2:42-46 CEB. I use here the new Common English Bible translation, as it makes clear in verse 24 the historical context for what the NRSV translates as "breaking bread." That is, it was a shared meal.

27 The degree to which the earliest communities actually practiced the communal sharing of goods is subject to question. Manuscripts from these texts in Acts, and their interpreters, indicate some disagreement on this. Contemporary readers of the accounts of this ideal in Acts, however, alongside Paul's preoccupation with social relations, are confronted with the sacred obligations inherent in our membership in the body of Christ. See Eric D. Barreto, " 'To Proclaim the Year of the Lord's Favor' (Luke 4:19): Possessions and the Christian Life in Luke-Acts," in *Rethinking Stewardship: Our Culture, Our Theology, Our Practices*, ed. Frederick J. Gaiser, Word and World, Supplement Series 6 (Saint Paul, Minn.: Luther Seminary, 2010); Luke Timothy Johnson, *Sharing Possessions: What Faith Demands*, 2nd ed. (Grand Rapids: Eerdmans, 2011).

28 Wirzba, *Food and Faith*, 149–53.

29 Walter Brueggemann, "The Liturgy of Abundance, The Myth of Scarcity," *Christian Century*, March 24–31, 1999.

30 "Special Days and Emphases: World Communion Sunday," General Assembly Mission Council, Presbyterian Church (USA), http://gamc .pcusa.org/ministries/worship/special-days-and-emphases/.

31 Steven M. Bender, *One Night in America: Robert Kennedy, César Chávez, and the Dream of Dignity* (Boulder, Colo.: Paradigm, 2008), 30–31.

32 "Eucharist," II.D.21.

33 Russell, *Church in the Round*, 78.

34 Here I have mentioned only briefly the moral issues inherent in the production of one of the elements of the Eucharist, wine. Norman Wirzba writes extensively about the changes and challenges in the production of bread in *Food and Faith*. See Wirzba, *Food and Faith*, 12–21.

35 "Eucharist," I.1.

36 "Eucharist," II.E.22.

37 Isaiah 25:6.

38 Jürgen Moltmann, *Theology of Hope: On the Ground and the Implications of a Christian Eschatology*, trans. James W. Leitch, 5th ed. (San Francisco: HarperSanFrancisco 1967), 21.

39 2 Corinthians 5:18-20.

40 Elisabeth Schüssler Fiorenza, "To Follow the Vision: The Jesus Movement as Basileia Movement," in Farley and Jones, *Liberating Eschatology*, 135.

41 Monika Hellwig, *The Eucharist and the Hunger of the World* (New York: Paulist Press, 1976), 10.

42 Theologian Michelle Clifton-Soderstrom once described the practice of Eucharist in the Evangelical Covenant tradition in precisely this way. Michelle Clifton-Soderstrom, at Forum on Faith and Food, North Park Theological Seminary, Chicago, 2010.

43 1 Corinthians 11:21-22. The new Common English Bible translation of *prolambanein en to phagein* as "goes ahead and eats a private meal" is, I argue, a better translation than the New Revised Standard Version ("goes ahead with your own supper"), representing more clearly what Paul perceives to be the challenges to the social meaning of the meal.

44 Hays, *First Corinthians*, 193–94. See also Wirzba, *Food and Faith*, 149–50.

45 Hays, *First Corinthians*, 204.

46 Hellwig, *The Eucharist and the Hunger of the World*, 87.

47 Leviticus 19:9-10; 23:22.

48 Ellen Davis compares the model of charity (and its exploitative potential) in gleaning with God's abundant provision in the provision of manna. Ellen F. Davis, *Scripture, Culture, and Agriculture: An Agrarian Reading of the Bible* (New York: Cambridge University Press, 2008), 71–72.

49 2 Kings 4:42-44. This story is mirrored in the feeding stories of the Gospels, where Jesus insists that the hungry receive food shared by the disciples. See Matthew 14:13-21; 15:32-39; Mark 6:31-44; 8:1-10.

50 Peter Rosset, "Lessons from the Green Revolution," Food First/Institute for Food and Development Policy, April 8, 2000, http://www.foodfirst .org/media/opeds/2000/4-greenrev.html.

51 *Strengthening Rural Communities: Hunger Report 2005: 15th Annual Report on the State of World Hunger* (Washington, D.C.: Bread for the World Institute, 2005).

52 "Major Crops Grown in the United States," United States Environmental Protection Agency, http://www.epa.gov/agriculture/ag101/cropmajor .html (2009).

53 See Corn, Background.

54 Davis, *Scripture, Culture, and Agriculture*, 3–4.

55 Theodore Hiebert, "The Human Vocation: Origins and Transformations in Christian Traditions," in Hessel and Ruether, *Christianity and Ecology*, 138–41. Of the two accounts of creation and humanity's role and responsibility within the created world, the Yahwist's account (presented in Genesis 2 and 3) is the oldest. Theodore Hiebert, *The Yahwist's Landscape* (New York: Oxford University Press, 1996), 23–26.

56 Hiebert, *Yahwist's Landscape*, 34–36.

57 Hiebert, "Human Vocation," 150–51.

58 Jeremiah 22:13.

59 Matthew 20:1-16.

60 Miguel De La Torre, "The Bible Demands Economic Justice," January 5, 2009, http://www.abpnews.com/content/view/3745/9/.

61 Gary W. Fick, *Food, Farming, and Faith* (New York: SUNY Press, 2008), 122.

62 Angela Mwaniki, *Achieving Food Security in Africa: Challenges and Issues* (United Nations Office of the Special Adviser on Africa), 2.

63 Holt-Giménez, Brent, and Shattuck, *Food Workers—Food Justice*.

64 Byron Pitts, " 'Harvest of Shame' 50 Years Later," CBS News, November 25, 2010, http://www.cbsnews.com/2100-18563_162-7087361.html.

65 Wendell Berry, "The Gift of Good Land," in *The Art of the Commonplace*, 304. Here, Wendell Berry touches on a key point of divergence between ecotheology and animal theology, despite some significant overlap between the two positions: whether killing another living being is ever morally justifiable. Berry here takes the broad view (which may allow for instances of killing) that frequently characterizes the perspective of ecotheology, but animal theologians like Andrew Linzey find such a perspective to be problematic, and that humans have a *special* responsibility

to adopt a strong moral position against violence (and killing). Linzey, *Creatures of the Same God*, 29–44.

66 John Calvin, *Institutes of the Christian Religion*, ed. John T. McNeill, trans. Ford Lewis Battles, Library of Christian Classics (Philadelphia: Westminster, 1960), I.5.8.

67 Calvin, *Institutes of the Christian Religion*, II.6.1.

68 Case-Winters, *Reconstructing a Christian Theology of Nature*, 49.

69 Case-Winters, *Reconstructing a Christian Theology of Nature*, 121.

70 White, "The Historical Roots of Our Ecologic Crisis."

71 Hiebert, *Yahwist's Landscape*, 65–66. Particularly to this point, environmental theology has emerged as a polarizing issue in political discourse at the time of this writing. Ironically, 2012 presidential candidate Rick Santorum accused President Barack Obama of holding a "phony theology" of "radical environmentalism," which promotes the "idea that man is here to *serve the earth*" (emphasis added). Leigh Ann Caldwell, "Santorum: Obama's World-View Upside-Down," CBS News, February 19, 2012, http://www.cbsnews.com/8301-3460_162-57381029/santorum-obamas-worldview-upside-down/.

72 See Leviticus 25:1-7 and Isaiah 28:24; Deuteronomy 24:19, Leviticus 19:9, and 23:22. Former Secretary of Agriculture Earl Butz has often been cited for his challenges to farmers to plant "fence-post to fence-post," which accompanied his warning, cited in chapter 2, to "get big or get out." See Beus and Dunlap, "Conventional versus Alternative Agriculture," 602; Barbara Wallace and Frank Clearfield, *Stewardship, Spirituality, and Natural Resources Conservation: A Short History* (Washington, D.C.: National Resources Conservation Service Social Sciences Institute, 1997), 4.

73 See Isaiah 28:25-26. The repetitive and intensive cultivation of one plant or one species of animal on the same land has long been shown to have adverse effects on soil health and the water supply. See Nancy M. Trautmann, Keith S. Porter, and Robert J. Wagenet, *Modern Agriculture: Its Effects on the Environment* (Ithaca, N.Y.: Cornell University Cooperative Extension, 1985).

74 Hiebert, "Human Vocation," 139.

75 Larry Rasmussen has described creation as "a commons to which we belong . . . [that] makes moral claims upon us." See Larry L. Rasmussen, "Creating the Commons," in *Justice in a Global Economy: Strategies for Home, Community, and World*, ed. Pamela Brubaker, Rebecca Todd Peters, and Laura A. Stivers (Louisville, Ky.: Westminster John Knox, 2006), 104.

76 Wirzba, *Food and Faith*, 151–52.

77 Wirzba, *Food and Faith*, 137, 150, 202. It is important to note that for Wirzba, the eucharistic potential of restoring health and membership resides in the meal's presentation of the sacrificial work of Jesus, and the posture of self-offering that is nurtured in participants as they partake of the sacrament: "When Jesus broke bread and shared the cup as the giving of his own body and blood . . . he instituted a new way of eating in which followers are invited to give their lives to each other, to turn themselves into food for others, and in so doing nurture and strengthen

the memberships of life." Wirzba, *Food and Faith*, 155. Although I have not emphasized the sacrificial meaning of the Eucharist in the way that he has, much of what Wirzba proposes with regard to the political, moral, and spiritual significance of eucharistic eating resonates with what I have written here.

78 Wendell Berry, "Health Is Membership," in *The Art of the Commonplace*, 146. See also Leopold, "The Land Ethic."

79 Wirzba, *Food and Faith*, 2–3.

80 Television chef Jamie Oliver had a difficult time, for example, getting elementary schoolchildren to properly identify common vegetables such as tomatoes and potatoes. See *Jamie Oliver's Food Revolution*, season 1, episode 2. A recently released study in Australia also indicates a lack of agricultural knowledge, finding that a majority of sixth-grade children thought that cotton comes from animals, and a notable minority thought that yogurt comes from plants. See Kylie Hillman and Sarah Buckley, *Food, Fibre and the Future: Report on Surveys of Students' and Teachers' Knowledge and Understanding of Primary Industries* (Primary Industries Education Foundation and Australian Council for Educational Research, 2011), 12. In response to this widespread agricultural educational gap, programs are popping up around the country to bring agriculture to schools in the National Farm to School Network, and to bring children to farms in innovative summer camp programs. See "National Farm to School Network"; Jan Ellen Spiegel, "Introducing Children to the Sources of Food," *New York Times*, May 11, 2012. Certainly adults, too, suffer from what Richard Louv has called "nature-deficit disorder." See Richard Louv, *The Last Child in the Woods: Saving Our Children from Nature-Deficit Disorder*, rev. and updated ed. (Chapel Hill, N.C.: Algonquin Books of Chapel Hill, 2008). During a recent trip to a local farm, one adult chaperone pointed to a long, slender, green fruit hanging from a plant and asked, "What is that?" When the farmer politely replied, "That's an okra plant," the chaperone replied, "Oh, really? I guess I've never seen okra in this form before. Usually it is in little round fried discs."

81 Wirzba, *Food and Faith*, 22.

82 David W. Orr, *Ecological Literacy: Education and the Transition to a Postmodern World*, SUNY Series in Constructive Postmodern Thought (Albany: SUNY Press, 1991), 92.

83 Craig Dykstra, "Reconceiving Practice," in *Shifting Boundaries: Contextual Approaches to the Structure of Theological Education*, ed. Barbara G. Wheeler and Edward Farley (Louisville, Ky.: Westminster John Knox, 1991), 45.

PART II

1 In addition to being limited in scope, the assumption that we might address injustices in our food system primarily through an ideational theological framework also implies that we are capable of discerning the "right" theological framework. On the contrary, one need only examine, for example, the anthropocentric readings of Genesis 1 (and Ellen Davis and Theodore Hiebert's corrections thereof) to grasp how limited our theological worldview can be. Although this book presents its own

theological framework, we do well to remember that such frameworks will always be limited and perspectival, and sometimes even destructive.

2   Dykstra, "Reconceiving Practice," 45.

3   See Alasdair MacIntyre, *After Virtue: A Study in Moral Theory*, 2nd ed. (Notre Dame, Ind.: University of Notre Dame Press, 1984), 187. MacIntyre's development of the concept of a social practice ("any coherent and complex form of socially established cooperative human activity through which goods internal to that form of activity are realized in the course of trying to achieve those standards of excellence which are appropriate to, and partially definitive of, that form of activity, with the result that human powers to achieve excellence, and human conceptions of the ends and goods involved, are systematically extended") has served as a foundational concept for a variety of scholars trying to account for how persons are equipped and inspired to contribute to positive social change. See, e.g., James M. Jasper, *The Art of Moral Protest: Culture, Biography, and Creativity in Social Movements* (Chicago: University of Chicago Press, 1999), 219; Orr, "Ecological Literacy," in *Ecological Literacy*, 92.

4   The social analysis introduced in chapters 1 and 2 and the theological and moral framework introduced in chapter 3 will be placed in mutually critical dialogue with all of the food practices described below. In a mutually critical dialogue, the practice gives new meaning and raises new challenges to theological and moral categories, and those theological and moral categories help us to see, enrich, and challenge our practices. See Chopp, "Practical Theology and Liberation."

5   Nancy Bedford describes the practice of discernment as "little moves against destructiveness," insofar as it comprises small, innovative, sometimes ambiguous, and disciplined responses to structural challenges: "For Latin American theology today, the small moves against destructiveness that are allowed by the practices of Christian faith open up glimpses of new horizons of hope in a time of apparently closed horizons." Bedford, "Little Moves against Destructiveness: Theology and the Practice of Discernment," in *Practicing Theology: Beliefs and Practices in Christian Life*, ed. Dorothy C. Bass and Miroslav Volf (Grand Rapids: Eerdmans, 2001), 180.

CHAPTER 4

1   Faith in Place is an interfaith environmental organization based in Chicago, Illinois. The organization and its work on sustainable food are detailed below.

2   These dimensions were discussed in some detail in chapters 1 and 2. This chapter (and chapters 5–7) assumes the social analysis conducted in chapters 1 and 2 as the context in which the practices described here take place.

3   Nancy Bedford describes small acts of resistance in the face of systemic injustice as "little moves against destructiveness." She argues that, in absence of wholesale structural change, persons and communities of faith still act in resistance to the suffering and oppression resulting from social injustice in small but significant and imaginative ways. See Bedford, "Little Moves against Destructiveness."

4   The distance between farmer and consumer is marked by many factors,

including the growing number of literal miles that food travels between farm and consumer; the increasing size of farm operations that, in turn, are reliant on vulnerable, transient migrant laborers; and the anonymity bred in a system in which farmers sell their produce to a large company that consolidates and sells the goods to consumers, who have virtually no way of tracing the origins of their food. See Davis, "From Agriculture to Agribusiness," 108; Gottlieb and Joshi, *Food Justice*, 18–21; Harper and Le Beau, *Food, Society, and Environment*; Patel, *Stuffed and Starved*, 11–13; Pirog, Van Pelt, Enshayan, and Cook, *Food, Fuel, and Freeways*, 9.

5   The very invocation of the category of "consumer" immediately presents moral questions. Although I will continue to use this term for clarity and because it is most descriptive of how many of us relate to food, we should bear in mind its limitations: when we become "patrons" of the food industry, Berry laments, we have "tended more and more to be *mere* consumers—passive, uncritical, and dependent" (emphasis in original). Berry, "The Pleasures of Eating," 322.

6   For discussion of debates on the viability of local, sustainable agricultural practices in meeting world food needs, see Mark Bittman, "Sustainable Farming Can Feed the World?" *New York Times*, March 8, 2011, http://opinionator.blogs.nytimes.com/2011/03/08/sustainable-farming/ (accessed July 18, 2012). For a discussion of the regulatory barriers to small-scale food production, see Arding, "Sally Jackson Closes Down." For discussions of the financial barriers to converting to more sustainable practices, see *Farming for the Future*, 10–11; Olmstead and Kleinschmit, *A Risky Proposition*.

7   Take, e.g., the case of Graham's Organics in central Michigan. Standing in the midst of a formidable herd of cows who, despite standing in the midst of a lush expanse of grass, hoped he would open yet another broad swath of pasture for them, farmer Matt Graham says, frankly, that his farm has been quite profitable since being certified organic in 1995. More profitable, he says, than many conventional beef cattle farms in the region. Without question, Graham cares deeply about the welfare of the animals on his farm, the condition of the land, and a more just food system. But many farmers like Graham have discovered that these modes of "alternative agriculture" (see below) are both ecologically *and* economically sustainable. Graham's anecdotal observations about his own farm are supported in research on the economic viability of organic agriculture. See Graham's Organics, http://www.grahamsorganics.com/ (accessed July 12, 2012).

8   *Transitioning to Organic Production* (College Park, Md.: Sustainable Agriculture Network/Sustainable Agriculture Research and Education, 2007), 14.

9   "Alternative agriculture" here represents the spectrum of agricultural practices and models that stand in contrast to the highly commodified and industrialized practices of conventional agriculture. As a broad category, it includes efforts like organics, biodynamics, sustainability, and localization. While practices may be diverse, the goals of the "alternative agrifood movement" are environmental soundness and social equity. Allen, *Together at the Table*, 16, 38.

10 John Drexhage and Deborah Murphy, *Sustainable Development: From*

Brundtland to Rio 2012: Background Paper (New York: United Nations High Level Panel on Global Sustainability, 2010), 2.

11 Vilsack, "Briefing on the Status of Rural America."

12 Patel, *Stuffed and Starved*, 26.

13 *Transitioning to Organic Production*, 3.

14 *Transitioning to Organic Production*, 14.

15 Among these risks are the loss of income stability offered through commodity subsidy payments, the loss (in many cases) of crop insurance assistance, and the payment of lingering debt accrued purchasing farm equipment in order to produce for large distributors. These risks and others were addressed in chapters 1 and 2.

16 For an account of one farming family's way of addressing the access to markets challenge, see Rebecca Todd Peters, "Supporting Community Farming," in Brubaker, Peters, and Stivers, *Justice in a Global Economy*, 17.

17 Since her contract with Perdue was terminated in 2009, Carole Morison has also continued to work in advocacy for area poultry workers. Caroline Abels, "*Food, Inc.* Chicken Farmer Has a New, Humane Farm," *Grist Magazine* (2012), http://grist.org/sustainable-farming/food-inc -chicken-farmer-has-a-new-humane-farm/ (accessed May 12, 2012).

18 Community-supported agriculture varies from farm to farm and will be discussed in more detail below. Here, however, a quick definition: in CSA, participants purchase a "share" at the beginning of the season and receive a box each week of produce, eggs, dairy products, and/or meats each week. The members pay for their shares in advance.

19 *Transitioning to Organic Production*, 17.

20 Readers will recall from chapter 2 that the Farm Bill does include some financial supports for farmers converting to organic operations, but that this amount was dwarfed by the amount designated for commodity supports and crop insurance assistance.

21 "The Amount Spent on Food."

22 Between 2002 and 2011, supermarket sales dropped by almost 23 percent. Annie Gasparro and Timothy W. Martin, "What's Wrong with America's Supermarkets?" *Wall Street Journal*, July 12, 2012.

23 See, e.g., "Budget Cooking: Feed 4 for $10," *Cooking Light*, http:// www.cookinglight.com/food/everyday-menus/healthy-budget-recipes -00400000056656/.

24 Stephanie Strom, "Has 'Organic' Been Oversized?," *New York Times*, July 8, 2012.

25 *The Organic Watergate: White Paper* (Cornucopia, Wis.: Cornucopia Institute, 2012).

26 In 2012, e.g., a proposition in California requiring identifying labeling of genetically modified foods was defeated by a margin of about six percentage points. Opponents of the measure spent about $45 million dollars to defeat it. See "State Ballot Measures—Statewide Results"; Sifferlin, "California Fails to Pass."

27 Or, as families and communities have begun to do in increasingly large numbers, grow their own produce, keep their own chickens (for eggs), and share with each other expertise in canning, baking, and preserving. These efforts toward "food sovereignty" are explored below in chapter 5.

28 Tom Beaudoin, *Consuming Faith: Integrating Who We Are with What We Buy* (Lanham, Md.: Sheed & Ward, 2003), xi.

29 The organization's other areas of emphasis are energy and climate change, water, and political advocacy. See "Programs," Faith in Place, http://faithinplace.org/programs.php (accessed July 15, 2012). Faith in Place began in 1999 as a project with the Center for Neighborhood Technology, with the goal of addressing urban sustainability needs by organizing community-based "interreligious sustainability circles." Before long, Clare realized that creating these additional organizations was "backwards. . . . What we want people to do is invest the energy they have from these issues in their own congregations." As a result, Faith in Place was born as an independent organization that works as a partner with religious communities, offering "tools to reflect deeply on these responsibilities (to one another and to creation), integrate the teachings of faith into practice, and work together for a just and sustainable future." See "Mission Statement," Faith in Place, http://faithinplace.org/about/mission-statement (accessed July 15, 2012).

30 "Sustainable Food," Faith in Place, http://faithinplace.org/programs .php?ID=9 (accessed July 15, 2012).

31 Some Muslims had been asking how their dietary laws accounted for (or failed to account for) the social, economic, and environmental conditions under which *halal* meat was raised and butchered. These questions prefigured those that arose regarding what constitutes "kosher" in the Jewish dietary laws arose following the 2008 immigration raid at the Postville, Iowa, kosher meat-processing plant, in which unjust labor conditions were uncovered, including child labor violations. Julia Preston, "Meatpacker May Lose Kosher Certification," *New York Times*, September 11, 2008. A group of Conservative Jewish leaders have established a new certification standard which augments traditional kosher standards of proper slaughter with some assessment of a company's performance according to other standards of Jewish ethics, including labor justice, animal welfare, and environmental concerns. The group of advocates now also includes leaders from the Reform movement. See "The Magen Tzedek Standard," Magen Tzedek Commission, http://www.magentzedek.org/ (accessed July 16, 2012).

32 "Winter Farmers Markets," Faith in Place, http://org2.democracyin action.org/o/6265/p/salsa/web/common/public/content?content_item _KEY=8942 (accessed July 15, 2012). Although Faith in Place is an interfaith organization that works with a wide range of religious communities, the goals of these markets have particular appeal for Christians who might embrace the eucharistic moral vision: dignity for farmers, tending the land, caring for the hungry, and building relationships of interdependence.

33 Although not itself a religious project, the Farm Crisis Fund is reminiscent of the earliest Christian communities, described in the book of Acts, in which community members strived to share their possessions, sometimes succeeding and sometimes failing to share their goods and to care for the most vulnerable among them. The Farm Crisis Fund provides economic stability to vulnerable community members, but it also, importantly, builds relationships of mutual obligation. See Acts 2:42-47, 4:32-37, and 5–6.

34 As further evidence of the major responsibility Erika has assumed for the markets, it is important to note her centrality in the development of the program. When the Lutheran Volunteer Corps placed her at Faith in Place as an intern, she brought with her a deep religious identity as a Lutheran pastor's kid, her interest in the sciences, growing interest in sustainable food systems, and an experience in Mexico that profoundly affected how she saw the relationship between ethics, ecology, and sustainability. She did not envision, however, how her presence at Faith in Place would prove so serendipitous. She joined one of her supervisors at an informal meeting with the Churches' Center for Land and People, which had been coordinating winter markets for local farmers in Wisconsin. During that meeting, she had a deep sense that "This is a natural fit! . . . It was good, because it really allowed me to flower in terms of having a project and making it my own. . . . It was something I was passionate about." With a staff person willing to coordinate the effort, an established program looking for a new home, and an organizational mission to work on sustainable food initiatives, the Faith in Place winter markets were born.

35 For a concise and helpful summary of the diverse approaches to CSAs, see Allen, *Together at the Table*, 67–68.

36 Another congregation that has taken this step is Berea Mennonite Church in Atlanta, Georgia. Berea is home to Oak Leaf Farm, featured in the documentary *Grow!* See Christine Anthony and Owen Masterson, *Grow!* (Anthony-Masterson Photography, 2011).

37 Christine Des Garennes, "Church's Latest Endeavor to Help Feed Hungry in East Central Illinois," *News Gazette*, March 11, 2012.

38 "Farm Updates," Sola Gratia Farm, http://www.solagratiafarm.org/blog.html (accessed July 18, 2012). Sola Gratia posts an update of pounds tithed to the Eastern Illinois Food Bank on their Facebook page, https://www.facebook.com/solagratiafarm (accessed July 18, 2012).

39 Dave Swensen, *Selected Measures of the Economic Values of Increased Fruit and Vegetable Production and Consumption in the Upper Midwest* (Ames: Department of Economics, Iowa State University, 2010), 35. The Leopold Center is named after Aldo Leopold, the conservationist, ecologist, and educator. Leopold's land ethic is discussed in more detail in chapter 7.

40 That is, 0.3 percent. The total acreage of Illinois farmland is taken from a report by the Illinois Local and Organic Food and Farm Task Force, which makes a case similar to Swensen's, calling for the shift of more farmland to grow food for consumption within the state of Illinois. See *Local Food, Farms and Jobs: Growing the Illinois Economy* (Springfield: Illinois Local and Organic Food and Farm Task Force, 2009).

41 Swensen, *Selected Measures*, 14.

42 Bedford, "Little Moves against Destructiveness."

43 Solia Gratia Farm, *By Grace Alone These Gifts Are Shared among Us* (Urbana, Ill.: Sola Gratia Farm, 2012).

44 Berry, "The Pleasures of Eating," 321.

45 Berry, "The Pleasures of Eating," 324–25.

46 Wirzba, *Food and Faith*, 145 (emphasis in original).

47 Cynthia, "Sola Gratia Farms Week Four: Beets Version 2.0," The Sandwich

Life, June 17, 2012, http://thesandwichlife.typepad.com/the_sandwich
_life/2012/06/sola-gratia-farms-week-four-beets-version-21.html.

48 "To be fully alive is to live sympathetically within the membership that
the community is called to be, suffering with those who suffer and rejoicing with those who rejoice." Wirzba, *Food and Faith*.

CHAPTER 5

1 Natalie Moore, "Chicago's Highest Murder Rate in Englewood,"
WBEZ91.5, January 5, 2012 (accessed August 19, 2012).

2 "About Us," Growing Home, Inc., http://growinghomeinc.org/learn
-more/about-us/ (accessed August 13, 2012).

3 Although not itself a religiously affiliated organization, Growing Home
has worked closely with religious communities such as the Su Casa Catho-
lic Worker House in Chicago.

4 This definition of food sovereignty developed by the Vía Campesina
movement is here applied on a more local level. Gottlieb and Joshi, *Food
Justice*, 116. For more information on the Vía Campesina movement, see
"La Via Campesina: International Peasant Movement," http://viacamp
esina.org/en/.

5 Many of these themes were introduced in chapter 1, and are here examined with more focused attention to the ways in which they make food
sovereignty, defined below, an elusive goal.

6 Food Security in the U.S., Key Statistics and Graphics.

7 Food insecurity is even more frequent in single-parent families with male
heads of household (24.9 percent) and female heads of household (36.8
percent). Food Security in the U.S., Key Statistics and Graphics.

8 In 1995, 12 percent of households were food insecure, compared with
almost 12 percent in 2010. In 2005, just before the recession, 11 percent
of households were food insecure. Food Security in the U.S., Key Statistics
and Graphics.

9 "U.S. Hunger: Introduction," WhyHunger, http://www.whyhunger.org/
getinfo/showArticle/articleId/2056 (accessed August 19, 2012).

10 "U.S. Hunger: Introduction."

11 This definition, from Mike Hamm and Anne Bellows, is used by the Food
Security Learning Center. See "What Is Community Food Security?"
WhyHunger, http://www.whyhunger.org/getinfo/showArticle/articleId/
639 (accessed August 19, 2012). The USDA defines the goals of community food security slightly differently: "To improve access of low-income
households to healthful nutritious food supplies; to increase the self-reliance of communities in providing for their own food needs; and to promote comprehensive responses to local food, farm, and nutrition issues."
Food Security in the U.S., Community Food Security. The USDA definition is somewhat vague with regard to the "comprehensive responses"
regarding food, farms, and nutrition, whereas Hamm and Bellows' definition emphasizes both economic and environmental sustainability in
the process of promoting community self-reliance. This invocation of
economic and environmental sustainability brings together parties who
sometimes see their goals as being in tension: food accessibility and hunger advocates, and sustainable agriculture practitioners and advocates.

See Allen, *Together at the Table*, 21–28; Gottlieb and Joshi, *Food Justice*, 83–86.

12 The racial dimension of food access has been documented by several scholars. See Gottlieb and Joshi, *Food Justice*, 43. In Chicago communities in which the majority of residents are African American, e.g., the distance to a grocery store tends to be *twice* as far the distance to a fast-food restaurant. See Gallagher, *Good Food*, 17.

13 Rachel Cromidas, "A Fresh Oasis Thrives in a Chicago Food Desert," *New York Times*, May 30, 2010.

14 "Food desert" is contested as a descriptive term, and the debate about it is described below. In this chapter, it appears in quotation marks in an effort to connect with some of the research that continues to use the term while acknowledging that it represents neither the full scope of social, economic, and cultural issues affecting these communities' access to healthy food nor the communities' own indigenous resources for responding to these issues. Robert S. Grossinger, "Introductory Letter," in *Good Food: Examining the Impact of Food Deserts on Public Health in Chicago*, ed. Mari Gallagher (Chicago: Mari Gallagher Research and Consulting Group and LaSalle Bank, 2006).

15 Across that time span, however, African Americans in Chicago continued to make up a disproportionate 78 percent of residents in "food deserts." Mari Gallagher, *The Chicago 2011 Food Desert Drilldown*, 5th anniversary ed. (Chicago: Mari Gallagher Research and Consulting Group, 2011).

16 In Detroit, e.g., Gallagher notes that 92 percent of stores accepting SNAP benefits should be considered "fringe" stores, focusing on junk food, soft drinks, lottery tickets, etc. See Gallagher, *The Chicago 2011 Food Desert Drilldown*, 3. Gallagher et al.'s research correlated diet-related health problems to residence in a "food desert." Although this correlation has, of late, been challenged, Gallagher has issued a rebuttal and a reaffirmation of the original findings. See Mari Gallagher, *Response to "Studies Question Pairing of Food Deserts and Obesity"* (Chicago: Mari Gallagher Research and Consulting Group, 2012); Gina Kolata, "Studies Question the Pairing of Food Deserts and Obesity," *New York Times*, April 18, 2012.

17 Gottlieb and Joshi, *Food Justice*, 44.

18 In 2011 Walmart announced a plan to open three hundred stores in USDA-identified "food deserts." "Walmart to Open up to 300 Stores Serving USDA Food Deserts by 2016; More than 40,000 Associates Will Work in These Stores," Walmart, http://news.walmart.com/news-archive/2011/07/20/walmart-to-open-up-to-300-stores-serving-usda-food-deserts-by-2016-more-than-40000-associates-will-work-in-these-stores (accessed August 20, 2012). Walmart, unlike other grocery store chains, has maintained a nonunion labor force.

19 The British company Tesco, for example, promised to build "neighborhood markets" in U.S. "food deserts." In addition to its business plan that would rely on a nonunion, part-time workforce, Tesco's promises have not come to pass in any great number. Gottlieb and Joshi, *Food Justice*, 48–51; Andrew Gumbel, "Tesco Still Searching for Magic Formula to Make America Pay," *Guardian*, January 18, 2012.

20 George Kaplan, foreword to Gallagher, *Good Food*, 5.

21 The six pillars of food sovereignty, established at the Nyéléni Forum for Food Sovereignty, held in 2007 in Sélingué, Mali, are the focus on food for people, the support of food providers, the localization of food systems, the establishment of local control over food systems, the nurture of knowledge and skill, and a sustainable way of working with nature. See *Synthesis Report*, Nyéléni 2007: Forum for Food Sovereignty, Sélingué, Mali, 2007.

22 The overarching goal of the food justice movement is "to achieve equity and fairness in relation to food system impacts and a different, more just, and sustainable way for food to be grown, produced, made accessible, and eaten." Gottlieb and Joshi, *Food Justice*, 223.

23 The story of Jesus' feeding of the multitude appears in all four Gospels. See Matthew 14:13-21, Mark 6:31-44, Luke 9:10-17, and John 6:5-15. For a comprehensive account of Protestant food ministries, see Daniel Sack, *Whitebread Protestants: Food and Religion in American Culture* (New York: Palgrave Macmillan, 2001).

24 Martin Luther King Jr., "A Time to Break Silence," in *A Testament of Hope: The Essential Writings and Speeches of Martin Luther King, Jr.*, ed. James M. Washington (New York: HarperCollins, 1991), 241.

25 Veronica Kyle is the Congregational Outreach Coordinator for Faith in Place. In 2009 she and Assistant Director Rosalyn Priester wrote a successful grant proposal for the Summer Youth Urban Gardening Program, and subsequently partnered with four local congregations to establish summer urban gardens in south and west Chicago. Although the grant funded the gardens for only one year, Veronica believes that the congregations will continue with the gardening projects. Some of the congregations had urban gardens already.

26 The congregations were Greater St. Paul African Methodist Episcopal Church in North Lawndale, Trinity United Church of Christ in South Chicago, Messiah–St. Bartholomew Episcopal Church in Avalon Park, and Lincoln Memorial Congregational United Church of Christ in West Woodlawn.

27 In 2000 the median family income was $24,495. See "Woodlawn," Voorhees Center for Neighborhood and Community Improvement, College of Urban Planning and Public Affairs, University of Illinois at Chicago, http://www.uic.edu/cuppa/voorheesctr/Gentrification%20Index%20Site/Woodlawn.htm.

   West Woodlawn is in Chicago's 20th ward, which has a history of violence dating back to the gang conflicts of the 1960s between the Blackstone Rangers and the Devil's Disciples. Rev. John Fry, pastor of First Presbyterian Church of Woodlawn, wrote a memoir about working with the Blackstone Rangers. See John R. Fry, *Locked Out Americans: A Memoir* (San Francisco: Harper & Row, 1973); James Alan McPherson, "Chicago's Blackstone Rangers, Part I," *Atlantic*, May 1969. After a long period of relative peace, the 20th ward in 2012 witnessed a major surge in violent crime, including twenty homicides, more than any other ward in the city. Garry McCarthy, "Neighborhoods See Spike in Violence," *Chicago Tribune*, July 9, 2012.

28 Gallagher, *The Chicago 2011 Food Desert Drilldown*.

29 The gardens in the Summer Youth Urban Gardening Program are innovative, but they are not the only efforts toward food sovereignty in communities affected by the "grocery gap." Gottlieb and Joshi, *Food Justice*, 39–43. Several recent books and essays have told the stories of congregations and other groups growing food, some of which also draw youth into the practice. See, e.g., Mallory McDuff, "Feeding the Hungry: Gardening for God's Children," in *Natural Saints*, 33–56.

30 "Yield of Dreams: Reflections, Hopes from Summer Youth Urban Gardeners," *Faith in Place Newsletter*, Autumn 2010.

31 Indeed, young people already are leaders in the movement toward food justice. See, e.g., the efforts of the Rethinkers, a group of youth in New Orleans who are challenging the local school system to distribute healthier and more sustainable foods in their cafeterias. Gottlieb and Joshi, *Food Justice*, 1–4, 181.

32 Dykstra, "Reconceiving Practice," 45.

33 "Community Gardens," Atlanta Community Food Bank, http://acfb.org/about/our-programs/community-gardens (accessed August 15, 2012).

34 "What We Do," Atlanta Community Food Bank, http://acfb.org/what-we-do (accessed December 15, 2012).

35 "Executive Staff and Boards," Atlanta Community Food Bank, http://acfb.org/executive-staff-boards (accessed December 15, 2012).

36 "Georgia Avenue Food Cooperative," Georgia Avenue Community Ministry, http://gacm.org/page1/page1.html (accessed December 10, 2012).

37 John 21:15-17.

38 Mark 8:1-9; Matthew 15:32-39.

39 In fact, the Atlanta Community Food Bank has sponsored the Plant a Row for the Hungry program, in which individuals and groups (including congregations) add one row to their summer gardens, donating the produce to the ACFB. These fresh produce supplements to food pantry offerings are crucial enhancements of food charity organizations. See "Community Gardens."

40 John McKnight, "Why 'Servanthood' Is Bad: Are We Service Peddlers or Community Builders?," *Other Side* 31, no. 6 (1995): 2. Scholars in the liberation theology movement, too, have critiqued ministries of charity, saying that charitable "aid remains a strategy for helping the poor, but treating them as (collective) objects of charity, not as subjects of their own liberation." See Leonardo Boff and Clodovis Boff, *Introducing Liberation Theology*, trans. Paul Burns (Maryknoll, N.Y.: Orbis, 1987), 4.

41 See Acts 2:42-47, 4:32-37, and 5–6.

42 See, e.g., 1 Corinthians 11:20-22.

43 Gottlieb and Joshi, *Food Justice*, 6.

44 Exodus 16.

45 Isaiah 43:19-21.

CHAPTER 6

1 The population in 2010 was less than 3,400. "Cuentepec (Temixco, Morelos, Mexico)," City Population, http://www.citypopulation.de/php/mexico-morelos.php?cityid=170180004 (accessed October 13, 2012).

2 "Visit Mexico: Cuernavaca," Mexico Tourism Board, http://www.isit mexico.com/en/cuernavaca (accessed September 15, 2012).

3   "Mexico," in *The World Factbook* (Washington, D.C.: Central Intelligence Agency, 2012).

4   For women in Mexico, this process requires hours of backbreaking labor. Although the women of Cuentepec are more than happy to teach the process to their guests, Karen Bassie-Sweet also describes it very succinctly. See Karen Bassie-Sweet, *Maya Sacred Geography and the Creator Deities* (Norman: University of Oklahoma Press, 2008), 30.

5   "Encuentros: Encounters in Latin America," Chicago Religious Leadership Network on Latin America, http://crln.org/delegations (accessed September 20, 2012).

6   Article 27 is the land sovereignty provision in the Mexican constitution, and is discussed below.

7   Loosely translated, "No to Monsanto Law." Because of the way that corn is farmed in Mexico, there is a very high probability that corn varieties cultivated over centuries could become crossbred with the transgenic seeds produced by Monsanto. The risk of crossbreeding is present even in the corn exported to Mexico from the United States, which contains both genetically modified and nonmodified corn. Peter Canby, "Retreat to Subsistence," *Nation*, June 16, 2010, http://www.thenation.com/article/36330/retreat-subsistence?page=0,4.

8   Lorne Matalon, "Mexico's Corn Farmers," *World*, January 15, 2008.

9   Earl Shorris, *The Life and Times of Mexico* (New York: W. W. Norton, 2004), 245–67.

10 The dismantling of *ejidos* in 1992, as NAFTA was being negotiated, is just one example of both the pressure from the United States and the Mexican government's failure to take advantage of opportunities to provide some agricultural protections. Frank Ackerman, Timothy A. Wise, Kevin P. Gallagher, Luke Ney, and Regina Flores, *Free Trade, Corn, and the Environment: Environmental Impacts of US—Mexico Corn Trade Under NAFTA.* (Medford, Mass.: Global Development and Environment Institute, 2003). E.g., instead of taking the full fifteen years allotted by NAFTA to remove tariffs on corn imports, the Mexican government stopped levying tariffs by 1994. See Alejandro Nadal, *The Environmental and Social Impacts of Economic Liberalization on Corn Production in Mexico* (Oxford: WWF Global, 2000), 26.

11 The tortillas produced in the traditional manner, described at the beginning of this chapter, are far more nutritious than the cheaper commercially produced tortillas made from masa flour in the United States. For more on the centrality of tortillas in the Mexican diet, see Roig-Franzia, "A Culinary and Cultural Staple in Crisis."

12 Roig-Franzia, "A Culinary and Cultural Staple in Crisis."

13 "Mexicans Stage Tortilla Protest," February 1, 2007, http://news.bbc.co.uk/2/hi/americas/6319093.stm (accessed September 25, 2012).

14 Nadal, *The Environmental and Social Impacts*, 4.

15 Harper and Le Beau, *Food, Society, and Environment*, 122.

16 Luis Hernández Navarro, "Mexico: The New Tortilla War," Worldpress.org, June 3, 2007, http://worldpress.org/Americas/2812.cfm (accessed December 12, 2012).

17 Nadal, *The Environmental and Social Impacts*, 10.

18 Shorris, *The Life and Times of Mexico*, 6.

19 Shorris, *The Life and Times of Mexico*, 6, 24.

20 "The Discovery of Maize," in *Popol Vuh*, 193 n. 457.

21 "The Discovery of Maize," 195.

22 Bassie-Sweet, *Maya Sacred Geography*, 21.

23 The organization hosted this program in 2009, 2010, and 2011. There was no Tortillas and Trade seminar in 2012, and there is no trip planned for 2013 as of this writing. Some of the themes addressed in the Mexico Tortillas and Trade program, however, are addressed in other trips organized by CRLN. See "Upcoming Travel Opportunities Latin America," Chicago Religious Leadership Network on Latin America, http://crln.org/delegations/upcomingtravel (accessed September 20, 2012).

24 "CAFTA-DR (Dominican Republic-Central America FTA)," Office of the United States Trade Representative, http://www.ustr.gov/trade-agree ments/free-trade-agreements/cafta-dr-dominican-republic-central -america-fta (accessed October 10, 2012).

25 The North American Free Trade Agreement entered into force in 1994. See "North American Free Trade Agreement (NAFTA)," Office of the United States Trade Representative, http://www.ustr.gov/trade-agree ments/free-trade-agreements/north-american-free-trade-agreement-nafta (accessed October 12, 2012).

26 Carman St. J. Hunter, "Commentary on Traveling for Transformation," in *Pedagogies for the Non-poor*, ed. Alice Frazer Evans, Robert A. Evans, and William Bean Kennedy (Maryknoll, N.Y.: Orbis Books, 1987), 177.

27 "About Us," Cuernavaca Center for Intercultural Dialogue on Development, http://www.ccidd.org/aboutus.htm (accessed September 25, 2012).

28 Paulo Freire, *Pedagogy of the Oppressed*, trans., Myra Bergman Ramos, 30th anniversary ed. (New York: Continuum, 2000), 79.

29 Since early 2011, when this exercise occurred, the Mexican minimum wage has increased twice. At the end of 2012, it was just over sixty pesos per day, or about $4.70 USD (the exchange value of the peso has deteriorated). Anthony Harrup, "Mexico's 2012 Minimum Wage Increase Set at 4.2%," *Wall Street Journal*, December 10, 2011, http://online.wsj .com/article/SB10001424052970203413304577091050495760194.html (accessed October 15, 2012).

30 In January 1994, when NAFTA entered into force, tortillas cost 0.50 pesos per kilogram. Nadal, *The Environmental and Social Impacts*, 38.

31 This comparison is based on observed costs of groceries in Mexico and average 2011 costs of food items according to the United States Bureau of Labor Statistics. "Average Retail Food and Energy Prices, U.S. City Average and Midwest Region," United States Bureau of Labor Statistics, http://www.bls.gov/ro3/apmw.htm (accessed October 20, 2012).

32 This comparison is calculated and provided to the participants in the "Cuernavaca Quest" by the staff of the CCIDD.

33 UNORCA is measured in its support even for "fair trade" models. Javier admits that fair trade is better than speculative trade (where corporations buy at low prices and sell at high prices, as is the case in the corn market), but problems with the fair trade model include a continued emphasis on the commodification of agriculture for export value, as well as the percentage of the profits that European and U.S. distributors keep.

34 The practice is rooted in a mythic story in which writer Ernest Heming-way accepts a challenge to write a short story in six words or less. He writes, "For sale. Baby shoes. Never worn." See Mark Juddery, "10 Works of Literature That Were Really Hard to Write," Mental Floss, January 16, 2011, http://www.cnn.com/2011/LIVING/01/16/mf.literature.hard .to.write/index.html (accessed November 10, 2012).

35 Many media outlets in Mexico are considered too favorably biased toward the government to be of use in providing an honest assessment of governmental policies, including those related to international trade. See Carmen Lira Saade, "Who Are We?" *La Jornada*, 2005.

36 "About Us," Cuernavaca Center for Intercultural Dialogue on Development.

37 "Encuentros."

38 The Peoples Movement Assembly (PMA) process has been used to strate-gize for social change in a variety of contexts and communities, including the United States Social Forum in Detroit, Michigan, and in events orga-nized specifically around immigration issues in Arizona and Texas. See "Assemblies," Peoples Movement Assembly Working Group, http://www .peoplesmovementassembly.org/assemblies (accessed October 15, 2012). For more about the PMA process, see Stephanie Guilloud and Ruben Solis, *The Peoples Movement Assembly Organizing Kit*, Peoples Move-ment Assembly Working Group, 2011.

39 For a full report, see "Principles of Food Justice," Institute for Agricul-ture and Trade Policy, http://www.iatp.org/documents/draft-principles -of-food-justice. Accessed March 26, 2013.

40 "Ecumenical Advocacy Days for Global Peace with Justice," Church World Service, http://advocacydays.org/ (accessed November 10, 2012).

41 Pat, "Group Journal from Tortillas and Trade Delegation to Mexico: Sunday, February 7," Chicago Religious Leadership Network on Latin America, http://crln.org/delegations/Mexico2010/journal (accessed Octo-ber 27, 2012).

42 Russell, *Church in the Round*, 75.

43 Russell, *Church in the Round*, 187.

44 Jacques Derrida has written extensively on the dynamics of hospitality and the ways in which radical hospitality disrupts assumptions regard-ing the roles of host and guest. See Jacques Derrida, *Adieu to Emmanuel Levinas*, trans. Pascale-Anne Brault and Michael Naas (Stanford, Calif.: Stanford University Press, 1999), 41.

45 Letty Russell argues that hospitality is thus predicated upon a basic orien-tation of philoxenia: love of the stranger. Letty M. Russell, *Just Hospital-ity: God's Welcome in a World of Difference*, ed. J. Shannon Clarkson and Kate M. Ott (Louisville, Ky.: Westminster John Knox, 2009), 90.

46 Derrida argues that this maintenance of rules fails the test of absolute hos-pitality. Jacques Derrida, *Of Hospitality: Anne Dufourmantelle Invites Jacques Derrida to Respond*, trans. Rachel Bowlby (Stanford, Calif.: Stanford University Press, 2000), 25.

47 Sharon Todd, *Learning from the Other: Levinas, Psychoanalysis, and Eth-ical Possibilities in Education* (Albany: SUNY Press, 2003), 28, 51–52.

48 Emmanuel Levinas, *Time and the Other: And Other Essays*, trans., Rich-ard A. Cohen (Pittsburgh: Duquesne University Press, 1987), 83.

49 Wild Goose Worship Group, *A Wee Worship Book,* Fourth incarnation (Glasgow, Scotland: Wild Goose Publications, 1999), 84.

50 Mark W. Westmoreland, "Interruptions: Derrida and Hospitality," *Kritike* 2, no. 1 (2008): 7–8.

51 Cláudio Carvalhaes, "Borders, Globalization and Eucharistic Hospitality," *Dialog* 49, no. 1 (2010): 48–49.

52 Melody, "Group Journal from Tortillas and Trade Delegation to Mexico: Wednesday, February 3," Chicago Religious Leadership Network on Latin America, http://crln.org/delegations/Mexico2010/journal (accessed October 27, 2012).

53 Levinas would argue that maintaining the alterity of the other is essential to responsible relationship. Todd, *Learning from the Other,* 51–52.

54 Calvin, *Institutes of the Christian Religion,* II.I.8.

55 For a more extended treatment of structural sin in the context of interdependence, see Jennifer R. Ayres, *Waiting for a Glacier to Move: Practicing Social Witness* (Eugene, Ore.: Wipf & Stock, 2011). Theologians and ethicists have wrestled with the moral significance of interrelatedness for a long time, including Friedrich Schleiermacher, Martin Luther King Jr., Desmond Tutu, and Marjorie Suchocki. See King, "Remaining Awake through a Great Revolution," 269; Friedrich Schleiermacher, *The Christian Faith,* ed. H. R. Mackintosh and James S. Stewart (Edinburgh: T&T Clark, 1989), 4.4; Marjorie Hewitt Suchocki, *The Fall to Violence* (New York: Continuum, 1995), 60; Desmond Tutu, *No Future without Forgiveness* (New York: Image Doubleday, 1999), 274.

56 Zelia Gregoriou, "How Hospitable Can Dwelling Be? The Folds of Spatiality in Levinas," in *Levinas and Education: At the Intersection of Faith and Reason,* ed. Denise Egéa-Kuehne (New York: Routledge, 2008), 214.

57 Luke 10:29-37.

58 Sometimes privileged Christians from the United States are perhaps too quick to claim "solidarity" with Christians on the margins without opening themselves to the deep challenge of their own privilege. Although it is beyond the scope of this book to fully explore just concepts of solidarity, it is important to note that for solidarity to avoid becoming a theoretical platitude, it must include efforts to relate authentically to vulnerable persons and communities.

59 Robert McAfee Brown, ed., *Kairos: Three Prophetic Challenges to the Church* (Grand Rapids: Eerdmans, 1990), 87–88.

60 See Dori Stone, *Beyond the Fence: A Journey to the Roots of the Migration Crisis* (Oakland, Calif.: Food First Books, 2009).

61 Elizabeth Palmberg and Ada María Isasi-Díaz, "Faith at the Tipping Point," *Sojourners,* March 2012.

62 Marcia, "Group Journal from Tortillas and Trade Delegation to Mexico: Saturday, February 6," Chicago Religious Leadership Network on Latin America, http://crln.org/delegations/Mexico2010/journal (accessed October 27, 2012).

CHAPTER 7

1 While Warren Wilson's program is unique and perhaps more comprehensive than most, liberal arts colleges like Berea College (Ky.), Green

Mountain College (Vt.), and Earlham College (Ind.) also maintain thriving farms and, in some cases, programs of study in sustainable agriculture. Traditional land grant universities—like Iowa State University with its Leopold Center, Clemson University (S.C.), Michigan State University, and Pennsylvania State University—have established emphases in sustainable agriculture as well. Some seminaries and theological schools have also taken on sustainable food and gardening avocationally. See, e.g., Jim Schaal, "Raising Our Gardens at LSTC," Lutheran School of Theology at Chicago, http://www.lstc.edu/voices/features/new-gardens.php (accessed September 7, 2012).

2   Neuman, "High Prices Sow Seeds of Erosion."
3   Personal conversation.
4   The "biotic pyramid" is a model developed by Aldo Leopold to express the ways in which the ecological structure is built layer upon layer, the very base layer being the soil. Leopold, "The Land Ethic," 182, 187.
5   Leopold, "The Land Ethic," 171.
6   Hiebert, *Yahwist's Landscape*, 65–66.
7   Hiebert, "Human Vocation," 139.
8   E.g., when a farmer clears forest land to allow for cattle grazing, he contributes to several problems in the ecosystem: he reduces the number of plants that can convert solar energy into nutrients for the soil and animals; he must introduce fertilizers and herbicides to make the hillside soil hospitable to the right plants (and inhospitable to the wrong ones); he exacerbates soil erosion; and relatedly, he empties the now-polluted rainfall running downhill into streams and rivers. Leopold, "The Land Ethic," 179. Of course, written in 1949, Leopold's work predates the advent of the concentrated animal feeding operation (CAFO), in which slopes are not turned to pasture (since animals are raised and fed in confined quarters) but are planted with corn and soybeans. Neuman, "High Prices Sow Seeds of Erosion."
9   Christopher M. Picone and David Van Tassel, "Agriculture and Biodiversity Loss: Industrial Agriculture," in *Life on Earth: An Encyclopedia of Biodiversity, Ecology, and Evolution*, ed. Niles Eldredge (Santa Barbara, Calif.: ABC-CLIO, 2002), 100–102.
10 For an exhaustive study of the conditions in CAFOs (or what they call Industrial Farm Animal Production), see the Pew Forum–commissioned study *Putting Meat on the Table*. A sow, e.g., might be kept in a "gestation crate" for the entire 124 days of her gestation period. These crates have sometimes been so small and so severely restrictive of movement that a sow cannot turn around or lie down comfortably inside one of them. *Putting Meat on the Table*, 85. The report notes that some states have passed legislation outlawing this most extreme animal confinement method. *Putting Meat on the Table*, 38.
11 Mark Bittman, "Some Animals Are More Equal than Others," *New York Times*, March 15, 2011, opinionator.blogs.nytimes.com/2011/03/15/some-animals-are-more-equal-than-others/ (accessed August 20, 2012).
12 One of the antibiotics found in two-thirds of the samples was fluoroquinolone, a class of drugs banned from poultry production since 2005. Flouroquinolones are reserved to treat severe bacterial infections in humans, prescribed sparingly in order to prevent the emergence of

antibiotic-resistant strains. D. C. Love, R. U. Halden, M. F. Davis, and K. E. Nachman, "Feather Meal: A Previously Unrecognized Route for Reentry into the Food Supply of Multiple Pharmaceuticals and Personal Care Products (PPCPs)," *Environmental Science and Technology* 46, no. 7 (2012), http://pubs.acs.org/doi/abs/10.1021/es203970e.

13 Respiratory problems, nausea, and weakness are among the most frequently reported symptoms associated with air and water pollution. Furthermore, pathogens sometimes present in the waste itself can cause illness such as listerosis, tetanus, and salmonella. Carrie Hribar, *Understanding Concentrated Animal Feeding Operations and Their Impact on Communities* (Bowling Green, Ohio: National Association of Local Boards of Health, 2010), 6, 9.

14 Steve Wing, Dana Cole, and Gary Grant, "Environmental Injustice in North Carolina's Hog Industry," *Environmental Health Perspectives* 108, no. 3 (2000), www.ncbi.nlm.nih.gov/pmc/articles/PMC1637958/ (accessed August 20, 2012).

15 Nicholas D. Kristof, "Arsenic in Our Chicken?" *New York Times*, April 5, 2012.

16 *Putting Meat on the Table*, viii.

17 The role of religious communities in directly supporting alternative agriculture was outlined in chapter 4.

18 See, e.g., Christine Anthony and Owen Masterson's documentary film about young farmers in Georgia, *Grow!* Corporations also are trying to harness the growing young adult enthusiasm for farming. Organic Valley, e.g., has launched the "Generation Organic" program, with the goal of nurturing future generations of organic farmers. See "Generation Organic: The Future Is Organic," Organic Valley Family of Farms, http://www.organicvalley.coop/about-us/generation-organic/about-gen-o/ (accessed August 23, 2012). See also Kirk Johnson, "Small Farmers Creating a New Business Model as Agriculture Goes Local," *New York Times*, July 2, 2012; Raftery, "In New Food Culture."

19 The economic and health challenges faced by farmers trying to maintain sustainable practices are documented above in chapter 4.

20 Davis, "From Agriculture to Agribusiness," 111.

21 Vilsack, Testimony.

22 Vilsack, "Briefing on the Status of Rural America."

23 2007 Census of Agriculture, Demographics, USDA–National Agricultural Statistics Service, http://www.agcensus.usda.gov/Publications/2007/Online_Highlights/Fact_Sheets/Demographics/demographics.pdf.

24 *Farming for the Future*, 9–10; *Putting Meat on the Table*, 5–6.

25 One farm that is responding to these challenges to farmer and farmworker dignity is Full Belly Farm, which, among its other commitments, has hired a permanent crew of fifty farmworkers, paying them a livable wage. They have, along the way, built the kind of place people want to visit, where they can connect to each other and to the land, says co-owner Judith Redmond: "It's alive with children, with all of us who work it and feel part of this land, the food we grow and the community of producers and eaters and community members who have created this special place." Gottlieb and Joshi, *Food Justice*, 141.

26 Leopold, "The Land Ethic," 171.

27 "Mission Statement," Warren Wilson College, http://www.warren -wilson.edu/info/plan/mission.php (accessed August 30, 2012). The school also hosts a graduate program in writing, but the "triad" model of academics, work, and service is particular to the undergraduate program.

28 The college recently revamped its service requirement, but the commitment to service remains. See "Community Engagement Commitment," Warren Wilson College, http://www.warren-wilson.edu/~service/Students/ CEcommitment/CEcommitment.php (accessed August 30, 2012).

29 "Warren Wilson College's Value: Scholarships, Financial Aid & Costs," Warren Wilson College, http://www.warren-wilson.edu/admission/ financial_aid/ (accessed September 7, 2012).

30 "A Triad of Academics, Work, and Service," Warren Wilson College, http:// www.warren-wilson.edu/triad/index.php (accessed September 7, 2012).

31 Denis Tippo, "Warren Wilson College On-Campus Work Program," address to Conference of Small Private Colleges February 9, 1977.

32 Reuben A. Holden and Mark T. Banker, *Warren Wilson College: A Centennial Portrait* (Swannanoa, N.C.: Warren Wilson College, 1994), 52. In the mid-1960s, Warren Wilson became a four-year liberal arts college. See the brief history of the school below.

33 "The Work Program: Mission Statement," in *2012–2013 Warren Wilson College Catalog* (Swannanoa, N.C.: Warren Wilson College, 2012).

34 "About Our Farm," Warren Wilson College, http://www.warren-wilson .edu/~farm/Aboutour_farm.php (accessed August 30, 2012).

35 Warren Wilson College Farm, *The Farm Brochure,* (Swannanoa, N.C.: Warren Wilson College, 2012).

36 Chase Hubbard and Jed Brown, *College Farm Crew Handout* (Swannanoa, N.C.: Warren Wilson College, 2011).

37 These schools made remarkable contributions and addressed real needs among the adolescents and young adults living in the region. At the same time, their origins can also be attributed to some cultural assumptions and stereotypes of "mountain folk," including "dismal picture[s] of the 'poverty, suffering, and ignorance'" among them, attributing it to both structural causes and personal moral failings such as lack of ambition, laziness, and even "disgusting snuff-dipping practices of the mountain women." See Mark T. Banker, *Toward Frontiers Yet Unknown: A Ninetieth Anniversary History of Warren Wilson College* (Swannanoa, N.C.: Warren Wilson College, 1984), 2–3; Holden and Banker, *Warren Wilson College,* 5.

38 Banker, *Toward Frontiers Yet Unknown,* 5.

39 Holden and Banker, *Warren Wilson College,* 9. For history of the Appalachian mission schools for girls, see 9–15.

40 Banker, *Toward Frontiers Yet Unknown,* 10. For a history of the Asheville Farm School's early years, see Holden and Banker, *Warren Wilson College,* 17–23.

41 The component of the triad now known simply as "service" historically had a more explicitly Christian dimension. Historical accounts of the language differ: the school's website describes this component as "morality," while Holden and Banker describe it as "Christian instruction and service." See "History of Warren Wilson, 1894–1942," Warren Wilson College, http://www.warren-wilson.edu/~advancement/wwc

history1894-1942.php (accessed August 30, 2012); Holden and Banker, *Warren Wilson College*, 10, 17–18.

42   Banker, *Toward Frontiers Yet Unknown*, 31; Holden and Banker, *Warren Wilson College*, 26.

43   Even today, students can design their own "integrative studies" major, a path chosen by several of the alumni interviewed.

44   Banker, *Toward Frontiers Yet Unknown*, 36.

45   Banker, *Toward Frontiers Yet Unknown*, 50–51.

46   Holden and Banker, *Warren Wilson College*, 35.

47   "Warren H. Wilson (1867–1937)," Warren Wilson College, http://www.warren-wilson.edu/~advancement/cr_WarrenWilson_theperson.php (accessed August 30, 2012).

48   Warren H. Wilson, *Rural Religion and the Country Church* (New York: Fleming H. Revell, 1917), 22.

49   Holden and Banker, *Warren Wilson College*, 10, 18, 28, 36.

50   Holden and Banker, *Warren Wilson College*, 53.

51   "Admissions: About Us," Warren Wilson College, http://www.warren-wilson.edu/admission/facts.php (accessed August 30, 2012).

52   John Curtis Ager, *We Plow God's Fields: The Life of James G. K. McClure* (Boone, N.C.: Appalachian Consortium Press, 1991), 242–76.

53   Ager, *We Plow God's Fields*, 356.

54   Hubbard and Brown, *College Farm Crew Handout*.

55   Abigail Bissette, "Unexpected Encounters with Faith and Piglets," *Presbyterian Outlook*, October 15, 2012, http://www.pres-outlook.com/infocus-features/current-features/17309-unexpected-encounters-with-faith-and-piglets.html.

56   Holden and Banker, *Warren Wilson College*, 55.

57   Wilson, *Rural Religion and the Country Church*, 22. Understanding the earth as a body, Sallie McFague argues, "takes the perspective of the whole and sees all parts, from the largest to the smallest, as interrelated and interdependent." Sallie McFague, *The Body of God: An Ecological Theology* (Nashville: Augsburg Fortress, 1993), 15.

58   Hubbard and Brown, *College Farm Crew Handout*.

59   Leopold, "The Land Ethic," 171.

60   Rasmussen, "Creating the Commons."

61   McFague, *The Body of God*, 19.

62   The actual quote from Jefferson is as follows: "Those who labour in the earth are the chosen people of God, if ever he had a chosen people, whose breasts he has made his peculiar deposit for substantial and genuine virtue. It is the focus in which he keeps alive that sacred fire, which otherwise might escape from the face of the earth." See Thomas Jefferson, "Query XIX," in *Notes on the State of Virginia* (1782), Electronic Text Center, University of Virginia Library.

63   Vilsack, Testimony.

64   J. Clarkson noted that a recent study by the United States Department of Agriculture found the agricultural products of the Southern Appalachian region to be among the most biodiverse in the country.

65   Wirzba, *Food and Faith*, 37 (emphasis in original).

66   Robert Wuthnow, *After the Baby-Boomers: How Twenty- and*

Thirty-Somethings are Shaping the Future of American Religion (Princeton, N.J.: Princeton University Press, 2007).

67 Wilson, *Rural Religion and the Country Church*, 22.

68 Wirzba, *Food and Faith*, 37.

CONCLUSION

1 Gottlieb and Joshi, *Food Justice*, 79.

2 Calvin, *Institutes of the Christian Religion*, II.I.8.

3 Bedford, "Little Moves against Destructiveness."

4 Julie, "Group Journal from Tortillas and Trade Delegation to Mexico: Sunday, January 30," Chicago Religious Leadership Network on Latin America, http://crln.org/delegations/Mexico2011/journal (accessed October 27, 2012).

5 See, e.g., the activists from the Central American peace movement interviewed by Christian Smith: Christian Smith, *Resisting Reagan: The U.S. Central America Peace Movement* (Chicago: University of Chicago Press, 1996).

6 In relationship to broader ecological concerns, Henry Simmons and Anne Marie Dalton argue that a new "social imaginary," as conceptualized by Charles Taylor, is precisely what is necessary. Anne Marie Dalton and Henry C. Simmons, *Ecotheology and the Practice of Hope* (Albany: SUNY Press, 2010), xi.

7 Jasper, *The Art of Moral Protest*, 340.

8 Letty Russell has called this a "spiritualty of connection," which is characterized by the "practice of bodily, social, political, and personal connectedness so that life comes together in a way that both transcends and includes the bits and pieces that make up our search for wholeness, freedom, relationality, and full human dignity." Russell, *Church in the Round*, 187.

9 McFague, *The Body of God*. When Christians participate in these food practices, both by tending to the brokenness and injustice in the system and by imagining another way, they demonstrate what Walter Brueggemann has called the "alternative consciousness," which "serves to *criticize* in dismantling the dominant consciousness. To that extent, it attempts to do what the liberal tendency has done: engage in a rejection and delegitimizing of the present order of things. On the other hand, that alternative consciousness to be nurtured serves to *energize* persons and communities by its promise of another time and situation toward which the community of faith may move. To that extent, it attempts to do what the conservative tendency has done, to live in fervent anticipation of the newness that God has promised and will surely give." Walter Brueggemann, *The Prophetic Imagination*, 2nd ed. (Minneapolis: Fortress, 2001), 3 (emphasis in original).

10 Ellen Ott Marshall, *Though the Fig Tree Does Not Blossom: Toward a Responsible Theology of Christian Hope* (Nashville: Abingdon, 2006), 105.

11 Farley and Jones, *Liberating Eschatology*, vii–viii.

12 Moltmann, *Theology of Hope*, 21.

13 King, "Letter," 291.

14 Maxine Greene, *Releasing the Imagination: Essays on Education, the Arts, and Social Change* (San Francisco: Jossey-Bass, 1995), 28.
15 Wirzba, *Food and Faith*, 37.
16 Martin Luther King Jr., "The Role of the Behavioral Scientist in the Civil Rights Movement," American Psychological Association, http://www.apa.org/monitor/features/king-challenge.aspx (accessed December 15, 2012).
17 M. Shawn Copeland, "Journeying to the Household of God," in Farley and Jones, *Liberating Eschatology*, 38–39.

Bibliography

2007 Census of Agriculture. Washington, D.C.: United States Department of Agriculture–National Agriculture Statistics Service, http://agcensus.usda.gov.

Abels, Caroline. "*Food, Inc.* Chicken Farmer Has a New, Humane Farm." *Grist Magazine* (2012). http://grist.org/sustainable-farming/food-inc-chicken-farmer-has-a-new-humane-farm/.

Abend, Lisa. "Meat-Eating vs. Driving: Another Climate Change Error?" *Time Magazine,* March 27, 2010. http://www.time.com/time/health/article/0,8599,1975630,00.html.

Ackerman, Frank, Timothy A. Wise, Kevin P. Gallagher, Luke Ney, and Regina Flores. *Free Trade, Corn, and the Environment: Environmental Impacts of US—Mexico Corn Trade Under NAFTA.* Medford, Mass.: Global Development and Environment Institute, 2003.

Ackerman, Laura, Don Bustos, and Mark Muller. *Disadvantaged Farmers: Addressing Inequalities in Federal Programs for Farmers of Color.* Minneapolis: Institute for Agriculture and Trade Policy, 2012.

Ager, John Curtis. *We Plow God's Fields: The Life of James G. K. McClure.* Boone, N.C.: Appalachian Consortium Press, 1991.

Ahn, Christine, and Albie Miles. *Free Trade Kills Korean Farmers.* Oakland, Calif.: Food First/Institute for Food Development and Policy, 2011.

Allen, Patricia. *Together at the Table: Sustainability and Sustenance in the American Agrifood System.* University Park: Pennsylvania State University Press, 2004.

"The Amount Spent on Food Rises with Income while the Proportion Falls." In *An Illustrated Guide to Research Findings from USDA's Economic Research Service*, 36–37. Washington, D.C.: USDA Economic Research Service, 2009.

"Animal Feeding Operations." Environmental Protection Agency. http://cfpub.epa.gov/npdes/faqs.cfm?program_id=7.

Anthony, Christine, and Owen Masterson. *Grow!* 60 min. Anthony-Masterson Photography, 2011.

App, Frank. "The Industrialization of Agriculture." *Annals of the American Academy of Political and Social Science* 142, Farm Relief (1929): 228–34.

Arding, Kate. "Sally Jackson Closes Down: With New Regulation, How Can Small Cheesemakers Stay in Business?" *Kate's Blog*, Culture: The Word on Cheese, December 22, 2010, http://www.culturecheesemag.com/blog/kate_sally_jackson_closes.

"Average Retail Food and Energy Prices, U.S. City Average and Midwest Region." United States Bureau of Labor Statistics. http://www.bls.gov/ro3/apmw.htm.

Ayres, Jennifer R. *Waiting for a Glacier to Move: Practicing Social Witness.* Eugene, Ore.: Wipf & Stock, 2011.

Babcock, Bruce A. "Cheap Food and Farm Subsidies: Policy Impacts of a Mythical Connection." *Iowa Ag Review Online* 12, no. 2 (2006). http://www.card.iastate.edu/iowa_ag_review/spring_06/article1.aspx.

Banker, Mark T. *Toward Frontiers Yet Unknown: A Ninetieth Anniversary History of Warren Wilson College.* Swannanoa, N.C.: Warren Wilson College, 1984.

Barreto, Eric D. " 'To Proclaim the Year of the Lord's Favor' (Luke 4:19): Possessions and the Christian Life in Luke-Acts." In *Rethinking Stewardship: Our Culture, Our Theology, Our Practices*, edited by Frederick J. Gaiser. Word and World, Supplement Series 6. Saint Paul, Minn.: Luther Seminary, 2010.

Bassie-Sweet, Karen. *Maya Sacred Geography and the Creator Deities.* Norman: University of Oklahoma Press, 2008.

Beaudoin, Tom. *Consuming Faith: Integrating Who We Are with What We Buy.* Lanham, Md.: Sheed & Ward, 2003.

Bedford, Nancy E. "Little Moves against Destructiveness: Theology and the Practice of Discernment." In *Practicing Theology: Beliefs and Practices in Christian Life*, edited by Dorothy C. Bass and Miroslav Volf, 157–84. Grand Rapids: Eerdmans, 2001.

Benbrook, Charles. *A Deeper Shade of Green: Lessons from Grass-Based Organic Dairy Farms.* Washington, D.C.: Organic Center, 2012.

Bender, Steven M. *One Night in America: Robert Kennedy, César Chávez, and the Dream of Dignity.* Boulder, Colo.: Paradigm, 2008.

Berkenkamp, JoAnn, and Bill Wenzel. *Everyone at the Table: Local Foods and the Farm Bill.* Minneapolis: Institute for Agriculture and Trade Policy, 2012.

Berry, Wendell. *The Art of the Commonplace: The Agrarian Essays of Wendell Berry.* Edited by Norman Wirzba. Berkeley, Calif.: Counterpoint, 2002.

———. "The Body and the Earth." In *The Art of the Commonplace*, 93–134.

———. "The Gift of Good Land." In *The Art of the Commonplace*, 293–304.

———. "Health Is Membership." In *The Art of the Commonplace*, 144–58.

———. "It All Turns on Affection." 2012 Jefferson Lecture, National Endowment for the Humanities, April 23, 2012.

———. "The Pleasures of Eating." In *The Art of the Commonplace*, 321–27.

Beus, Curtis E., and Riley E. Dunlap. "Conventional versus Alternative Agriculture: The Paradigmatic Roots of the Debate." *Rural Sociology* 55, no. 4 (1990): 590–616.

"Biodynamic® Farm Standard." Demeter Association, Philomath, Ore., 2012.

Bissette, Abigail. "Unexpected Encounters with Faith and Piglets." *Presbyterian Outlook*, October 15, 2012. http://www.pres-out look.com/infocus-features/current-features/17309-unexpected -encounters-with-faith-and-piglets.html.

Boff, Leonardo, and Clodovis Boff. *Introducing Liberation Theology.* Translated by Paul Burns. Maryknoll, N.Y.: Orbis, 1987.

Breimyer, Harold F. "The Three Economies of Agriculture." *Journal of Farm Economics* 44, no. 3 (1962): 679–99.

Brown, Robert McAfee, ed. *Kairos: Three Prophetic Challenges to the Church.* Grand Rapids: Eerdmans, 1990.

Brubaker, Pamela K., Rebecca Todd Peters, and Laura A. Stivers, eds. *Justice in a Global Economy: Strategies for Home, Community and World.* Louisville, Ky.: Westminster John Knox, 2006.

Brueggemann, Walter. "The Liturgy of Abundance, the Myth of Scarcity." *Christian Century,* March 24–31, 1999, 342–47.

———. *The Prophetic Imagination.* 2nd ed. Minneapolis: Fortress, 2001.

Burkholder, JoAnn, Bob Libra, Peter Weyer, Susan Heathcote, Dana Kolpin, Peter S. Thorne, and Michael Wichman. "Impacts of Waste from Concentrated Animal Feeding Operations on Water Quality." *Environmental Health Perspectives* 115, no. 2 (2007): 308–12.

"CAFTA-DR (Dominican Republic-Central America FTA)." Office of the United States Trade Representative. http://www.ustr.gov/trade-agreements/free-trade-agreements/cafta-dr-dominican-republic-central-america-fta.

Calvin, John. *Institutes of the Christian Religion.* Edited by John T. McNeill. Translated by Ford Lewis Battles. Library of Christian Classics. Philadelphia: Westminster, 1960.

Canby, Peter. "Retreat to Subsistence." *Nation,* June 16, 2010. http://www.thenation.com/article/36330/retreat-subsistence?page=0,4.

Carlsen, Laura. "NAFTA Is Starving Mexico." Foreign Policy in Focus, October 20, 2011. http://www.fpif.org/articles/nafta_is_starving_mexico.

Carvalhaes, Cláudio. "Borders, Globalization and Eucharistic Hospitality." *Dialog* 49, no. 1 (2010): 45–55.

Case-Winters, Anna. *Reconstructing a Christian Theology of Nature: Down to Earth.* Ashgate Science and Religion Series. Edited by Robert Trigg and J. Wentzel van Huyssteen. Burlington, Vt.: Ashgate, 2007.

"Chairwoman's Summary of the 2012 Farm Bill." U.S. Senate Committee on Agriculture, Nutrition and Forestry. http://www.ag.senate.gov/newsroom/press/release/2012-farm-bill-committee-print.

Chopp, Rebecca. "Practical Theology and Liberation." In *Formation and Reflection: The Promise of Practical Theology*, edited by Lewis S. Mudge and James N. Poling, 120–38. Minneapolis: Augsburg Fortress, 2009.

Commodity Foods and the Nutritional Quality of the National School Lunch Program: Historical Role, Current Operations, and Future Potential. Washington, D.C.: Food Research and Action Center, 2008.

Copeland, M. Shawn. "Journeying to the Household of God." In Farley and Jones, *Liberating Eschatology*, 26–44.

Corn. USDA Economic Research Service. http://www.ers.usda.gov/topics/crops/corn/background.aspx#.UVMNsVtC7Wt. 2009.

Cowan, Tadlock, and Jody Feder. *The Pigford Cases: USDA Settlement of Discrimination Suits by Black Farmers.* Washington, D.C.: Congressional Research Service, 2011.

Cynthia. "Sola Gratia Farms Week Four: Beets Version 2.0." The Sandwich Life, June 17, 2012. http://thesandwichlife.typepad.com/the_sandwich_life/2012/06/sola-gratia-farms-week-four-beets-version-21.html.

Dalton, Anne Marie, and Henry C. Simmons. *Ecotheology and the Practice of Hope.* Albany: SUNY Press, 2010.

Davis, Ellen F. *Scripture, Culture, and Agriculture: An Agrarian Reading of the Bible.* New York: Cambridge University Press, 2008.

Davis, John H. "From Agriculture to Agribusiness." *Harvard Business Review* 34, no. 1 (1956): 107–15.

De La Torre, Miguel. "The Bible Demands Economic Justice." January 5, 2009. http://www.abpnews.com/content/view/3745/9/.

Derrida, Jacques. *Adieu to Emmanuel Levinas.* Translated by Pascale-Anne Brault and Michael Naas. Stanford, Calif.: Stanford University Press, 1999.

———. *Of Hospitality: Anne Dufourmantelle Invites Jacques Derrida to Respond.* Translated by Rachel Bowlby. Stanford, Calif.: Stanford University Press, 2000.

"The Discovery of Maize." In *Popol Vuh: The Sacred Book of the Maya.* Norman: University of Oklahoma Press, 2007.

Double Value Coupon Program: 2011 Outcomes. Bridgeport, Conn.: Wholesome Wave Foundation, 2012.

Drexhage, John, and Deborah Murphy. *Sustainable Development: From Brundtland to Rio 2012: Background Paper.* New York: United Nations High Level Panel on Global Sustainability, 2010.

Dykstra, Craig. "Reconceiving Practice." In *Shifting Boundaries: Contextual Approaches to the Structure of Theological Education,* edited by Barbara G. Wheeler and Edward Farley. Louisville, Ky.: Westminster John Knox, 1991.

Easley, Jonathan. "Gingrich: Poor Kids Have Bad Work Habits 'Unless It's Illegal.'" The Hill, December 1, 2011. http://thehill.com/video/campaign/196663-gingrich-poor-children-have-bad-work-habits-unless-its-illegal.

Eslami, Esa, Kai Filion, and Mark Strayer. *Characteristics of Supplemental Nutrition Assistance Program Households: Fiscal Year 2010.* Alexandria, Va.: USDA Food and Nutrition Service, Office of Research and Analysis, 2011.

"Eucharist." In *Baptism, Eucharist and Ministry: Faith and Order Paper 111.* Geneva: World Council of Churches, 1982.

Farley, Margaret A., and Serene Jones, eds. *Liberating Eschatology: Essays in Honor of Letty M. Russell.* Louisville, Ky.: Westminster John Knox, 1999.

Farming for the Future: A Sustainable Agriculture Agenda for the 2012 Food and Farm Bill. Washington, D.C.: National Sustainable Agriculture Coalition, 2012.

"Fat Mexico: Sins of the Fleshly." *Economist,* December 16, 2004. http://www.economist.com/node/3507918?Story_ID=3507918.

Fernández-Armesto, Felipe. *Near a Thousand Tables: A History of Food.* New York: Free Press, 2002.

Fick, Gary W. *Food, Farming, and Faith.* Albany: SUNY Press, 2008.

Fiorenza, Elisabeth Schüssler. "To Follow the Vision: The Jesus Movement as Basileia Movement." In Farley and Jones, *Liberating Eschatology,* 123–55.

Food Access in Central and South Los Angeles: Mapping Injustice, Agenda for Action. Los Angeles: Center for Food and Justice, Urban and Environmental Policy Initiative, Occidental College, 2007.

Food CPI and Expenditures. USDA Economic Research Service. http://www.ers.usda.gov/data-products/food-expenditures.aspx.

Food Marketing to Children and Youth: Threat or Opportunity? New York: Institute of Medicine of the National Academies, 2005.

Food Security in the U.S. USDA Economic Research Service. http://www.ers.usda.gov/topics/food-nutrition-assistance/food -security-in-the-us.aspx.

Freire, Paulo. *Pedagogy of the Oppressed.* Translated by Myra Bergman Ramos. 30th anniversary ed. New York: Continuum, 2000.

Friendly, Fred W. *Harvest of Shame.* 55 min. CBS News, 1960.

Fry, John R. *Locked out Americans: A Memoir.* San Francisco: Harper & Row, 1973.

Gallagher, Mari. *The Chicago 2011 Food Desert Drilldown.* 5th anniversary ed. Chicago: Mari Gallagher Research and Consulting Group, 2011.

———, ed. *Good Food: Examining the Impact of Food Deserts on Public Health in Chicago.* Chicago: Mari Gallagher Research and Consulting Group and LaSalle Bank, 2006.

———. *Response to "Studies Question Pairing of Food Deserts and Obesity."* Chicago: Mari Gallagher Research and Consulting Group, 2012.

Glazer, Eliot. "See Gallagher (Yes, That Gallagher) in a Geico Commercial." Vulture, 2012. http://www.vulture.com/2012/07/ gallagher-in-a-geico-commercial.html.

Gottlieb, Robert, and Anupama Joshi. *Food Justice.* Food, Health, and the Environment. Cambridge, Mass.: MIT Press, 2010.

Greene, Gael. "What's Nouvelle? La Cuisine Bourgeoise." *New York*, June 2, 1980, 32–41.

Greene, Maxine. *Releasing the Imagination: Essays on Education, the Arts, and Social Change.* San Francisco: Jossey-Bass, 1995.

Gregoriou, Zelia. "How Hospitable Can Dwelling Be? The Folds of Spatiality in Levinas." In *Levinas and Education: At the Intersection of Faith and Reason*, edited by Denise Egéa-Kuehne, 213–27. New York: Routledge, 2008.

Grossinger, Robert S. "Introductory Letter." In Gallagher, *Good Food.*

Guilloud, Stephanie, and Ruben Solis. *The Peoples Movement Assembly Organizing Kit.* Peoples Movement Assembly Working Group, 2011.

Hansen-Kuhn, K., Sophia Murphy, and David Wallinga. *Exporting Obesity: How U.S. Farm and Trade Policy Is Transforming the Mexican Food Environment.* Minneapolis: Institute for Agriculture and Trade Policy, 2012.

Harper, Alethea, Annie Shattuck, Eric Holt-Giménez, Alison Alkon, and Frances Lambrick. *Food Policy Councils: Lessons Learned*. Oakland, Calif.: Food First/Institute for Food and Development Policy, 2009.

Harper, Charles L., and Bryan F. Le Beau. *Food, Society, and Environment*. Upper Saddle River, N.J.: Prentice Hall, 2003.

Hays, Richard B. *First Corinthians*. Interpretation, A Bible Commentary for Teaching and Preaching. Louisville, Ky.: Westminster John Knox, 1997.

Hellwig, Monika. *The Eucharist and the Hunger of the World*. New York: Paulist Press, 1976.

Henning, Brian G. "Standing in Livestock's 'Long Shadow': The Ethics of Eating Meat on a Small Planet." *Ethics and the Environment* 16, no. 2 (2011): 63–93.

Hessel, Dieter T., and Rosemary Radford Ruether, eds. *Christianity and Ecology*. Cambridge, Mass.: Harvard University Center for the Study of World Religions, 2000.

Hiebert, Theodore. "The Human Vocation: Origins and Transformations in Christian Traditions." In Hessel and Ruether, *Christianity and Ecology*, 135–54.

———. *The Yahwist's Landscape*. New York: Oxford University Press, 1996.

Hillman, Kylie, and Sarah Buckley. *Food, Fibre and the Future: Report on Surveys of Students' and Teachers' Knowledge and Understanding of Primary Industries*. Primary Industries Education Foundation and Australian Council for Educational Research, 2011.

Holden, Reuben A., and Mark T. Banker. *Warren Wilson College: A Centennial Portrait*. Swannanoa, N.C.: Warren Wilson College, 1994.

Holt-Giménez, Eric, Zoe Brent, and Annie Shattuck. *Food Workers—Food Justice: Linking Food, Labor and Immigrant Rights*. Oakland, Calif.: Food First/Institute for Food and Development Policy, 2010.

hooks, bell. *Belonging: A Culture of Place*. New York: Routledge, 2009.

Hribar, Carrie. *Understanding Concentrated Animal Feeding Operations and Their Impact on Communities*. Bowling Green, Ohio: National Association of Local Boards of Health, 2010.

Hubbard, Chase, and Jed Brown. *College Farm Crew Handout*. Swannanoa, N.C.: Warren Wilson College, 2011.

Hunter, Carman St. J. "Commentary on Traveling for Transformation." In *Pedagogies for the Non-poor*, edited by Alice Frazer Evans, Robert A. Evans, and William Bean Kennedy, 177–80. Maryknoll, N.Y.: Orbis Books, 1987.

Imhoff, Daniel. "Overhauling the Farm Bill: The Real Beneficiaries of Subsidies." *Atlantic*, March 21, 2012. http://www.theatlantic.com/health/archive/2012/03/overhauling-the-farm-bill-the-real-beneficiaries-of-subsidies/254422/.

Jaffe, Sarah. "McJobs Should Pay, Too: Inside Fast-Food Workers' Historic Protest for Living Wages." *Atlantic*, November 29, 2012. http://www.theatlantic.com/business/archive/2012/11/mcjobs-should-pay-too-inside-fast-food-workers-historic-protest-for-living-wages/265714/#.

Jasper, James M. *The Art of Moral Protest: Culture, Biography, and Creativity in Social Movements*. Chicago: University of Chicago Press, 1999.

Jefferson, Thomas. "Query XIX." In *Notes on the State of Virginia*. 1782. Electronic Text Center, University of Virginia Library, 1782.

Johnson, Luke Timothy. *Sharing Possessions: What Faith Demands*. 2nd ed. Grand Rapids: Eerdmans, 2011.

Johnson, Renée. *The 2008 Farm Bill: Major Provisions and Legislative Action*. Washington, D.C.: Congressional Research Service, 2008.

Johnson, Renée, and Jim Monke. *What Is the Farm Bill?* CRS Report for Congress, September 26, 2019. Washington, D.C.: Congressional Research Service.

Juddery, Mark. "10 Works of Literature That Were Really Hard to Write." Mental Floss, January 16, 2011. http://www.cnn.com/2011/LIVING/01/16/mf.literature.hard.to.write/index.html.

Julie. "Group Journal from Tortillas and Trade Delegation to Mexico: Sunday, January 30." Chicago Religious Leadership Network on Latin America. http://crln.org/delegations/Mexico 2011/journal.

Jung, L. Shannon. *Food for Life: The Spirituality and Ethics of Eating*. Minneapolis: Augsburg Fortress, 2004.

Kaplan, George. Foreword to Gallagher, *Good Food*.

Katz, Sandor Ellix. *The Art of Fermentation: An In-Depth Exploration of Essential Concepts and Processes from Around the World*. White River Junction, Vt.: Chelsea Green, 2012.

Kenner, Robert. *Food, Inc.* Magnolia Pictures, 2008.

Key, Nigel, and Michael J. Roberts. *Commodity Payments, Farm Business Survival, and Farm Size Growth.* Washington, D.C.: USDA Economic Research Service, 2007.

King, Martin Luther Jr. "Remaining Awake through a Great Revolution." In *A Testament of Hope: The Essential Writings and Speeches of Martin Luther King, Jr.,* edited by James M. Washington, 268–78. New York: HarperCollins, 1991.

———. "The Role of the Behavioral Scientist in the Civil Rights Movement." American Psychological Association. http://www.apa.org/monitor/features/king-challenge.aspx.

———. "A Time to Break Silence." In *A Testament of Hope,* 231–44.

Leopold, Aldo. "The Land Ethic." In *A Sand County Almanac,* 237–63. New York: Oxford University Press, 2001.

Levaux, Ari. "The War between Organic and Conventional Farming Misses the Point." *Atlantic,* May 14, 2012.

Levinas, Emmanuel. *Time and the Other: And Other Essays.* Translated by Richard A. Cohen. Pittsburgh: Duquesne University Press, 1987.

Levy, Paul. "What Is a Foodie?" *The Guardian: Word of Mouth Blog,* June 14, 2007. http://www.guardian.co.uk/lifeandstyle/wordofmouth/2007/jun/14/whatisafoodie.

Levy, Paul, and Ann Barr. *The Official Foodie Handbook: Be Modern—Worship Food.* New York: Arbor House, 1985.

Liese, Angela D., Kristina E. Weis, Delores Pluto, Emily Smith, and Andrew Lawson. "Food Store Types, Availability, and Cost of Foods in a Rural Environment." *Journal of the American Dietetic Association* 107, no. 11 (2007): 1916–23.

Lilliston, Bill. *What's at Stake in the 2012 Farm Bill?* Minneapolis: Institute for Agriculture and Trade Policy, 2012.

Linzey, Andrew. *Creatures of the Same God: Explorations in Animal Theology.* Brooklyn, N.Y.: Lantern Books, 2009.

———. "Is Christianity Irredeemably Speciesist?" In *Animals on the Agenda: Questions about Animals for Theology and Ethics,* edited by Andrew Linzey and Dorothy Yamamoto, xi–xx. Chicago: University of Illinois Press, 1998.

Liu, Yvonne Yen, and Dominique Apollon. *The Color of Food.* New York: Applied Research Center, 2011.

Local Food, Farms and Jobs: Growing the Illinois Economy. Springfield: Illinois Local and Organic Food and Farm Task Force, 2009.

Louv, Richard. *The Last Child in the Woods: Saving Our Children from Nature-Deficit Disorder.* Rev. and updated ed. Chapel Hill, N.C.: Algonquin Books of Chapel Hill, 2008.

Love, D. C., R. U. Halden, M. F. Davis, and K. E. Nachman. "Feather Meal: A Previously Unrecognized Route for Reentry into the Food Supply of Multiple Pharmaceuticals and Personal Care Products (PPCPs)." *Environmental Science and Technology* 46, no. 7 (2012). http://pubs.acs.org/doi/abs/10.1021/es203970e.

MacIntyre, Alasdair. *After Virtue: A Study in Moral Theory.* 2nd ed. Notre Dame, Ind.: University of Notre Dame Press, 1984.

Manning, Rita. "Corporate Responsibility and Corporate Personhood." *Journal of Business Ethics* 3, no. 1 (1984): 77–84.

Marcia. "Group Journal from Tortillas and Trade Delegation to Mexico: Saturday, February 6." Chicago Religious Leadership Network on Latin America, http://crln.org/delegations/Mexico2010/journal.

Marshall, Ellen Ott. *Though the Fig Tree Does Not Blossom: Toward a Responsible Theology of Christian Hope.* Nashville: Abingdon, 2006.

Marx, Karl. "Estranged Labour." In *The Marx-Engels Reader,* edited by Robert C. Tucker, 70–81. New York: W. W. Norton, 1978.

Matalon, Lorne. "Mexico's Corn Farmers." *World,* January 15, 2008.

McDuff, Mallory. "Feeding the Hungry: Gardening for God's Children." In *Natural Saints,* 33–56.

———. *Natural Saints: How People of Faith Are Working to Save God's Earth.* New York: Oxford University Press, 2010.

McFague, Sallie. *The Body of God: An Ecological Theology.* Nashville: Augsburg Fortress, 1993.

McKnight, John. "Why 'Servanthood' Is Bad: Are We Service Peddlers or Community Builders?" *Other Side* 31, no. 6 (1995): 56–59.

McPherson, James Alan. "Chicago's Blackstone Rangers, Part I." *Atlantic,* May 1969.

Mehren, Philip T. von, and Eduardo Ruiz Vega. "The Interrelationship between NAFTA and Mexican Law." (Excerpt from Curtis, Mallet-Prevost, Colt, and Mosle, International Report July 1996.) Institute for Agriculture and Trade Policy, April 3, 2000. http://iatp.org/documents/interrelationship -between-nafta-and-mexican-law-the.

Melody. "Group Journal from Tortillas and Trade Delegation to Mexico: Wednesday, February 3." Chicago Religious Leadership Network on Latin America. http://crln.org/delegations/ Mexico2010/journal.

Miller, Daniel K. *Animal Ethics and Theology: The Lens of the Good Samaritan.* New York: Routledge, 2012.

Miller-McLemore, Bonnie J. *Christian Theology in Practice: Discovering a Discipline.* Grand Rapids: Eerdmans, 2012.

Moltmann, Jürgen. *Theology of Hope: On the Ground and the Implications of a Christian Eschatology.* Translated by James W. Leitch. 5th ed. San Francisco: HarperSanFrancisco 1967.

"Music: 'I'm Gonna Sit at the Welcome Table.'" PBS Online. http://www.pbs.org/wgbh/amex/eyesontheprize/story/04_non violence.html#music.

Mwaniki, Angela. *Achieving Food Security in Africa: Challenges and Issues.* United Nations Office of the Special Adviser on Africa.

Nadal, Alejandro. *The Environmental and Social Impacts of Economic Liberalization on Corn Production in Mexico.* Oxford: Oxfam; Gland, Switzerland: WWF Global, 2000.

National School Lunch Program Fact Sheet. Washington, D.C.: USDA Food and Nutrition Service, 2011.

Navarro, Luis Hernández. "Mexico: The New Tortilla War." Worldpress.org. June 3, 2007. http://worldpress.org/Americas/2812. cfm.

Nestle, Marion. *Food Politics: How the Food Industry Influences Nutrition and Health.* Berkeley: University of California Press, 2002.

———. "Surprise! Food Companies Still Market to Children." *Atlantic,* August 26, 2011.

———. *What to Eat.* New York: North Point Press, 2006.

"Newt and the 'Food-Stamp President.'" *Economist,* January 2, 2012. http://www.economist.com/blogs/democracyinamerica/ 2012/01/newt-gingrichw.

Nord, Mark, and Mark Prell. "Food Security of SNAP Recipients Improved Following the 2009 Stimulus Package." *Amber Waves* (June 2011).

Olmstead, Julia, and Jim Kleinschmit. *A Risky Proposition: Crop Insurance in the Face of Climate Change*. Minneapolis: Institute for Agriculture and Trade Policy, 2012.

The Organic Watergate: White Paper. Cornucopia, Wis.: Cornucopia Institute, 2012.

Orr, David W. "Ecological Literacy." In *Ecological Literacy*, 85–96.

———. *Ecological Literacy: Education and the Transition to a Postmodern World*. SUNY Series in Constructive Postmodern Thought. Albany: SUNY Press, 1991.

Paarlberg, Robert. "The Inconvenient Truth about Cheap Food and Obesity: It's Not Farm Subsidies." *GOOD* (2011). http://www .good.is/post/the-inconvenient-truth-about-cheap-food-and -obesity-it-s-not-farm-subsidies/.

Page, Kathleen A., Owen Chan, Jagriti Arora, Renata Belfort-DeAguiar, James Dzuira, Brian Roehmholdt, Gary W. Cline, Sarita Naik, Rajita Sinha, R. Todd Constable, and Robert S. Sherwin. "Effects of Fructose vs Glucose on Regional Cerebral Blood Flow in Brain Regions Involved with Appetite and Reward Pathways." *Journal of the American Medical Association* 309, no. 1 (2013). http://jama.jamanetwork.com/article.aspx?articleid=1555133.

Palmberg, Elizabeth, and Ada María Isasi-Díaz. "Faith at the Tipping Point." *Sojourners*, March 2012.

Park, Alice. "All Sugars Aren't the Same: Glucose Is Better, Study Says." *Time Magazine*, April 21, 2009.

Pat. "Group Journal from Tortillas and Trade Delegation to Mexico: Sunday, February 7." Chicago Religious Leadership Network on Latin America. http://crln.org/delegations/Mexico2010/journal.

Patel, Raj. *Stuffed and Starved: The Hidden Battle for the World Food System*. Brooklyn, N.Y.: Melville House, 2008.

Peters, Rebecca Todd. "Supporting Community Farming." In Brubaker, Peters, and Stivers, *Justice in a Global Economy*, 17–28.

Philpott, Tom. "Is Cooking Really Cheaper Than Fast Food?" *Mother Jones*, October 4, 2011.

Picone, Christopher M., and David Van Tassel. "Agriculture and Biodiversity Loss: Industrial Agriculture." In *Life on Earth: An Encyclopedia of Biodiversity, Ecology, and Evolution*, edited by Niles Eldredge, 99–105. Santa Barbara, Calif.: ABC-CLIO, 2002.

Pirog, Rich, Timothy Van Pelt, Kamyar Enshayan, and Ellen Cook. *Food, Fuel, and Freeways*. Ames: Leopold Center for Sustainable Agriculture, Iowa State University, 2001.

Pollan, Michael. "Farmer in Chief," *New York Times Magazine*, October 12, 2008. http://www.nytimes.com/2008/10/12/magazine/12policy-t.html.

"Principles of Food Justice." Institute for Agriculture and Trade Policy. http://www.iatp.org/documents/draft-principles-of-food-justice.

"Program Synopsis: Community Food Projects." USDA National Institute of Food and Agriculture. http://www.nifa.usda.gov/funding/cfp/cfp_synopsis.html.

Pui-lan, Kwok. "Mending of Creation: Women, Nature, and Eschatological Hope." In Farley and Jones, *Liberating Eschatology*, 144–55.

Putting Meat on the Table: Industrial Farm Animal Production in America. Pew Commission on Industrial Farm Animal Production and Johns Hopkins Bloomberg School of Health, 2006.

"Questions and Answers about Food Biotechnology." International Food Information Council Foundation. http://www.foodinsight.org/Resources/Detail.aspx?topic=Questions_and_Answers_About_Food_Biotechnology.

Rasmussen, Larry L. "Creating the Commons." In Brubaker, Peters, and Stivers, *Justice in a Global Economy*, 101–12.

Rhodes, V. James. "Industrialization of Agriculture: Discussion." *American Journal of Agricultural Economics* 75, no. 5 (1993): 1137–39.

Ritzer, George. *The McDonaldization of Society 6*. 6th ed. Thousand Oaks, Calif.: Pine Forge Press, 2011.

Romo, Rafael. "Mexico's Other Enemy: Obesity Rates Triple in Last Three Decades." CNN.com, January 4, 2011. http://articles.cnn.com/2011-01-04/world/mexico.obesity_1_obesity-rates-obese-people-junk-food?_s=PM:WORLD.

Rosset, Peter. "Lessons from the Green Revolution." Food First/Institute for Food and Development Policy, April 8, 2000. http://www.foodfirst.org/media/opeds/2000/4-greenrev.html (2009).

Rossing, Barbara R. "River of Life in God's New Jerusalem: An Eschatological Vision for Earth's Future." In Hessel and Ruether, *Christianity and Ecology*, 205–24.

Russell, Letty M. *Church in the Round: Feminist Interpretation of the Church*. Louisville, Ky.: Westminster John Knox, 1993.

———. *Just Hospitality: God's Welcome in a World of Difference.* Edited by J. Shannon Clarkson and Kate M. Ott. Louisville, Ky.: Westminster John Knox, 2009.

Saade, Carmen Lira. "Who Are We?" *La Jornada*, 2005.

Sack, Daniel. *Whitebread Protestants: Food and Religion in American Culture*. New York: Palgrave Macmillan, 2001.

Schaal, Jim. "Raising Our Gardens at LSTC." Lutheran School of Theology at Chicago. http://www.lstc.edu/voices/features/new-gardens.php.

Scherer, Glenn. "Christian-Right Views Are Swaying Politicians and Threatening the Environment." *Grist Magazine* (2004).

Schleiermacher, Friedrich. *The Christian Faith*. Edited by H. R. Mackintosh and James S. Stewart. Edinburgh: T&T Clark, 1989.

Schlosser, Eric. "Still a Fast-Food Nation: Eric Schlosser Reflects on 10 Years Later." *Daily Beast*, March 12, 2012. http://www.thedailybeast.com/articles/2012/03/12/still-a-fast-food-nation-eric schlosser-reflects-on-10-years-later.html.

Shiva, Vandana. *The Violence of the Green Revolution*. New York: Zed Books, 1991.

Shorris, Earl. *The Life and Times of Mexico*. New York: W. W. Norton, 2004.

Siebert, Charles. "Food Ark." *National Geographic*, June 2011.

Siegel, Taggart. *The Real Dirt on Farmer John*. 82 min. CAVU Pictures, 2005.

Simon, Michele, and Siena Chrisman. *Enough to Eat: Food Assistance and the Farm Bill*. Minneapolis: Institute for Agriculture and Trade Policy, 2012.

Singer, Peter. *Animal Liberation*. San Francisco: HarperCollins, 2001.

Smith, Christian. *Resisting Reagan: The U.S. Central America Peace Movement*. Chicago: University of Chicago Press, 1996.

Sola Gratia Farm. *By Grace Alone These Gifts Are Shared among Us*. Urbana, Ill.: Sola Gratia Farm, 2012.

State Fact Sheets: United States. USDA Economic Research Service. http://www.ers.usda.gov/data-products/state-fact-sheets/state -data.aspx?StateFIPS=00#.UVJYeltC7Ws.

Steinfeld, Henning, Pierre Gerber, Tom Wassenaar, Vincent Castel, Mauricio Rosales, and Cees de Haan. *Livestock's Long Shadow: Environmental Issues and Options*. Rome: Food and Agriculture Organization of the United Nations, 2006.

Stier, Ken. "How Frankenfood Prevailed." *Time Magazine*, June 28, 2010.

Stone, Dori. *Beyond the Fence: A Journey to the Roots of the Migration Crisis*. Oakland, Calif.: Food First Books, 2009.

Strengthening Rural Communities: Hunger Report 2005: 15th Annual Report on the State of World Hunger. Washington, D.C.: Bread for the World Institute, 2005.

Suchocki, Marjorie Hewitt. *The Fall to Violence*. New York: Continuum, 1995.

Supplemental Nutrition Assistance: Average Monthly Participation (Households). USDA Food and Nutrition Service. http://www.fns .usda.gov/pd/16SNAPpartHH.htm.

"Supplemental Nutrition Assistance Program (Monthly Data— National Level)." Alexandria, Va.: Supplemental Nutrition Assistance Program (USDA Food and Nutrition Service), 2011.

Swensen, Dave. *Selected Measures of the Economic Values of Increased Fruit and Vegetable Production and Consumption in the Upper Midwest*. Ames: Department of Economics, Iowa State University, 2010.

Synthesis Report. Nyéléni 2007: Forum for Food Sovereignty, Sélingué, Mali, 2007.

Todd, Sharon. *Learning from the Other: Levinas, Psychoanalysis, and Ethical Possibilities in Education*. Albany: SUNY Press, 2003.

Transitioning to Organic Production. College Park, Md.: Sustainable Agriculture Network/Sustainable Agriculture Research and Education, 2007.

Trautmann, Nancy M., Keith S. Porter, and Robert J. Wagenet. *Modern Agriculture: Its Effects on the Environment*. Ithaca, N.Y.: Cornell University Cooperative Extension, 1985.

Tutu, Desmond. *No Future without Forgiveness*. New York: Image Doubleday, 1999.

Vilsack, Tom. "Agriculture Secretary Vilsack Makes Case for Stronger Rural America." News release, United States Department of Agriculture, 2010.

———. "Briefing on the Status of Rural America." United States Department of Agriculture, 2010.

———. Testimony at U.S. Senate Committee on Agriculture, Nutrition, and Forestry, Farm Bill Oversight Hearing, June 30, 2010.

Wallace, Barbara, and Frank Clearfield. *Stewardship, Spirituality, and Natural Resources Conservation: A Short History.* Washington, D.C.: National Resources Conservation Service Social Sciences Institute, 1997.

Wallinga, David. "Agricultural Policy and Childhood Obesity: A Food Systems and Public Health Commentary." *Health Affairs* 29, no. 3 (2010): 405–10.

Walsh, Brian. "Getting Real about the High Price of Cheap Food." *Time Magazine*, August 21, 2009, http://www.time.com/time/magazine/article/0,9171,1917726,00.html.

Warren Wilson College Farm. *The Farm Brochure.* Swannanoa, N.C.: Warren Wilson College, 2012.

Welch, Sharon D. *A Feminist Ethic of Risk.* Rev. ed. Minneapolis: Fortress, 2000.

Westmoreland, Mark W. "Interruptions: Derrida and Hospitality." *Kritike* 2, no. 1 (2008): 1–10.

White, Lynn. "The Historical Roots of Our Ecologic Crisis." *Science*, March 10, 1967, 1203–7.

Wild Goose Worship Group. *A Wee Worship Book.* Fourth incarnation. Glasgow, Scotland: Wild Goose Publications, 1999.

Wilson, Warren H. *Rural Religion and the Country Church.* New York: Fleming H. Revell, 1917.

Wing, Steve, Dana Cole, and Gary Grant. "Environmental Injustice in North Carolina's Hog Industry." *Environmental Health Perspectives* 108, no. 3 (2000). http://www.ncbi.nlm.nih.gov/pmc/articles/PMC1637958/.

Wirzba, Norman. *Food and Faith: A Theology of Eating.* New York: Cambridge University Press, 2011.

Wuthnow, Robert. *After the Baby-Boomers: How Twenty- and Thirty-Somethings Are Shaping the Future of American Religion.* Princeton, N.J.: Princeton University Press, 2007.

"Yield of Dreams: Reflections, Hopes from Summer Youth Urban Gardeners." *Faith in Place Newsletter*, Autumn 2010.

Young, Edwin, Victor Oliveira, and Roger Claassen. "2008 Farm Act: Where Will the Money Go?" *Amber Waves* (November 2008). http://webarchives.cdlib.org/sw1vh5dg3r/http://ers.usda.gov/AmberWaves/November08/DataFeature/.

Index

agribusiness, 17–18, 27, 29, 39, 42, 45, 47, 84, 142, 169n15, 171n22, 176n83, 179n23, 182n67

agriculture, x, 152–54, 161, 175n67, 178n9; alternative, xii, 5, 18, 32–33, 34, 41, 45–46, 52, 71, 75, 82–85, 89–90, 91, 93, 94, 97, 99, 109, 118, 126, 138, 141–42, 143, 144–47, 154, 159, 165n3, 165–66n4, 169n14, 176n78, 176n84, 191n6, 191n7, 194n40, 195–96n11, 202–3n1, 204n18; alternative, defined, 191n9; consolidation in, 15, 17–18, 27, 30, 32, 171n22, 191n4, 200n33; and eating, 3–4, 6, 21, 23, 28–29, 32, 34, 39, 57–59, 69, 70, 73, 80, 82, 85–86, 88, 95–97, 108, 188n77, 191n5; global, 24, 25–26, 39, 47, 67, 76, 118, 122, 126, 133–36, 174n56, 176n77, 177–78n93; industrialization of, 5, 26, 27–28, 30–34, 139–42, 176n78, 177n87, 188n72, 188n73, 191n4; in Mexico, 7, 47–49,

118–19, 120–22, 126, 135, 172n35, 199n10

Agriculture Reform, Food, and Jobs Act (2012); *see* Farm Bill

alienation in global food system; *see* interdependence in food system, and alienation

analysis of food system; as part of grounded practical theology, xi, xii, 3, 5, 7–8, 14, 47, 52, 75, 76, 77, 102, 159, 165n2, 190n4, 190n2; components of 14, 26, 35

animals, x, 3, 5, 6, 8, 10, 14, 15, 26, 29, 31–32, 35, 40, 54, 69–70, 80, 86, 137, 139–42, 143, 146, 149, 152–53, 164, 165–67n4, 169n4, 169n15, 174n62, 174–75n63, 175n73, 187–88n65, 188n73, 191n7, 193n91; concentrated animal feeding operations (CAFOs), 32, 33, 42, 63, 71, 140–41, 175n72, 176–77n85, 177n87, 177n88, 203n8, 203n10, 204n13; livestock farming, 27, 29, 31, 33–34, 42,

227

CPSIA information can be obtained
at www.ICGtesting.com
Printed in the USA
LVHW040208081221
705585LV00002B/169

9 781602 589858